I0088765

Nathan Eubank
Wages of Cross-Bearing and Debt of Sin

Beihefte zur Zeitschrift für die neutestamentliche Wissenschaft

und die Kunde der älteren Kirche

Herausgegeben von
James D. G. Dunn · Carl R. Holladay
Hermann Lichtenberger · Jens Schröter
Gregory E. Sterling · Michael Wolter

Band 196

De Gruyter

Nathan Eubank

Wages of Cross-Bearing
and Debt of Sin

The Economy of Heaven in Matthew's Gospel

De Gruyter

ISBN 978-3-11-048798-5
e-ISBN 978-3-11-030407-7
ISSN 0171-6441

Library of Congress Cataloging-in-Publication Data

A CIP catalog record for this book has been applied for at the Library of Congress.

Bibliographic information published by the Deutsche Nationalbibliothek

The Deutsche Nationalbibliothek lists this publication in the DeutscheNationalbibliografie; detailed bibliographic data are available in the Internet at http://dnb.dnb.de.

© 2013 Walter de Gruyter GmbH, Berlin/Boston

Printing: Hubert & Co. GmbH & Co. KG, Göttingen
∞ Printed on acid-free paper
Printed in Germany
www.degruyter.com

For Jessie

Acknowledgements

I would like to thank Duke University and the James B. Duke Fund for providing the financial support that allowed me to devote most of my time to this project. The members of my committee were all enormously helpful to me in one way or another. Ellen Davis read the entire dissertation during a very busy semester and offered invaluable feedback and encouragement. I am also grateful to Professor Davis for her extraordinary help in navigating the mercurial requirements of the Graduate Program in Religion. Mark Goodacre's unparalleled knowledge of the Gospels and of the relevant secondary literature was a great help to me, and I am grateful to him for taking the time to provide detailed feedback. Surely it is rare that a dogmatic theologian shows up at a dissertation defense with Greek New Testament in hand, ready to discuss both conceptual matters and the minutiae of the Greek text, but Reinhard Hütter is one such theologian. His advice on matters theological and practical has helped me in more ways than I can express. Kavin Rowe has been a constant source of wise counsel. I am grateful for that and for his willingness to help me tease out the significance of my arguments. Finally, thanks are due to my advisor, Richard Hays. When I first came to Duke as a MTS student I took Professor Hays's Introduction to the New Testament class. It only took a few weeks of listening to him talk about the New Testament for me to decide that this is what I wanted to do with my life. I have enjoyed learning from him in the years since then, and I am grateful to him for his brilliant and incisive comments on this study – comments given while he was also working as Dean of the Divinity School – as well as for his enthusiasm for the project.

Thanks are due also to a number of friends who helped me with this project either by reading some portion of it or by talking through some aspect of it with me, including Gary Anderson, Hans Arneson, Douglas Campbell, Stephen Carlson, Carl-Magnus Carlstein, Natalie Carnes, Joel Decker, Sarah Decker, Rebekah Eklund, Ben Gordon, Bradley C. Gregory, Paul Griffiths, Nancy Hütter, John Kincaid, Joel Marcus, Tom McGlothlin, Dave Moffitt, Brant Pitre, John Sehorn, Matthew Thiessen, and Msgr. John Williams. Rodrigo Morales and Matthew

Whelan both read the entire dissertation and offered helpful comments. A special thank you is due to T. J. Lang who has been a great friend and colleague since we both arrived at Duke in 2003. T.J. discussed this project with me day in and day out, and he read every chapter as I wrote them and provided extensive and insightful comments.

My parents, Geoffrey and Pamela Eubank, have been indefatigable in their support of and enthusiasm for my work. From reading the dissertation to praying for its daily progress, they have helped me in more ways than I can name. I also want to mention my grandmother, Mary Jean Moore, who has encouraged me with her generosity and love. My parents-in-law, Kent and Connie Arthur, helped get me started by buying me my first laptop and have continued to support me with cigars and good conversations, among other things. My children, Mary, Scott, Benjamin, and Thomas (who arrived when I had only one chapter left to write) have an unmatched ability to help me think about something other than my work. I am grateful for their support and especially for their goofiness. The biggest debt of all is due to my wife Jessie. Her love, patience, and sense of humor seem to know no bounds. As a small gesture of my gratitude I dedicate this project to her.

Contents

Introduction

1. Justification for the Study

In comparison to Mark and Luke, Matthew's Gospel contains a striking preponderance of economic imagery, especially in passages dealing with sin, righteousness, and divine recompense.[1] This cluster of economic terms is found in every strand of tradition in Matthew's Gospel, and frequently appears to be the result of Matthean redaction. A good chunk of this language occurs in five uniquely Matthean parables dealing either with the pricelessness of the kingdom or judgment and reward (the hidden treasure in 13:44; the pearl in 13:45–46; the parable of the unforgiving servant in 18:23–35; the parable of the workers in the vineyard 20:1–16; the sheep and the goats in 25:31–46). Matthean additions to the triple tradition also tend to contain economic language. For instance, in 16:27 Matthew alone mentions that when the Son of Man comes in the glory of his Father he will render what is due (ἀποδώσει) to each according to his deeds (cf. Mark 8:38; Luke 9:26). Likewise, economic language is frequently found in Matthean "pluses" in the double tradition. For instance, much of the Sermon on the Mount deals with the wage due to one who practices righteousness without attempting to receive credit from other people (e.g., 6:1–19). Most of this material is absent from Luke. Similarly, Matthew 5:46 speaks of the "wage" (ὁ μισθός) which is due one who loves her enemies, whereas Luke 6:33 speaks of the "favor" (χάρις) of such a person. While there have been studies of recompense in Matthew, I am aware of no study of any length that has examined Matthew's understanding of wages

---

1 E.g., ὁ μισθός (wages): 9/1/3; κερδαίνω (to acquire by effort or investment): 6/1/1; ἀπέχω in the sense of receiving in full what is due: 3/0/1; ἀποδίδωμι in the sense of rending what is due: 14/1/8; συναίρω (to settle accounts): 3/0/0. Συναίρω never appears in anywhere else in the NT or LXX. There is a cluster of words describing debt: τό δάνειον: 1/0/0; τό ὀφείλημα: 1/0/0; ὁ ὀφειλέτης: 2/0/1. There is also ὁ θησαυρός and θησαυρίζω (treasure/to store up treasure): 11/1/5; πιπράσκω (to sell): 3/1/0. For a helpful study of economics in Luke see Halvor Moxnes, *The Economy of the Kingdom: Social Conflict and Economic Relations in Luke's Gospel* (OBT; Philadelphia: Fortress Press, 1988).

and debts and the import of this language for Matthew's narrative as a whole.

This lacuna becomes more conspicuous in light of Gary Anderson's recent study, *Sin: A History*.[2] Anderson shows that financial language provided the conceptual framework for speaking of good and bad deeds beginning in the later strata of the Hebrew Bible and stretching on into early Judaism and Christianity. In Aramaic, Anderson notes, "the word for a debt that one owes a lender, *ḥôbâ*, is the standard term for denoting sin. This term comes into Second Temple Hebrew and has the same double meaning. The earlier idea of sin as a weight is rarely found in rabbinic Hebrew, having been replaced by the idea of sin as a debt."[3] Anderson illustrates this transformation by showing how the Targumim almost always translate the phrase נשא עון when it refers to sin with the Aramaic idiom קבל חובא. For instance, Leviticus 5:1 ("If a person should sin…he shall bear the weight of his sin [ונשא עונו]") is translated "If a person becomes obligated [by sin]…he assumes a debt (ויקביל חוביה)." Perhaps the most famous instance of sin as debt in the New Testament is in the Matthean version of the Our Father: "Forgive us our debts (τὰ ὀφειλήματα) as we also forgive our debtors (τοῖς ὀφει-λέταις)." Matthew's restatement of the petition in verses 14−15 ("For if you forgive people their trespasses, your heavenly Father will also forgive you") shows that "debt" is used here to refer to sin. Closely related to the idea of sin as debt was the notion of righteous deeds as earning credit –שכר or זכות, as the rabbis called it, or, in Matthew's idiom, wages (μισθός) or treasures in heaven (θησαυροὶ ἐν οὐρανῷ).

The basic claims of Anderson's insightful and far-reaching study are difficult to contest.[4] Still, even if one should quibble with Anderson's contention that the language of debt and credit formed the basic building blocks for understanding sin and righteousness in early Judaism and Christianity, the Gospel according to Matthew, which receives scant attention in *Sin*, is replete with such language.[5] Previous scholarship has

---

2 (New Haven: Yale University Press, 2009).

3 Ibid., 27.

4 Cf. Joseph Lam's assessment: "There is not much with which to quarrel in terms of Anderson's broad historical argument. The metaphorical transition from sin as burden to sin as debt is highly conspicuous in the primary sources, and it is perhaps the fault of biblical scholarship that this conceptual shift has not been adequately emphasized in previous discussions." Review of Gary A. Anderson, *Sin: A History*, RBL [http://www.bookreviews.org] (2010).

5 Anderson's treatment of the Synoptic Gospels is largely limited to Mark.

not been unaware that Matthew has much to say about sin, righteousness, and divine recompense, but this scholarship has failed to attend to the particularities of this language and its role in the narrative. The result of this, as I shall argue, is that these studies have, in significant respects, failed to understand what Matthew is about. I shall outline three deficiencies in previous treatments of Matthew's financial language.

First, many studies have focused on the teaching of Jesus as a whole, or even the entire New Testament, and have not attended to Matthew's narrative dynamics. For instance, Paul S. Minear's 1941 monograph, *And Great Shall Be Your Reward: The Origins of Christian Views of Salvation*, treats selected Synoptic pericopae,[6] as does Wilhelm Pesch's *Der Lohngedanke in der Lehre Jesu: Verglichen mit der religiösen Lohnlehre des Spätjudentums*.[7] Studies that have focused exclusively on Matthew have tended to treat the question of recompense without reference to its role in the story as a whole.[8]

Second, previous work on recompense in Matthew has ignored the specific conceptual register of much of this language, the grammar that gave these concepts meaning in Matthew's day – that of debt and wages. For instance, some studies of recompense in Matthew frame the question in terms of his relationship to Paul and his understanding of grace (χάρις) – a word-group that never appears in Matthew.[9] Yet, the only way to understand what Matthew says about what we might call "grace" is to enter into Matthew's own field of discourse. Another example is Blaine Charette's 1992 study, *The Theme of Recompense in Matthew's Gospel*, which situates Matthew against the background of Old Testament promises of reward for observing God's commandments and punishment for failing to do so, but does not attend to the partic-

---

6   (YSR 12; New Haven: Yale University Press, 1941).
7   (Munich: Karl Zink, 1955). See also Bo Reicke, "The New Testament Conception of Reward," in *Aux sources de la tradition chréttienne: Mélanges offerts à M. Maurice Goguel* (Bibliothèque théologique; Paris: Delachaux and Niestlé, 1950), 195–206; Günther Bornkamm, "Der Lohngedanke im Neuen Testament," in *Studien zu Antike und Urchristentum: Gesammelte Aufsätze* (2 vols.; Munich: Kaiser Verlag, 1963), 2.69–92.
8   E.g., recently, Sigurd Grindheim, "Ignorance is Bliss: Attitudinal Aspects of the Judgment according to Works in Matthew 25:31–46," *NovT* 50 (2008): 313–31.
9   E.g. Grindheim, "Ignorance is Bliss," 313–31; Donald A. Hagner, "Law, Righteousness, and Discipleship in Matthew," *WW* 18 (1998): 364–71; Roger Mohrlang, *Matthew and Paul: A Comparison of Ethical Perspectives* (SNTSMS 48; Cambridge: Cambridge University Press, 1984).

ularities of first-century understandings of sin and righteousness.[10] Charette moves directly from recompense as found in the Hebrew Bible to Matthew, though there were broad shifts in the way recompense was understood throughout the strata of the Hebrew Bible and in the second temple period.[11]

Third, many, if not most, discussions of the wages of sin and righteousness in Matthew have treated the issue as a theological embarrassment that needs to be explained and have produced predictably one-sided results.[12] Günther Bornkamm offers a candid summary of the consternation that New Testament scholars have faced with the *Lohngedanken* of the New Testament:

> We find ourselves with a marked bias against the idea of wage [or "reward"] in the New Testament. Educated in the Kantian conception of duty [*Pflicht*], we immediately connect with the idea of wage the prospect of a debased eudaemonism that clouds the purity of a moral ethos. The idea of wage in ethics, so it is said, makes people's deeds dependent on extrinsic ends. The human will can no longer govern freely only by the suitability of its maxims. It strains after the outcome of its actions and no longer does the good for its own sake. The idea of wage is opposed to the high ideal, on which Plato, the Stoics, and Idealism agree, that justice is its own wage.

---

10 (JSNTSup 79; Sheffield: Sheffield Academic Press, 1992).

11 It is not uncommon for NT scholars to make "the Old Testament" – as circumscribed by the text and canon of the Masoretic tradition – the context for understanding the NT, thereby ignoring the manifold versions and interpretations of Israel's Scriptures that were actually in play in the first century. To his credit, Charette is unusually clear that this is what he is doing, though this clarity brings the anachronism into sharp relief. In Charette's own words, "The question as to whether (and if so, how) other writings subsequent to the Old Testament may have influenced Matthew is not of interest to the present study. For that reason, parallels to other materials (e.g. Deutero-canonical writings, Qumran texts, Rabbinic works) have not been cited. Since it is indisputable that Matthew was influenced by the Old Testament, it makes for a sound methodology to turn first to the Old Testament for insight before looking elsewhere" (*Theme of Recompense*, 19). There is a kernel of truth here: there can be no doubt that, say, Genesis or the Psalms were important to the Evangelist, whereas a text like *Joseph and Aseneth* is of questionable significance. The problem is that Charette et al. imagine a canonical and textual stability that did not exist in the first century. Worse yet is the fact that Charette's approach ignores the crucial question of how texts such as Genesis or the Psalms were interpreted in the first century.

12 Minear's *And Great Shall Be Your Reward* and Charette's *Theme of Recompense* are notable exceptions to this rule, though the former treats Matthew only sparingly.

Hence our *moral* misgivings against the idea of wage. The role played by the idea of wage in Catholic teaching on morals and justification strengthens our aversion to it even more. The concept of wage sanctions the concept of merit, and indeed, as it seems, with an undeniable logical consistency. For what can the concept of wage mean other than the payment that is due for work done? Do not wage and effort, wage and merit belong together in an indestructible relationship, so that whoever says the one [sc. "wage"] must also say the other [sc. "merit"]? And do not late Judaism and Catholicism, with their doctrine of the merit of good works, take the concept of "wage," which the Bible of the Old and New Testaments offers to them, just at its word? And do they not have the courage to draw out the implications for ethics and the doctrine of justification?… Hence our *religious* misgivings against the idea of wage.[13]

Indeed, Kant's conception of duty (*Pflicht*) – as well as the characteristically Protestant concerns behind it – cast a surprisingly long shadow over studies of wage in the New Testament.[14] For Kant, duty cannot

---

13 "Der Lohngedanke im Neuen Testament," 2.69–92. The original: "Wir befinden uns dem Lohngedanken des Neuen Testamentes gegenüber in einer merklichen Befangenheit. Erzogen in dem Kantischen Begriff der Pflicht, verbinden wir sofort mit dem Begriff Lohn die Vorstellung eines unterwertigen Eudamonismus, der die Reinheit sittlicher Gesinnung trübt. Der Lohngedanke in der Ethik, so heisst es, macht das Handeln des Menschen abhangig von fremden Zwecken, der menschliche Wille lässt sich nicht mehr in Freiheit bestimmen einzig von der Tauglichkeit seiner Maximen, er schielt nach dem Erfolg seines Tuns und tut das Gute nicht mehr um seiner selbst willen. Der Lohngedanke ist dem hohen Grundsatz, in dem Plato, die Stoa und der Idealismus einig sind, entgegengesetzt, dass nämlich die Gerechtigkeit ihren Lohn in sich selbst trage. Von daher unser *moralisches* Bedenken gegen den Lohngedanken. In der Abneigung gegenüber dem Lohngedanken bestärkt uns aber erst recht seine Verwendung in der katholischen Moral und Rechtfertigungslehre. Der Begriff des Lohnes sanktioniert ja hier den Begriff des Verdienstes, und zwar, wie es scheint, mit einer unbestreitbaren logischen Folgerichtigkeit. Denn was kann der Begriff des Lohnes anderes meinen, als ein schuldiges Entgelt für eine geleistete Arbeit? Gehoren nicht Lohn und Leistung, Lohn und Verdienst in einer unzerstorbaren Korrelation zusammen, so daß, wer das eine sagt, auch das andere sagen muß? Und nehmen nicht etwa das späte Judentum und der Katholizismus mit ihrer Lehre von der Verdienstlichkeit der guten Werke den Begriff „Lohn", den ihnen die Bibel Alten und Neuen Testamentes bietet, einfach nur beim Wort, und haben sie nicht eben nur den Mut, die Konsequenzen aus ihm für die Ethik und Rechtfertigungslehre zu ziehen? …Von daher unser *religiöses* Bedenken gegenüber dem Lohngedanken." (2.69–70)

14 E.g., F. C. Baur, *Vorlesungen über neutestamentiche Theologie* (Darmstadt: Wissenschaftliche Buchgesellschaft, 1864), 60–3; Ulrich Luz on Kant's influence on the interpretation of Matt 20:1–16 (*Das Evangelium nach Matthäus* [4 vols.; EKKNT; Düsseldorf: Benziger, 1985–2002], 3.144).

be based on anything hypothetical or contingent, such as the promise of
some happy outcome.[15] No deed can have moral worth if it is done to
attain something extrinsic to the deed itself. As Kant himself put it, "Die
Tugend in ihrer eigentlichen Gestalt erblicken, ist nichts anderes als die
Sittlichkeit von aller Beimischung des Sinnlichen und allem unechten
Schmuck des Lohns oder der Selbstliebe entkleidet darzustellen."[16]

Kant's seminal contention that the pursuit of *Lohn* is antithetical to
virtue placed New Testament scholars in an awkward position, for Jesus
seemed to have a lot to say about how to receive a *Lohn bei eurem Vater
im Himmel* (Matt 6:1), as Luther's translation put it. In 1950 Bo Reicke
noted that earlier generations of scholars were so influenced by Kant
that they tended to deny that the New Testament said anything at all
about rewards; twentieth century scholars, while less apt to deny outright the existence of rewards in the New Testament, still faced "great
problems as to how this reward should be conceived."[17] Those who
have attempted to deal with these problems have tended to rely on
one or more of the following claims: (1) Jesus did not use wages to motivate his followers. His commands, therefore, still qualify as "duty." (2)
Jesus admittedly talked about rewards from God, but only to transcend
and subvert the notions of reward that were current in his day. (3) The
parable of the workers in the vineyard is the key to understanding Jesus'
conception of wage, and its significance in the NT as a whole.

Strack and Billerbeck, who devote a chapter to the parable of the
workers in the vineyard and its significance for understanding the contrast between the New Testament teaching on wage and that of ancient
Judaism, illustrate this approach.[18] They aver that Jews thought that humans could do meritorious deeds that God would reward, whereas Jesus
taught that one must leave behind every thought of reward and simply
do one's duty. The question posed to the workers hired at the 11th hour

---

15 Duty is "eine Nötigung zu einem ungern genommenen Zweck." *Metaphysik
    der Sitten* (Philosophische Bibliothek 42; Leipzig: Dürr'schen, 1907), 386.
    And again, "Wir haben soviel also wenigstens dargetan, dass, wenn Pflicht
    ein Begriff ist, der Bedeutung und wirkliche Gesetzgebung für unsere Hand-
    lungen enthalten soll, diese nur in kategorischen Imperativen, keineswegs
    aber in hypothetischen ausgedrückt werden könne." *Grundlegung zur Metaphy-
    sik der Sitten* (Philosophische Bibliothek 41; Leipzig: Felix Meiner, 1925), 425.
16 *Grundlegung zur Metaphysik der Sitten*, 426.
17 "The New Testament Conception of Reward," 196.
18 *Kommentar Zum Neuen Testament zum Neuen Testament aus Talmud und Midrasch*
    (6 vols.; Munich: C. H. Beck, 1928), 4:484–500.

("Why are you standing here idle all day?") shows that "zur Mitarbeit im Reiche Gottes jeder ohne Ausnahme verpflichtet ist. Die Lohnfrage spielt dabei keine Rolle, sie wird gar nicht berührt; nur die Arbeitspflicht ist von prinzipieller Bedeutung."[19] Similarly, the remark of the landowner in 20:15 to the grumblers ("Am I not allowed to do what I choose with what belongs to me? Or are you envious because I am generous?") shows that:

> Work for God's kingdom does not proceed on the basis of a legal agreement between God and humans, so that the divine wage would correspond to human achievement, but rather the work is simply the duty of humans to be done without any regard for wages... This is the cornerstone and headstone of the New Testament teaching on wages, which is closely related to the New Testament teaching on justification.[20]

Like most scholars who address the issue up to the present day, Strack and Billerbeck assume without argument that the parable of the workers in the vineyard is the key to the New Testament understanding of wage. While detailed exegesis of the parable must wait until chapter 2, it is worth noting that the drama of the parable springs from the fact that those who were paid a standard wage for their work are offended by the master's decision to pay those who were hired late in the day more than they deserve. The scandal, in other words, is in the master's decision to be generous to those who had not worked the whole day; there is little hint that the workers are to forget the very concept of payment in favor of the pure *Pflicht* that is its own reward.[21]

The history of scholarship since Strack and Billerbeck reveals more of the same. In the mid-twentieth century Preisker and Würthwein placed a special emphasis on the workers in the vineyard in their article on μισθός in *TWNT*, arguing that Jesus admittedly spoke of reward, but this was only to transcend and free himself from the Jewish concept of

---

19 Ibid., 485
20 Ibid. "Die Arbeit für Gottes Reich vollzieht sich nicht auf Grund eines Rechtsvertrages zwischen Gott u. Mensch, so dass der göttliche Lohn der menschlichen Leistung entspräche, sondern die Arbeit ist einfach des Menschen Pflicht, die zu leisten ist ohne jede Rücksicht auf Lohn.... Das ist der Grund- u. Eckstein der neutestamentlichen Lohnlehre, die aufs engste mit der neutestamentlichen Rechtfertigungslehre zusammenhängt."
21 H. Heinemann ("The Conception of Reward in Mat. XX. 1 16," *JJS* 1 [1948]: 85–9) offers a very brief but incisive refutation of Strack and Billerbeck's exegesis as well as of their treatment of rabbinic literature.

merit.[22] Commenting on Matthew 6, Jeremias averred, "Hier ist deutlich, dass Jesus zwar die Vokabel 'vergelten' aufnimmt, dass er aber sa-
chlich voraussetzt, dass seine Jünger sich völlig von dem Lohnstreben
gelöst haben; sie sollen ja vergessen, was sie Gutes taten."[23] Bornkamm
claimed that the New Testament is free of eudaemonism, which "macht
ja das Urteil über Gut und Böse abhängig von den Folgen, die unser
Handeln hat."[24] Though Jesus spoke of reward in the Sermon on the
Mount, his command "do not let your left hand know what your
right hand is doing" (6:3) shows that Jesus forbade his followers to
make heavenly reward a motive for their actions.[25] Similarly, in
25:31–46 the surprise of the "sheep" when the Lord tells them they
have inherited the kingdom because of their deeds shows that one
must do meritorious deeds without realizing they are such.[26]

---

22 "μισθός," TWNT, 4.725.
23 Neutestamentliche Theologie (2 vols.; Gütersloh: Gütersloher Verlagshaus, 1971),
    1.209. It is not apparent how Jeremias knows that the disciples have detached
    themselves from striving for a reward; indeed, this speculation would seem to
    run against the grain of Jesus' command to "Store up for yourselves treasure in
    heaven" (6:20), and his instructions on how to avoid losing one's heavenly
    wage by seeking a wage from people (6:1–18). Cf., also on the preceding
    page: "Nun darf man aber nicht übersehen, dass Jesus an die Sprechweise der
    Zeit anknüpft, wenn er vom Lohn redet. Die religiöse Sprache ist konservativ,
    und vor allen Dingen in polemischen Zusammenhängen muss man von der
    Sprache der Gegner ausgehen" (208).
24 "Der Lohngedanke im Neuen Testament," 79.
25 "Wenn die Rechte nicht wissen darf, was die Linke tut, so heisst das ja nichts
    anderes, als dass nicht nur die andern, nein, nicht einmal der Handelnde selbst
    sich berechnend über sein eigenes Tun erheben darf. Wer den Lohn zum Motiv
    seines Gehorsams macht, der tut eben das, was Jesus verwehrt; er lässt die Re-
    chte wissen, was die Linke tut; während die Linke die Tat vollbringt, streckt
    schon die Rechte sich aus, den sicheren Lohn zu erhalten" (Ibid., 80). Perhaps
    it is unnecessary to point out that this interpretation of 6:3 is a literalistic con-
    fusion of Matthew's hyperbole; not letting the left hand know what the right is
    doing is a restatement of the main thesis of 6:1–21: do not perform your right-
    eousness for show or you will "have no wage with your Father in heaven"
    (6:1).
26 Ibid., 80. Grindheim ("Ignorance is Bliss"), Reicke ("The New Testament
    Conception of Reward," 203), and Jeremias (Neutestamentliche Theologie 209),
    make the same argument. I note in passing that the surprise of the "sheep" is
    not in response to the fact that work is rewarded. The surprise concerns who
    gets the wages; not those you might expect, but those who helped "the least
    of these." This interpretation is particularly puzzling in light of the fact that
    the parable itself uses the picture of the Last Judgment to motivate the readers
    to help "the least of these."

This Kantian stream of interpretation appears almost everywhere that "reward" in the teaching of Jesus is discussed until the present day.[27] In his 1966 article, "The Conception of Reward in the Teaching of Jesus," G. de Ru concluded:

> Service "for reward" is decisively rejected by Jesus. In that sense Kant and Idealism were right, when, because of their rigorous conception of "duty", they connected with the "conception of reward" the idea of an inferior eudaemonism, that defaces the purity of true morality. Everything that is done with an eye to a reward is egotistic, a residue of hedonism. ... A good deed brings its own reward. As the well-known aphorism of Kant has it: "Die Eudamonie ist die Euthanasie aller rechten Sittlichkeit".[28]

Similarly, Florian Voss's article, "Der Lohn der guten Tat," suggested that in the Sermon on the Mount wages "dient also nicht dazu, den Menschen zum gerechten Handeln zu motivieren, sie wird hier vielmehr mit der Frage verknüpft, von woher der Lohn, d. h. das dem Tun entsprechende 'Ergehen', erwartet wird: von den Menschen oder von Gott."[29] If this were the case, however, one wonders what hortatory force would be left in Jesus' warning "Beware of doing your righteousness before others in order to be seen by them; for then you have no reward with your Father in heaven" (6:1).

---

27 This is not to say that all these scholars are dependent on Kant, but that they share the post-Kantian doubt that good deeds should be motivated by hope for recompense of any kind. Explicit anti-Judaism and anti-Catholicism becomes increasingly rare in the latter part of the twentieth century. Cf., also James I. H. McDonald, "The Concept of Reward in the Teaching of Jesus" *ExpTim* 89 (1978): 269–73; Daniel Marguerat (*Le Jugement dans L'Évangile de Matthieu* [2nd ed.; *MdB* 6; Genève: Labor et Fides, 1995], 473) "*Le salaire, pas plus que la crainte du jugement, n'est le mobile de la fidélité éthique*" (emphasis original); Craig Blomberg ("Degrees of Reward in the Kingdom of Heaven?" *JETS* 35 [1992]: 159–72) treats as self-evident the pre-eminent place of the parable of the workers in the vineyard.

28 *NovT* 8 (1966): 202–22, 220. In 1968 Klaus Koch began his essay "Der Schatz im Himmel" (in *Leben Angesichts des Todes: Beiträge zum theologischen Problem des Todes: Helmut Thielicke zum 60. Geburtstag* [eds. Berhard Lohse and H. P. Schmidt; Tübingen: Mohr Siebeck, 1968), 47–60) noting that "Ein Ergebnis historischer Schriftforschung, das uns heute fremdartig berührt, ist die Rolle des Lohngedankens im Neuen Testament, scheint doch hier die Idee einer berechenbaren Korrespondenz von Leistung und Lohn aufzutauchen, die der Freiheit Gottes hohnspricht" (47–48).

29 "Der Lohn der guten Tat: Zur theologischen Bestimmung der Beziehung zwischen Matthäus und Paulus," *ZTK* 103 (2006): 333.

A final recent example should suffice to show the enduring influence of this line of interpretation. In his 2007 commentary, R. T. France wrote the following about Matthew 6:19–20:

> The verb "store up for yourselves" (literally, "make a treasure for yourselves") might suggest that these heavenly treasures are to be earned by the disciples' own efforts, and the frequent language of "reward" in this gospel easily conveys the same impression…[I]n 19:21 it is by giving to the poor that "a treasure in heaven" is to be secured; in 19:29 eternal life is spoken of as compensation for earthly losses, and in 25:21, 33, 34, 46 the heavenly rewards are directly linked to the disciples' use of earthly opportunities. But while the theme of reward is important in this gospel, we must remind ourselves again that in the parable which most directly addresses the issue (20:1–15) there is a deliberate discrepancy between the effort expended and the recompense received: God does not leave anyone unfairly treated, but his grace is not limited to human deserving. In a kingdom in which the first are last and the last first (19:30; 20:16) there is no room for computing one's "treasures in heaven" on the basis of earthly effort. *Those treasures are "stored up" not by performing meritorious acts (and certainly not only by almsgiving) but by belonging to and living by the priorities of the kingdom.*[30]

Few would quibble with France's contention that, for Matthew, God's "grace" is not limited to human deserving – though God's "repayment" would have better fit the Matthean idiom. Nevertheless, like most scholars who comment on reward in Matthew, France provides no rationale for his claim that the parable of the workers in the vineyard is the lens through which all the other passages – including the programmatic Sermon and the climactic 25:14–46 – must be read. Similarly problematic is France's rather oblique claim that heavenly treasure is not stored up by doing meritorious acts but by "belonging to and living by the priorities of the kingdom." It is not clear what "belonging to and living by" means in contradistinction to meritorious deeds; one is left with the general impression that for Matthew heavenly treasure is not stored up by selling one's possessions and giving the money to the poor (19:21) or by any other discrete good deed, but by identifying oneself with the kingdom. Ironically, this construal is close to an inversion of 25:31–46 where it is those who did not know they were serving Jesus but who did in fact do works of mercy who receive the kingdom. That is, those who actually did "meritorious deeds" enter into the kingdom rather than those who assume they belong (cf. also 7:21–22 and 21:28–32).

---

30 *The Gospel of Matthew* (NICNT; Grand Rapids: Eerdmans, 2007), 258–59. Emphasis added.

This brief examination of what one might call the Kantian stream of interpretation is not intended to suggest that whereas previous interpreters of heavenly wages in Matthew have been influenced by their prior commitments, I will now provide *das Ding an sich*. Rather, I hope to show only that much of the scholarship relevant to this study has been manifestly influenced by post-Kantian anxieties about recompense for righteousness which are foreign to Matthew.[31] It should also be noted that the purpose of this study is not to wrest Matthew from a Kantian and Protestant interpretative matrix only to insert it into some other modern framework, still less to engage in inter-confessional polemics. Rather, the goal of the study is to situate Matthew's debt and wage language firmly in its late first-century Jewish context. Indeed, the full force of the critique of previous readings of Matthew will not be apparent until chapter 2 when Matthew's debt and wage language is described against the backdrop of similar language in other early Jewish and Christian literature.[32]

---

31 This is not an endorsement of Kantian epistemology but only an admission of my own situatedness as an interpreter.

32 Not all who have been discomfited by Matthew's economic language have attempted to downplay it or deny its existence. See, e.g., Jacques Derrida's close reading and critique of Matthew in *The Gift of Death* (2d ed.; trans. David Wills; Chicago: University of Chicago Press, 2008), esp. 82–116. Derrida famously argued that true gift giving is impossible because humans always maintain some expectation of recompense, such as the gratitude of the recipient or even the personal satisfaction of being a gift-giver. For Derrida Matthew, which enjoins one not to let one's left hand know what one's right hand is doing etc., comes tantalizingly close to finding a way around such calculation only to spoil it in the end by succumbing to another sort of calculation: the hope of heavenly treasure. Thus, Matthew's economy begins by renouncing "earthly wages (*merces*) and a finite, accountable, exterior, visible market... only to capitalize on it by means of a profit or surplus value that was infinite, heavenly, incalculable, interior, and secret. A sort of secret calculation would continue to wager on the gaze of a God who sees the invisible, and who sees in my heart what I decline to have seen by my fellow humans" (109). David Bentley Hart's response to Derrida (*The Beauty of the Infinite: The Aesthetics of Christian Truth* [Grand Rapids, MI: Eerdmans, 2003], 260–68) is particularly relevant to Matthew. Hart suggests that "the inhuman extremism of a Kantian dogmatism regarding ethical disinterestedness has burdened Derrida with a definition of the gift that is simply a category mistake." The axiom that any desire or self-interest destroys the gift "assumes in some sense the priority of a subjectivity that possesses a moral identity prior to the complex exchanges of moral practices, of gift and gratitude[.] Or, if one has not assumed such a subjectivity, why allow the idea of the gift no wider ambit than is provided by this myth of the punctiliar

2. "Atonement"

A central burden of this study will be to show that Matthew's conception of sin and righteousness is not simply a theme which is more or less incidental to the narrative, but rather that some of the Gospel's central claims about Jesus emerge from this conceptual matrix and should be understood in light of it. To be more specific, a complete account of Matthew's grammar of sin and righteousness must ultimately deal with what is traditionally referred to as "atonement." No study of any length of which I am aware has examined atonement in Matthew in light of Matthew's economic language. I shall argue that this economic language is the idiom that Matthew uses to describe *how* Jesus saves "his people from their sins" (1:21).[33]

It would not be incorrect to say, therefore, that this is a study of atonement in Matthew. Nevertheless, to describe the project this way would be misleading in two respects. First, the word "atonement" privileges the default conception of sin of modern westerners: that of alienation or separation.[34] The conceptual framework of salvation from sins as at-one-ment (and thus also its obverse, sin as separation) is based in a

---

self whose ethical integrity consists in a kind of self-sufficient responsibility before an ethical sublime?" (262). Hart problematizes Derrida's argument by pointing out Derrida's implicit modernist commitment to disinterestedness. One might take this critique a step further by historicizing disinterestedness itself as a possibility sustained by the anonymity of capitalist markets. Rather than assuming a univocity in "market" or "exchange," it is necessary to attend to what valences "wages", "repayment", and "exchange" take on in different economic contexts: capitalism, local markets, bartering, the home, etc. In Matthew, the heavenly economy presupposes covenant (26:26–29), divine sonship (5:45; 6:9 etc.), the empowering presence of the Holy Spirit and Jesus (10:18–20; 18:19–20; 28:20), and the prior gift of Jesus' life for the many, which is not only vicarious, but also generative of a similar giving back on the part of the many. Payment on earth is indeed renounced in favor of another, heavenly repayment. Yet the more important question of what sort of economy of exchange such heavenly repayment participates in is far from resolved by easy accusations of the tainting influence of market and exchange. See also John Milbank, "Can a Gift be Given?", *Modern Theology* 11 (1995): 119–61.

33   This is perhaps not a surprise considering the relative paucity of discussions of atonement tout court in Matthean studies. E.g., Luz's *The Theology of the Gospel of Matthew* (Cambridge; New York: Cambridge University Press, 1995) contains no discussion of the topic.

34   Matthew does use images of separation to describe the final destination of the reprobate (22:13; 25:41).

spatial metaphor and is not simply a literal description of what sin *is*, despite the fact that atonement/separation has lost its evocative power due to its familiarity. Thus, as regrettable as it may be to marginalize the English language's one lasting contribution to our theological lexicon, I shall attempt to steer clear of the word "atonement" in order to avoid reinforcing the conception of sin and salvation embedded in much modern theology and in hope of enabling a more careful examination of Matthew's own conceptual framework.

Second, to speak of "atonement" or "soteriology" in Matthew is to risk implying that Matthew has something like an "atonement theory" – that is, a systematic, second order description – when there is nothing of the sort in Matthew. If this is a study of atonement, it is from below. To be sure, I shall argue that careful attention to Matthew's grammar of divine recompense in its late first-century Jewish context reveals a coherent description of how Jesus saves his people from their sins.[35] In other words, Matthew does not simply assert that Jesus saves his people from their sins and leave the reader to cook up an explanation as to how this happened. Nevertheless, if judged by the standards of subsequent systematic theology, this narrative soteriology leaves many loose ends.

This relatively modest claim, however, goes against the grain of most recent scholarship which has tended to conclude that Matthew's "atonement" language has no apparent meaning or significance. Davies and Allison's expression of bewilderment at 20:28 is frequently cited as representative:

> As it stands in Matthew, 20.28 states that Jesus was – note the one-time aorist – an atonement offering, a substitution, a ransom for sins. But almost every question we might ask remains unanswered. What is the condition of 'the many'? Why do they need to be ransomed? To whom is the ransom paid…?….Even when 1.21 and 26.26–9 are taken into account it is impossible to construct a Matthean theory of the atonement. We have in the Gospel only an unexplained affirmation.[36]

Likewise, Luz writes the following about 20:28: "Der genaue Sinn der Aussage bleibt also relativ unbestimmt. Für Mt ist hier wahrscheinlich weniger der Loskauf- oder 'Ersatz'gedanke wichtig als die Radikalität

---

35 I use the word "coherent" in contradistinction to "systematic," following the distinction made by E. P. Sanders, ("Did Paul's Theology Develop?" in *The Word Leaps the Gap: Essays in Scripture and Theology in Honor of Richard B. Hays* [ed. J. Ross Wagner et al.; Grand Rapids: Eerdmans, 2008], 325–50).

36 *A Critical and Exegetical Commentary on the Gospel according to Saint Matthew* (3 vols; ICC; Edinburgh: T&T Clark, 1988–1997), 3.100.

des Dienstes Jesu: So ernst nahm Jesus den Dienst an anderen Menschen, daß er sein eigenes Leben für 'viele' gab."[37] This passage raises
many questions about the meaning of Jesus' death, but "[s]ie sind von
Mt her kaum zu beantworten."[38] John T. Carroll and Joel B. Green
offer a similarly vague formulation: "Somehow, in the mystery of the
divine action, the death of Jesus fulfills his mission, embodied in his
very name, to effect the salvation of the people through the forgiveness
of their sins (cf. 1:21)."[39] John Nolland avers that "what exactly is
thought to be involved in the Son of Man giving his life as a ransom
for many remains quite imprecise."[40] Matthean scholarship faces a curious situation: there is general agreement that a central concern of the
Gospel is to present Jesus as the one who saves his people from their
sins, but there is little if any idea about what this means.[41]

A few more recent studies have attempted to describe atonement in
Matthew with greater specificity. Warren Carter and Boris Repschinski
provide rich descriptions of the biblical resonances of Matthew's descriptions of Jesus' saving activity.[42] In a recent monograph Leroy Huizenga suggests that Matthew presents Jesus as a new Isaac and that his

---

37 *Matthäus*, 3.166.
38 Ibid.
39 "His Blood on Us and On Our Children: The Death of Jesus in the Gospel
    according to Matthew" in *The Death of Jesus in Early Christianity* (John T. Car-
    roll and Joel B. Green, eds.; Peabody, Mass.: Hendrickson, 1995), 44.
40 *The Gospel of Matthew: A Commentary on the Greek Text* (NIGTC; Grand Rap-
    ids, MI.: Eerdmans, 2005), 826.
41 Even a cursory side-glance at Matthew's redaction of Mark demonstrates the
    Gospel's special interest in relating Jesus to salvation from sins; there are, argu-
    ably, three key statements in Matthew relating either to sin or the purpose of
    Jesus' death, all at critical junctures in the narrative: 1:21, 20:28, and 26:26–
    28. While the ransom saying is nearly identical to the Markan version, there
    are two important changes here vis-à-vis Mark. First, 1:21 is unique; Matthew
    alone begins his gospel by connecting Jesus' mission and name to salvation from
    sins. Second, Matthew omits any mention of John's baptism being εἰς ἄφεσιν
    ἁμαρτιῶν, but adds that same phrase at the Last Supper to describe the purpose
    for which Jesus' blood is poured out.
42 Warren Carter, *Matthew: Storyteller, Interpreter, Evangelist* (Peabody, Mass.: Hen-
    drickson Publishers, 1996), 211–25; Boris Repschinski, "For He Will Save His
    People from Their Sins (Matthew 1:21): A Christology for Christian Jews,"
    CBQ 68 (2006): 248–67. Oddly, Repschinski never mentions 20:28. Cf.,
    also Daniel M. Gurtner, *The Torn Veil: Matthew's Exposition of the Death of
    Jesus* (SNTSMS 139; Cambridge: Cambridge University Press, 2007),
    esp.126–37.

death inaugurates a new divinely ordained sacrifice just as the Akedah was seen as the basis of the temple and its sacrifices.[43] Petri Luomanen analyzes key passages dealing with God's demand on human beings in order to analyze the relationship between "getting in" and "staying in."[44] For all the many insights of these studies, none of them examines how Jesus "saves his people from their sins" in light of what sin and righteousness mean in the narrative. This omission leads to a tendency to deal with Jesus' saving work, on the one hand, and divine recompense for human behavior, on the other, in abstraction from each other.

3. Interpretive Method

Having described the need for this project, I shall now offer a brief explanation and defense of the methodology to be employed. The main methodology employed in this study is a form of narrative criticism. Defined simply, the sweep of the story as a whole is the main object of study and the primary frame of reference for understanding any part therein. In chapters one and two it will be necessary to describe Matthew's wage and debt language and its relationship to similar language in other early Jewish and Christian texts. This initial, thematic description is, however, a preliminary step toward an exposition of the significance of wages and debts for understanding the narrative in its entirety.

Narrative studies of the Gospels have a reputation, perhaps not undeserved, for ignoring history. Yet, there is nothing intrinsic in the attempt to read ancient narratives as narratives that requires one to pretend there is no world outside the story. Indeed, feigned ignorance of Matthew's *Sitz im Leben*, if followed through rigorously, would make it impossible to read the Greek. To read a narrative well – that is, to read with the sympathy and patience necessary to have a sense of how the implied authorial audience would have read it – is to immerse oneself in the "cultural encyclopedia" of the narrative's production.[45] Indeed,

---

43 *The New Isaac: Tradition and Intertextuality in the Gospel of Matthew* (NovTSup 131; Leiden: Brill, 2009), 263–91.

44 *Entering the Kingdom of Heaven: A Study on the Structure of Matthew's View of Salvation* (WUNT 11/101; Tübingen: Mohr Siebeck, 1998).

45 Mark Allan Powell notes that narrative criticism "demands that the modern reader have the historical information that the text assumes of its implied reader. Attention must be paid to what Iser calls 'the reader's repertoire.'" *What is Narrative Criticism* (Minneapolis: Augsburg Fortress, 1990), 97. Cf., Graham Stan-

one of the main axes to grind in this study is that previous work on the Gospel has not paid sufficient attention to the way its wage and debt language would have been heard in a late first-century Jewish-Christian setting. What separates a narrative approach from much other work on the Gospels is that the main object of study is the story itself, rather than the prehistory of its parts or the authorial *Sitz*. Matthew's Gospel is after all the principal source of all we might know about the Evangelist's setting in life or about how he used sources; one could argue, therefore, that careful attention to the sweep of the narrative as a whole can only enrich one's understanding of these other, more remote objects of study. In other words, far from being ahistorical, narrative analysis attends to the artifact history has actually bequeathed us: the story.[46]

---

ton: "Close attention to the 'story world' of Matthew alone will not enable us to appreciate why and how he uses apocalyptic imagery. Many individual sayings and incidents will baffle us unless they are set in the context of first century Jewish (or Christian) teaching." *A Gospel for a New People: Studies in Matthew* (Louisville: Westminster John Knox, 1993),73.

46 There is good evidence in the Gospel itself that it is written to be read with attention to the sweep of the entire story. To name just a few examples out of many, the fulfillment quotation in 1:23 ("…they will call his name Emmanuel, which is translated God with us") and the final words of the risen Jesus in 28:20 ("Behold I am with you always until the end of the age") form an inclusio around the whole of the Gospel. Matthew is also replete with narrative foreshadowing; for instance, the first four chapters foreshadow many of the high points of the story; the threat to Jesus' life from the chief priests, scribes, and "all Jerusalem" point forward to Jesus' arrest and crucifixion, the coming of the magi and the preaching of John the Baptist presage the Gentile mission which is not announced until the resurrection (see also 4:15), and John the Baptist's arrest anticipates Jesus' (Davies and Allison, *Matthew*, 1.93–94). Not without reason does Luz affirm that "Das Matthäusevangelium ist eine Geschichte, die von Anfang bis zum Schluss gelesen werden will. Sie erschliesst sich erst einer – wenn möglich mehrmaligen – Lektüre des Ganzen" ("Eine thetische Skizze der matthäischen Christologie," in *Anfänge der Christologie: Festschrift für Ferdinand Hahn zum 65. Geburtstag* [ed. Ferdinand Hahn et al.; Göttingen: Vandenhoeck & Ruprecht, 1991], 221).
      The current debate concerning the genre of the Gospels also suggests that they were written to be understood as coherent wholes. Richard Burridge, following David Aune and Charles Talbert among others, has shown that the Gospels resemble Greco-Roman *bioi* as much as works which are commonly acknowledged as examples of this genre resemble each other (Richard Burridge, *What Are the Gospels? A Comparison with Greco-Roman Biography* [2d ed.; Grand Rapids: Eerdmans, 2004]; David Aune, *The New Testament in its Literary Environment* [Philadelphia: Westminster Press, 1987]; Charles Talbert, *What is a Gospel? The Genre of the Canonical Gospels* [Philadelphia: Fortress

A narrative study that takes the historical setting of the Gospel seriously cannot ignore the question of sources, even if it insists on keeping the narrative horse firmly in front of the source and redaction-critical cart.[47] I regard Markan priority as a serviceable hypothesis and will, therefore, not prescind from making note of Matthew's redaction of Mark when it illuminates the story. At the same time, however, I am not persuaded that the Q hypothesis is the best explanation of the synoptic double tradition material.[48] In light of the fact that Q skepticism remains a minority position it is necessary to point out that the absence of Q rarely influences the exegesis in this study, and, on the few occasions when it does, I will make note of the differences that might follow. It is also worth noting that Q skepticism offers at least one serious advantage in a narrative-critical study: rather than comparing Matthew to a hypothetical source, I will compare Matthew to the actual, extant Gospel of Luke.

Press, 1977]). Burridge's arguments have not convinced everyone; Adela Collins, for instance, has stressed the similarity between the Gospels and Greco-Roman histories (*Mark: A Commentary* [Hermeneia; Minneapolis: Fortress Press, 2007], 15–43). Others have noted that the Septuagintal style of the gospels would seem to indicate that the Evangelists were imitating biblical narratives. Though consensus remains elusive, an important datum emerges from the debate: the Gospels share characteristics with *bioi*, Old Testament narratives, and Greco-Roman histories, all of which are, generally speaking, coherent narratives which are best understood in light of their whole. For the purposes of this discussion, then, it may be of little import which type of narrative Matthew's first auditors would have seen as Matthew's closest relative; all of the main contenders would have indicated that Matthew was a coherent narrative. Matthew identifies itself as a story, whatever else it might be.

47 C. Kavin Rowe's comments on Luke's use of Mark apply, *mutatis mutandis*: "Luke did have sources, and to ignore known sources is actually to forfeit insight into Luke's narrative. One need not think in the manner of 'old-school' *Redaktionsgeschichte* that we can detect Luke's theology – broken up, no less, into pericope-size theologies – solely on the basis of his departure from Mark to recognize that Luke's departure from Mark is of potential interpretive significance." *Early Narrative Christology* (Berlin: Walter de Gruyter & Co., 2006), 16.

48 The definitive defense of Markan priority without Q is found in Mark Goodacre, *The Case Against Q: Studies in Markan Priority and the Synoptic Problem* (Harrisburg, PA: Trinity Press International, 2002). See also E. P. Sanders and Margaret Davies, *Studying the Synoptic Gospels* (London: SCM Press, 1989), 51–119.

4. Distinguishing *ab quo*, *ad quem*, and *de quo* (Or: What is Matthew about?)

I have argued here for the legitimacy if not supremacy of a narrative critical approach to Matthew's Gospel, in contradistinction to diachronic investigations of Matthew's component traditions. But what is the narrative about? Many recent treatments of Matthew have assumed that the Gospel is in large part about "the Matthean community." Luz, for example, calls Matthew an *inklusive Geschichte*, that is, a story that "ihre eigenen Erfahrungen einschließt" by interweaving the experiences of the community of the author into a narrative that ostensibly concerns events in the past. It is, Luz writes, "ähnlich wie die johanneische Jesusgeschichte, ein 'two-level-drama', in dem die vergangene Geschichte Jesu zugleich die Geschichte und Gegenwartssituation der Gemeinde darstellt und verstehbar macht."[49]

One must concede that all narratives about events in the past are "inclusive stories" in the sense that even the most antiquarian author is indelibly shaped by her own experiences. An account of the Vietnam War written by a veteran of the Iraq War would see the former conflict through the lens of the experience of the latter; an account written after 70 C.E. of a prophet who had overturned tables in the temple could hardly fail to be shaped by the experience of the destruction of the temple. But Luz, whom I take here to be representative of a sizable stream of Matthean scholarship, occasionally goes beyond the modest hermeneutical observation that all narratives about past events are shaped by the experiences surrounding their composition and reads Matthew's Gospel as if it were *about* the experiences of the Matthean community, despite the fact that the narrative is ostensibly about Jesus of Nazareth. For instance, commenting on 19:28–29, where Jesus promises twelve thrones to the twelve apostles for having left all their possessions, Luz asserts that these thrones are in fact promised to the whole Matthean community which the apostles represent. Matthew's depiction of the twelve is not just influenced by the concerns of "the community"; the twelve *are* the community. The textual representation of the twelve contains little or no historical referentiality. They recall no memory of a

---

49 *Matthäus*, 1.37. cf. J. Louis Martyn, *History and Theology in the Fourth Gospel* (3d ed.; NTL; Louisville: Westminster John Knox Press, 2003).

group of people distinguishable from Matthew's community. They are, in this passage at least, only a cipher.[50]

To be sure, there are numerous hints suggesting Matthew was written in the late first century by a Jewish-Christian who was in conflict with pharisaic Judaism and who supported a Gentile mission, and who may have hailed from Antioch.[51] What redaction critics have tended to assume rather than argue, however, is that the *a quo* of the Gospel is the same thing as its *ad quem* and *de quo*.[52] All narratives which purport to convey past events are influenced by the circumstances of their composition, and some are better than others at concealing tell-tale anachronisms. But there is an important difference between the sort of detective work that goes against the grain of the *intentio operis* by using such tell-tale signs to attempt a reconstruction of the world behind the text and an interpretation of the text on its own terms. This distinction is of no little significance for interpreting the First Gospel because there is good evidence within Matthew itself that it was not written exclusively for – let alone *about* – the community of its origin.

In the 1990s a growing number of scholars began questioning aspects of the dominant community-centered approach of redaction criticism. In 1993 Graham Stanton pointed out that there may have been no

---

50   The Markan parallel (10:28–31) illuminates the difficulty of reading the twelve as a symbol of "the community." In Mark, after the young man goes away Peter points out "Behold, *we* have left everything" (28). Jesus gives a generic reply rather than promising any specific recompense for the disciples: *no one who leaves his possessions behind will fail to receive a hundred times as much.* The Matthean version, in contrast, draws attention to the twelve in particular. Peter points out "Behold, we have left everything and followed you" and then asks pointedly, "What then will there be for us?" Jesus gives a two-part answer, promising twelve thrones for the apostles (ἀμὴν λέγω ὑμῖν ὅτι ὑμεῖς οἱ ἀκολουθήσαντές μοι ἐν τῇ παλιγγενεσίᾳ, ὅταν καθίσῃ ὁ υἱὸς τοῦ ἀνθρώπου ἐπὶ θρόνου δόξης αὐτοῦ, καθίσεσθε καὶ ὑμεῖς ἐπὶ δώδεκα θρόνους κρίνοντες τὰς δώδεκα φυλὰς τοῦ Ἰσραήλ). He then goes on to promise that whoever (πᾶς ὅστις) leaves his possessions will receive a hundred times as much and eternal life. Cf. the twelve foundations of the new Jerusalem on which are written the names of "the twelve apostles of the Lamb" (Rev 21:14) as well as the twenty-four elders which appear to represent the twelve apostles and the twelve tribes. See also Luke 22:28–30.

51   Luz's own discussion of the issue is sober and insightful (*Matthäus*, 1.84–104).

52   Richard Bauckham, "For Whom Were Gospels Written," in *The Gospels for All Christians: Rethinking the Gospel Audiences* (ed. by Richard Bauckham; Grand Rapids: Eerdmans, 1998), 9–48.

"Matthean community" at all, but rather "Matthean communities."[53] In his study on books and readers in early Christianity, Harry Gamble noted that the careful literary crafting the Gospels combined with "the small size of individual Christian congregations in the first century make it unlikely that any of the Gospels was composed for the strictly local and intramural use of a single community."[54] A few years later Richard Bauckham and others mounted a more expansive challenge to the community-centered tradition of gospel interpretation.[55] According to Bauckham, the ease of travel and communication in the empire and the ecumenical consciousness of the early church, combined with the globe-trotting tendency of early Christian leaders, militate against the

---

53 Stanton, *Gospel for a New People,* 51. Cf. also Stanton's cautionary note: "Matthew is writing a gospel, not a letter. The literary genre chosen by Matthew indicates to his readers or listeners the expectations they should have. The evangelist's primary aim is to set out the story of Jesus. That he does so from a particular perspective is undeniable. What is less clear is the extent to which that perspective is *directly* related to the views and circumstances of the addressees" (45); And again: "the older view that the individual gospels circulated only in limited geographical areas is no longer tenable: the papyri…indicate clearly that there was a great deal of contact between different regions around the Mediterranean" ("The Fourfold Gospel," *NTS* 43 [1997]: 317–46, 336).

54 *Books and Readers in the Early Church: A History of Early Christian Texts* (New Haven: Yale University Press, 1995), 102.

55 "For Whom Were Gospels Written." Though Bauckham cites Streeter (*The Four Gospels: A Story of Origins* [London: MacMillan, 1924], 12) as the origin of the "community" approach (14), Wrede had already made the needs of "the community" a cornerstone of his argument about the messianic secret: "Das Bewusstsein, dass ich Darstellungen vor mir habe, deren Autoren spätere – wenn auch noch so frühe – Christen sind, Christen, die das Leben Jesu nur mit den Augen ihrer Zeit ansehen konnten, *die es aus dem Glauben der Gemeinde, mit allen Anschauungen der Gemeinde, für die Bedürfnisse der Gemeinde beschrieben –* dies Bewusstsein darf mich keinen Augenblick verlassen" (*Das Messiasgeheimnis in den Evangelien: Zugleich ein Beitrag zum Verständnis des Markusevangeliums* [Göttingen: Vandenhoeck und Ruprecht, 1963], 2, emphasis added). While commenting on Jacob Neusner's application of the community-centered approach to rabbinic literature, Seth Schwartz (*Imperialism and Jewish Society, 200 B.C.E. to 640 C.E.* [Princeton: Princeton University Press, 2001], 8–9) argues that in both rabbinic and NT scholarship, what started as a cautious, skeptical position (i.e., read a document in light of the circumstances of its composition) metastasized into an implausible positivism that reifies the hermeneutical models "into real communities, which are supposed to have existed more or less in isolation from each other, so that each literary work is approached as if it here the hypostasis of a single monadic community" (9).

view that the evangelists wrote about and for their own communities.[56] Bauckham may have exaggerated certain aspects of his argument, but few would deny that his proposal deserves serious consideration.[57]

More importantly, however, there are a number of points specific to Matthew that complement and fill out these rather broad observations, suggesting that Matthew was intended for a wide audience. First, in 28:19–20 the risen Jesus commands the disciples to teach all nations "to obey all that I have commanded you." This shows the Evangelist was concerned with spreading his message far and wide. It seems likely that one of the ways Matthew thought his audience should teach new peoples all that Jesus had commanded was by disseminating this very Gospel with its heavy emphasis on the authoritative teachings of Jesus. Thus, 28:19–20 suggests that Matthew was written in part as catechesis for wider consumption.

Second, Matthew's probable use of Mark is illuminating in a number of respects. Unless Mark and Matthew belonged to the same community, it would have been natural for Matthew to assume that his Gospel would circulate beyond his immediate situation just as Mark's had

---

56 E.g., Peter, Paul and his cohorts, the seer of Revelation, the Johannine letters, Ignatius, Polycarp, and the leaders mentioned in the Didache 11–13. See also Michael Thompson, "The Holy Internet: Communication Between Churches in the First Christian Generation," in *The Gospels for All Christians*, 49–70.

57 E.g., Margaret Mitchell has taken issue with Bauckham's claim that no one read the gospels as if they were addressed to particular communities until modernity, noting that patristic writers already thought the gospels were directed toward particular audiences ("Patristic Counter-evidence to the Claim that 'the Gospels were Written for All Christians,'" *NTS* 51 [2005]: 36–79). While the evidence adduced by Mitchell nuances some of Bauckham's claims, it is of questionable significance for understanding Matthew; the patristic evidence does not suggest that Matthew wrote for a single, insular community, but that he wrote in Hebrew for Jews. Moreover, it is not clear that this testimony is based on actual knowledge of the evangelists' situations rather than the exigencies of early Christian apologetics. For example, in his homilies on Matthew, cited by Mitchell, Chrysostom emphasized Matthew's supposed Hebrew audience in order to explain its divergences from the other Gospels (*Hom. Matt.* 1.3). See now Bauckham's rebuttal: "Is there Patristic Counter-Evidence? A Response to Margaret Mitchell," in *The Audience of the Gospels: The Origin and Function of the Gospels in Early Christianity* (ed. Edward W. Klink III; LNTS; London: T & T Clark, 2009), 68–110. See also the objections raised by David C. Sim ("The Gospel for All Christians?" A Response to Richard Bauckham," *JSNT* 84 [2001]: 3–27) and the rebuttal of Sim by Mike Bird ("Bauckham's *The Gospel for All Christians* Revisited," *EuroJTh* 15 [2006]: 5–13, esp.7–9).

from his. In other words, when Matthew wrote his Gospel the only existing template was a circulating Gospel; this makes it unlikely that Matthew was written with only a single, local community in mind.

Third, the fact that Matthew repeats almost all of Mark suggests that Matthew is not the product of a highly insular community of Christians, but is rather the product of an author who was willing to base his Gospel largely on traditions handed down from another author or community. To be sure, there is little doubt that Matthew found Mark unsatisfactory in certain respects (e. g., Mark 7:19; Matt 15:17). Yet, despite notable disagreements, Matthew remains a deeply Markan Gospel, a fact which attests both to Matthew's openness to influences from outside his local church and to his conservatism with the traditions he received.[58]

Fourth, the Gospel according to Matthew received fairly speedy and widespread dissemination and acceptance in the early church.[59] It is certainly possible that this was contrary to the Evangelist's intentions, but considered alongside of the fact that Matthew was modeled after Mark, which was a circulating Gospel, and that Matthew ends with the Great Commission, it is likely that Matthew was written for the widespread dissemination that it in fact achieved.

Finally, Matthew lacks any reference to circumcision. It is not certain whether or not Matthean Christians circumcised Gentile converts. John P. Meier and John Kenneth Riches, for example, say they did not;

---

58 Matthew repeats some 90 % of Mark and, as Christopher Tuckett wisely notes, material copied from a source may be just as indicative of the writer's views as the changes the he makes (*Reading the New Testament: Methods of Interpretation* [London: SPCK, 1987], 12). Mark Goodacre has shown that the sloppy application of redaction criticism has obscured the fact that Matthew's portrayal of Peter is remarkably similar to Mark's ("The Rock on Rocky Ground: Matthew, Mark and Peter as Skandalon" in *What Is It That the Scripture Says?: Essays in Biblical Interpretation, Translation, And Reception in Honour of Henry Wansbrough OSB* [ed. Philip McCosker; LNTS; London & New York: Continuum, 2006], 61–7.

59 E.g., Ignatius (c. 110) seems to know Matthew (*inter alia, Smyrn.* 1); Papias (c. 130) knows of a Gospel of Matthew, though he claims it was written in Hebrew (*Hist. Eccl.* 3.39); Justin Martyr (c. 150) cites Matthew's birth narrative (*Dial.* 106.4); Celsus (c. 178) critiqued passages found only in Matthew; both *Did.* (c. 100?) and 1 Peter (c. 80) may be based in part on Matthew. For a detailed discussion see E. Massaux, *The Influence of the Gospel of Saint Matthew on Christian Literature before Saint Irenaeus* (3 vols.; New Gospel Studies 5; Macon, GA: Mercer University Press, 1990).

David C. Sim argues to the contrary.[60] Regardless of which side Matthew himself actually came down on, it seems likely that this was a controversial issue for him and his community/ies. If Matthean Christians had insisted that Gentile converts be baptized but not circumcised (see 28:19–20) it would have caused conflict with Jewish Christian groups, as well as non-Christian Jews. But if Matthean Christians had insisted on circumcision they would have been at loggerheads with Pauline Christianity. In any case, the fact that the Matthean Jesus never addresses this issue at all, despite his many sayings about the Law, further underscores Matthew's conservatism with his sources and raises serious questions about our ability to perform mirror readings.[61]

The hermeneutical upshot of these observations is a justification of a narrative critical reading of Matthew that makes every effort to situate the Gospel in its historical setting without equating *Sitz* and *Sache*. This is not to deny that the subject of a narrative and the setting in life of the author are closely related. Differently put, it is undeniable that every story is told from the perspective of the story-teller. For example, it is commonly and rightly argued that 26:26–28 and 28:19 presuppose and reinforce the eucharistic and baptismal practices with which Matthew was familiar; bearing this in mind allows one to read the narrative with more sympathy for how its first auditors might have heard it. But if the distinction between the pastness of the narrative and the pres-

---

60   John P. Meier, *Matthew* (Collegeville, Minn.: Liturgical Press, 1990), 371–72; John Kenneth Riches, *Conflicting Mythologies: Identity Formation in the Gospels of Mark and Matthew* (Studies of the New Testament and Its World; Edinburgh: T&T Clark, 2000), 216–22; David C. Sim, "Christianity and Ethnicity in the Gospel of Matthew," in *Ethnicity and the Bible* (ed. G. Brett; Biblical Interpretation Series 19; Leiden: Brill, 1996), 171–95.

61   Cf., N. T. Wright's observation that "a good many matters were debated prominently in the early church which have left no record in the gospels at all. There is nothing in the gospels about circumcision; nothing about food offered to idols; nothing about speaking in tongues; about incest; about, in fact, the multitude of matters discussed in 1 Corinthians (a good example, since it is something of a repository of pressing early Christian issues). The only exception, a point at which something discussed in the letter occurs also in the gospel narratives, is divorce; and, precisely at that point, Paul refers explicitly to a word of Jesus" (*Jesus and the Victory of God* [Minneapolis: Fortress Press, 1996], 373). The force of Wright's argument lessens when one considers other issues which are common to Paul and the Synoptics, such as food more generally (Rom 14; Gal 2; Matt 15:1–20), Sabbath and calendar (Gal 4:9–10; Matt 12:1–14), and Jesus' return (1 Thess 4; 2 Thess 2; Matt 24).

ent experiences of Matthew's first auditors were collapsed, the etiological power of the narrative would disappear.

1 Heavenly Treasure and Debts in Early Judaism and Christianity

1.1 Introduction

How would a late first-century Jewish-Christian audience understand Jesus' claim that "Everyone who has left houses or brothers or sisters or father or mother or children or fields for my name's sake will receive a hundredfold, and will acquire eternal life" (19:29), or his advice to the rich young man: "Go, sell your possessions, and give the money to the poor, and you will have treasure in heaven" (19:21)? Did this heavenly treasure have anything do with the "debts" that one asks God to forgive (6:12)? In order to facilitate a historically sensitive response to these questions, it is important to provide some context by examining heavenly treasure and debts in other early Jewish and Christian texts. I shall not attempt to provide a comprehensive account of heavenly treasure in early Judaism and Christianity. Such a venture is unnecessary in the wake of Anderson's work and would at any rate be impossible in a monograph devoted to Matthew.[1] Nevertheless, by sampling texts from the Hebrew Bible, Septuagint, apocryphal and pseudepigraphical literature, as well as early Christianity and rabbinic Judaism, one can see broad agreements across distances of time, geography, and sect that make it is possible to give a thicker account of heavenly treasure in Matthew.

One note before beginning in earnest: a question these texts inevitably raise is how literal they are. Were these authors envisioning actual physical treasures and debts with scales and ledgers in some heavenly space, or are these metaphorical descriptions intended to sharpen understanding of God's just recompense of good and bad deeds?[2] There is no simple answer to this question, and there is no answer that applies with equal suitability to all the texts considered here. For now, it must suffice

---

1   See also Tzvi Novick, "Wages from God: The Dynamics of a Biblical Metaphor," *CBQ* 73 (2011): 708–22.

2   Jonathan T. Pennington argues convincingly that the phrase ἡ βασιλεία τῶν οὐρανῶν has spatial connotations in Matthew (*Heaven and Earth in the Gospel of Matthew* (NovTSup 126; Leiden: Brill, 2007), 279–99. See the discussion in chapter 2.

to mention two convictions that will guide the analysis. First, the border between literal and metaphorical language tends to be blurry. Much of what one might consider literal language was once metaphorical (does electricity *literally* "flow" and move in a "current"?). In ancient Jewish and Christian texts images that were once metaphorical can over time become the basis of quite literal doctrines.[3] It follows from this that images and expressions can be in a state of flux somewhere between strictly literal and metaphorical language. If it is difficult to ascertain whether a particular statement is literal or metaphorical it may be that there is no clear cut answer, even in the speaker's own mind. Second, the economic language which gained such prevalence in texts such as Matthew could hardly be purely ornamental. When a cluster of metaphors forms part of the essential grammar for describing a particular thing it inevitably shapes the way that thing is understood. For instance, the varying metaphors for sin in the Hebrew Bible – sin as burden, stain, or debt – shape the way sin is understood in those texts at a fundamental level.[4] Thus, even if a text uses "metaphorical" descriptions of treasure in heaven, these metaphors cannot simply be set aside for some other conceptual register.

---

3   See, e.g., Ps 22:30, where the even the dead ("all those who go down to the dust…who cannot keep themselves alive") are included in the praise of God. Noting that this prayer emerges in a period before the doctrine of an afterlife began to play a significant role in Jewish thought, Ellen F. Davis comments: "…the psalmist's joyful confidence that God is responsive to his plea demands that the dead above all may not be excluded from celebration and worship. It is the exuberance of the poetic vision that explodes the limits of Israel's traditional understandings. The shift in thought occurs first within the linguistic sphere, when a poet's productive imagination glimpses a possibility that only later (perhaps even centuries later) will receive doctrinal formulation as the resurrection of the dead" ("Exploding the Limits: Form and Function in Psalm 22," in *The Poetical Books* [The Biblical Seminar 41; ed. David J. A. Clines; Sheffield, 1997], 135–46, 144).

4   Gary Anderson *Sin: A History* (New Haven: Yale University Press, 2009), esp. 3–14. Anderson draws on George Lakoff and Mark Johnson's *Metaphors We Live By* (Chicago: University of Chicago Press, 1980).

1.2 Heavenly Treasures and Debts before the First Century

Some of the earliest hints of treasure in heaven appear in the book of Proverbs. For instance, Proverbs 19:17 says "He who is generous to the poor makes a loan (מלוה/δανίζει) to the LORD, and he will repay (ישלם/ἀνταποδώσει) him." This verse is as simple as it is surprising: when giving money to the poor, one not only makes a gift to God but a loan that God will repay.[5] In sharing one's earthly treasure one gains treasure with God. While this verse does not specify what form God's repayment of the loan will take, Proverbs 10:2 may shed light on the matter: "Treasuries of the wicked person do not profit, but righteousness (צדקה/δικαιοσύνη) delivers from death." Similarly, 11:4 says "Riches do not profit in the day of wrath, but righteousness delivers from death." Though צדקה could refer to righteousness in general, the antithetical parallel with the "treasuries of the wicked person" and "riches" suggests that צדקה may refer here to riches stored up by almsgiving.[6] The wicked store up wealth, but such earthly treasure cannot save a person from death. Righteousness funds a more reliable treasury that does protect one from death, which may be the "repayment" envisioned in 19:17.[7]

Skipping ahead to the first century for just a moment, it is noteworthy that these proverbs are read in precisely the manner suggested here in book two of the Sibylline Oracles:

> To beggars freely give, nor put them off.
> To the needy give with hands dripping with grain.
> The one who gives alms knows how to make a loan to God [Prov 19:17].

---

5   See also Prov 14:21, 31; 28:8 and Anderson's discussion in *Sin*, 139–146. Anderson (*Sin*, 140) notes that in the Babylonian Talmud, R. Yohanan comments "Had it not been written in scripture, it would have been impossible to say it! It is as though the borrower becomes a slave to the one who offers the loan [Prov 22:7]." BT *B. Bathra*, 10a.

6   Bradley C. Gregory (*Like an Everlasting Signet Ring: Generosity in the Book of Sirach* [DCLS 2; Berlin: Walter de Gruyter, 2010], 178) shows that Ben Sira is the first author to use the Hebrew צדקה to refer unambiguously to almsgiving, though Tobit had already used to the Aramaic cognate to do so. Second Temple and rabbinic texts tend to read this shift in meaning back into the HB (180). See also Yael Wilfand Ben Shalom, "Poverty, Charity and the Image of the Poor in Rabbinic Texts from the Land of Israel" (Ph.D. diss., Duke University, 2011), 64–70.

7   See also Ps 62, where God's steadfast repayment of all according to their deeds is contrasted with the ephemerality of wealth.

Alms deliver from death (ῥύεται ἐκ θανάτου ἔλεος [Prov 10:2/11:4]) when judgment comes.

Not sacrifice, but mercy (ἔλεος) God desires in place of sacrifice [Hos 6:6].[8]

The oracle reads the proverbs in light of each other and Hosea 6:6 to clarify how God repays the loan given to him by almsgiving; God will pay back the loan by saving the one who gives alms on the day of judgment.[9]

The book of Tobit, which was written in the third or second century B.C.E., shows that this line of interpretation had been around for some time. When Tobit summarizes for his son how to live righteously he stresses the saving power of almsgiving:

> Revere the Lord all your days, my son, and refuse to sin or to transgress his commandments. Live uprightly all the days of your life, and do not walk in the ways of wrongdoing; for those who act in accordance with truth will prosper in all their activities. To all those who practice righteousness give alms (צדקות/ἐλεημοσύνην) from your possessions, and do not let your eye begrudge the gift when you make it. Do not turn your face away from anyone who is poor, and the face of God will not be turned away from you. If you have many possessions, make your gift from them in proportion; if few, do not be afraid to give according to the little you have. So you will be laying up a good treasure for yourself against the day of necessity. *For almsgiving delivers from death* (ἐλεημοσύνη ἐκ θανάτου ῥύεται) and keeps you from going into the Darkness. Indeed, almsgiving, for all who practice it, is an excellent offering in the presence of the Most High. (NRSV 4:5 – 11).[10]

The Hebrew text from Qumran is missing v.10 where the phrase ἐλεημοσύνη ἐκ θανάτου ῥύεται appears, but it is clear from the rest of the text that צדקה stands behind the Greek ἐλεημοσύνη (alms).[11] The words ἐλεημοσύνη ἐκ θανάτου ῥύεται are therefore a verbatim quotation of Proverbs 10:2 and 11:4. This passage draws out what is hinted at in these

---

8   2.78–82. Text and translation, here slightly altered, from J. L. Lightfoot, *The Sibylline Oracles: With Introduction, Translation, and Commentary on the First and Second Books* (New York/Oxford, Oxford University Press: 2007), 315.

9   See J. J. Collins on the eschatology of books 1–2 of *Sib. Or.*, *OTP* 1.330–33. For a similar interpretation of Prov 19:17 see *T. Zeb.* 6:4–7.

10   Hebrew text from 4QTobit^e as found in Fitzmyer, "Tobit" in *Qumran Cave 4.XIV: Parabiblical Texts, Part 2* (ed. Broshi, M., et al; DJD XIX; Oxford: Clarendon Press, 1995), 65.

11   צדקה is found in v. 10 in the later Hebrew manuscripts documented in Stuart Weeks et al., eds., *The Book of Tobit: Texts from the Principal Ancient and Medieval Traditions* (FoSub 3; Berlin/New York: Walter de Gruyter, 2004), 143.

proverbs; almsgiving delivers from death because it funds a "good treasure" in heaven that delivers from death and keeps one from going into the darkness.[12]

The book of Sirach, which is roughly contemporaneous with Tobit, similarly describes almsgiving as a bulwark against disaster:

> Help the poor for the commandment's sake, and in their need do not send them away empty-handed. Lose your silver for the sake of a brother or a friend, and do not let it rust under a stone and be lost. Lay up your treasure according to the commandments of the Most High, and it will profit you more than gold. Store up almsgiving in your treasury, and it will rescue you from every disaster; better than a stout shield and a sturdy spear, it will fight for you against the enemy. (29:9–13 NRSV)

Like all the texts considered thus far, this passage stresses the superior reliability of treasuries funded by almsgiving in comparison to earthly treasures.[13] Some texts attribute the efficacy of heavenly treasure to its ability to deal with sin. Sirach says that the one who honors his father atones for sins (ὁ τιμῶν πατέρα ἐξιλάσκεται ἁμαρτίας 3:3) and that "as water extinguishes a flaming fire, so almsgiving atones for sins (ἐλεημοσύνη ἐξιλάσεται ἁμαρτίας)" (3:30). In the same chapter alms are said to "replace" one's sins: "Alms given to a father will not be forgotten; it will be established in place of your sins. In the day of your distress it will be remembered for you; like fair weather against frost, your sins will melt away" (3:14–15).[14] The image here is of alms establishing a foundation for the future (cf. Tob 4:9; 1 Tim 6:19) by doing away with sins. In light of the post-exilic tendency to view sin as incurring a debt with God, it is possible that Sirach envisions alms replacing sins by being credited against them, but no such claim is made explicit.[15]

---

12 Anderson, *Sin*, 144–46. See also 12:8–9. Note that both Tobit and *Sib. Or.* liken almsgiving to sacrifice.

13 On this and related texts in Sirach see Gregory's rich study, *Generosity in the Book of Sirach*.

14 See also Prov 16:6 LXX (15:27 in Rahlfs): "Sins are cleansed by almsgiving and acts of faithfulness (ἐλεημοσύναις καὶ πίστεσιν ἀποκαθαίρονται ἁμαρτίαι)." In Greek and Aramaic cleansing language frequently refers to the clearing of a debt or obligation. E.g., Gen 24:8 LXX.

15 *Pace*, the NRSV and NETS, both of which say almsgiving "will be credited to you against your sins." The texts of Sirach are not so clear. The LXX (καὶ ἀντὶ ἁμαρτιῶν προσανοικοδομηθήσεταί σοι) uses the rare word προσανοικοδεμέω, which appears to mean something like "establish (in place of)" in conjunction with ἀντί. Hebrew ms A reads תנע, presumably a misspelling of נטע (to plant) and C has תנצב from נצב (to set up). In all these texts the sense seems to be that

The book of Daniel, which was written around the same time as Tobit and Sirach, makes the connection between alms and the debt of sin clearer. In 4:24 (4:27 LXX) Daniel advises Nebuchadnezzar to avoid his coming punishment by giving alms: "Therefore, O king, may my counsel please you: redeem your sins with righteousness, and your   iniquities   with   mercy   to   the   oppressed (וחטיך בצדקה פרק ועויתך במחן ענין), so that your prosperity may be lengthened." פרק is the Aramaic term used to translate גאל in the Targumim when it refers to redeeming someone from debt slavery.[16] If this is the sense of פרק here, the implication would be that Nebuchadnezzar is offered the possibility of repaying the debt of his sins through almsgiving. The Old Greek and Theodotion translate וחטיך בצדקה פרק accordingly as καὶ τὰς ἁμαρτίας σου ἐν ἐλεημοσύναις λύτρωσαι.[17] Liddell and Scott define λυτρόω in the middle voice as "release by payment of ransom." One may object that the verb λυτρόω, like the English word "redeem," does not necessarily refer to the act of freeing someone by paying money. In many places in the LXX λυτρόω is used in an extended sense, referring simply to "deliverance" without any exchange of currency (e. g., Exod 6:6). Yet, the context shows that the usual sense of λυτρόω is in view here; Nebuchadnezzar is advised to pay money in order to "redeem" himself from his coming loss of freedom.[18] The sense here would seem to be then that Nebuchadnezzar's alms could be the ransom-price that would free him from his coming punishment. It is as if he is being offered an opportunity to pay off his creditor before he is thrown into debt-slavery.

Second Maccabees, which is roughly contemporaneous with Tobit, Sirach, and Daniel, depicts sin as a debt that piles up and resurrection as a reward stored up in heaven. In chapter 6 the author addresses the readers and begs them not to lose confidence in God's faithfulness while reading

---

ἐλεημοσύνη/צדקה given to one's father is established as a foundation in place of one's sins. See the discussion in Johannes Marböck, *Jesus Sirach 1–23* (HThKAT; Freiburg im Breisgau: Herder, 2010), 72, 76. See also Novick, "Wages from God," 712–15.

16 Anderson, *Sin*, 143.

17 The OG has ἀδικίας rather than ἁμαρτίας.

18 This was a common interpretation of the verse in ancient Judaism and Christianity. See, e. g., Jacob Z. Lauterbach, *Mekhilta Ishmael: A Critical Edition, Based on the Manuscripts and Early Editions, with an English Translation, Introduction, and Notes* (2 vols.; Philadelphia: JPS, 1933; repr., 2004), 2.415–16; Augustine connects this verse with Matt 25:31–46 (*Homily* 389.5).

about the atrocities committed against the Jewish people under the Seleucids and offers a remarkable theodical explanation:

> In fact, it is a sign of great kindness not to let the impious alone for long,
> but to punish them immediately. For in the case of the other nations the
> Lord waits patiently to punish them until they have reached the full meas-
> ure of their sins (πρὸς ἐκπλήρωσιν ἁμαρτιῶν); but he does not deal in this
> way with us, in order that he may not take vengeance on us afterward
> when our sins have reached their height (πρὸς τέλος ἀφικομένων ἡμῶν τῶν
> ἁμαρτιῶν). Therefore he never withdraws his mercy from us. Although
> he disciplines us with calamities, he does not forsake his own people.
> (6:13–16 NRSV)

Anderson argues that the phrase "to complete/fulfill sins" in the Hebrew Bible, Dead Sea Scrolls, and elsewhere refers to the moment
when debt reaches the point where the creditor must step in to collect,
or, depending on context, to the time when the debtor has fulfilled his
obligation by repaying the debt.[19] The point here would be that God
allowed the persecutions under the Seleucids in order to prevent the
debts of the Jewish people from piling too high.[20] Regardless of whether
one accepts Anderson's reading, this passage introduces the martyrdoms
of Eleazar (6:18–31) and the seven brothers with their mother (7:1–
42), which are a critical turning point in the narrative; by faithfully
dying for God's Law, the martyrs bring an end to the punishment
(e. g., 7:18, 32–33, 37–38) and the revolt of Judas Maccabeus begins
to pick up steam. Interestingly, however, the martyrs not only bring
an end to God's punishment of the people, but also merit their own resurrection from the dead (see 7:9, 23, 29, 36).[21]

In chapter 12 the author describes resurrection as the "splendid reward which is stored up (κάλλιστον ἀποκείμενον χαριστήριον) for those
who sleep in godliness" (12:45). The passive ἀπόκειμαι is a standard
term for storing away money, and, like its near-synonym θησαυρίζω,

---

19 *Sin*, 75–94. See Gen 15:16; Dan 8:23; 9:24; 4Q388 col. 2 frag. 9:4–6; 1
    Thess 2:15–16; L.A.B. 26:13; 36:1; 41:1. The clearest instance of this meta-
    phor is perhaps Matt 23:32, which Anderson does not discuss. See chapter 2.
20 Cf. 1 Cor 11:32: "When we are judged by the Lord we are being disciplined
    (παιδευόμεθα) in order that we may not be condemned with the world."
21 Verse 29 actually refers to the life the martyrs experienced immediately after
    their deaths, and presumably before resurrection. See Daniel R. Schwartz, *2
    Maccabees* (CEJL; Berlin/New York: Walter de Gruyter, 2008), 317.

was used to describe the recompense for good behavior that is stored up in the heavens.[22] The passage as a whole is revealing:

> On the next day, as had now become necessary, Judas and his men went to take up the bodies of the fallen and to bring them back to lie with their kindred in the sepulchres of their ancestors. Then under the tunic of each one of the dead they found sacred tokens of the idols of Jamnia, which the law forbids the Jews to wear. And it became clear to all that this was the reason these men had fallen. So they all blessed the ways of the Lord, the righteous judge, who reveals the things that are hidden; and they turned to supplication, praying that the sin that had been committed might be wholly blotted out. The noble Judas exhorted the people to keep themselves free from sin, for they had seen with their own eyes what had happened as the result of the sin of those who had fallen. He also took up a collection, man by man, to the amount of two thousand drachmas of silver, and sent it to Jerusalem to provide for a sin offering. In doing this he acted very well and honorably, taking account of the resurrection. For if he were not expecting that those who had fallen would rise again, it would have been superfluous and foolish to pray for the dead. But if he was looking to the splendid reward that is laid up for those who sleep in godliness, it was a holy and pious thought. Therefore he made atonement for the dead, so that they might be delivered from their sin (εἴτε' ἐμβλέπων τοῖς μετ' εὐσεβείας κοιμωμένοις κάλλιστον ἀποκείμενον χαριστήριον ὁσία καὶ εὐσεβὴς ἡ ἐπίνοια ὅθεν περὶ τῶν τεθνηκότων τὸν ἐξιλασμὸν ἐποιήσατο τῆς ἁμαρτίας ἀπολυθῆναι). (12:39–45 NRSV)[23]

There are a number of noteworthy items here. First, though Proverbs, Tobit, and Sirach say that heavenly treasure preserves one from "death," or from "going into the darkness," these texts lack a clear depiction of the afterlife.[24] In Daniel, Nebuchadnezzar is advised to give alms in order to prevent an imminent earthly punishment. Here, however, the reward "stored up" for the pious is associated with – or perhaps even equated with – resurrection from the dead. Wisdom of Solomon 2:22 similarly describes life after death as the "wages of holiness" (μισθός ὁσιότητος), and *Psalms of Solomon* 9:5 says that "The one who does righteousness treasures up life for himself with the Lord (ὁ ποιῶν δικαιοσύνην θησαυρίζει ζωὴν αὐτῷ παρὰ κυρίῳ)."[25] By doing righteous-

---

22 Liddell and Scott. E.g., Col 1:5; 2 Tim 4:8.

23 I have altered the translation of τοῖς μετ' εὐσεβείας κοιμωμένοις for reasons that will be clear in a moment.

24 Though see Tob 3:6.

25 See also *T. Levi* 13:5. N. T. Wright overstates his case when he argues that Wisdom depicts the resurrection of bodies, *The Resurrection of the Son of God* (Minneapolis: Fortress Press, 2003), 162–75. David Winston's contention that Wis-

ness one treasures up life for the world to come. As we shall see, the link between heavenly treasure and one's fate in the afterlife becomes common in the first century C.E.

Second, in this passage those who die in sin may still achieve the heavenly reward through the prayer and sacrifices of those who are still alive. This point is obscured by most English translations which render τοῖς μετ' εὐσεβείας κοιμωμένοις in 12:45 as "those who fall asleep in godliness," thereby suggesting that it is necessary to die in a state of godliness to receive the heavenly reward. The euphemism "to sleep" or "to fall asleep" can refer to dying (e. g., Acts 7:60). Yet, as BDAG notes, in the present and perfect participle it often denotes the state of being dead (e. g., 1 Thess 4:13; 1 Cor 15:20). The NRSV, NAB, and NETS all take τοῖς μετ' εὐσεβείας κοιμωμένοις in 2 Macc 12:45 in the former sense (i. e., "those who have fallen asleep in godliness"), but this cannot be correct. The point of this passage is that the men with the idols did *not* fall asleep in godliness, but may nevertheless come to be able to "sleep" in godliness (i. e., exist as a dead person in a state of godliness) and so receive resurrection. According to the author this is precisely why Judas and his men prayed and made sacrifices on behalf of their comrades who had died with idols: so that those who had fallen asleep in sin could be "released from their sin," and so sleep in godliness and receive the reward which is stored up for them. This is similar to what we saw in Sirach and Daniel, where righteous deeds are able to deal with sin and help one avoid punishment. The difference is that this passage presupposes belief in some kind of purgatorial state prior to the resurrection and that the heavenly reward is based not only on one's own righteous deeds but also on the righteous deeds of others on one's behalf. In other words, this passage, like the martyrdoms in chapters 6–

dom was written in the first century C.E. has found wide acceptance (*The Wisdom of Solomon: A New Translation with Introduction and Commentary* [AB 43; Garden City, NY: Doubleday, 1979], 20–25). The lynchpin of his argument, however, was his claim that Wisdom contains 35 words that do not appear in Greek literature until the first century, a claim that has now been decisively refuted by Hans Arneson ("Vocabulary and Date in the Study of Wisdom: A Critical Review of the Arguments" [Paper presented at the SBL annual meeting, New Orleans, 23 November 2009]). Greek text of *Pss. Sol.* from Robert B. Wright, *The Psalms of Solomon: A Critical Edition of the Greek Text* (New York, New York: T & T Clark, 2007), 128. Wright argues that *Pss. Sol.* was composed in Hebrew in the last half of the first century B.C.E. and translated into Greek not long afterward (1–13).

7, presupposes the possibility of what is usually called "vicarious atonement"; the reward stored up in heaven is not simply based on one's own deeds.[26]

In sum, prior to the first century treasure loaned to God was thought to provide protection for the future. In texts without a clear sense of life after death or resurrection, such as Proverbs and Tobit, such treasure is said simply to keep one from going into darkness, whereas texts with more developed eschatologies associate wages from God with life after death, including resurrection. Though it would be tempting to assume that these texts imagine heavenly treasure paying down the debt of sin, nothing like this is made explicit, though Sirach describes alms replacing sins and Daniel tells Nebuchadnezzar to "redeem" his sins with alms.

1.3 First and Second Century Apocalypses

Jewish apocalypses frequently depict heavenly treasure as what determines one's fate in the coming day of judgment.[27] Good and bad deeds are sometimes depicted being weighed in a scale.[28] For instance, in *1 Enoch* 61:1−5 angels are sent out with ropes to measure the righteous ones. God will place the Elect one on his "throne of glory" where he will sit and "judge all the works of the holy ones in heaven above, weighing in the balance their deeds," with good deeds presumably being weighed against the debts of sin.[29] Similarly, in *2 Enoch*, a text

---

26 Cf. Sir 7:33: "Give graciously to all the living, and withhold not kindness from the dead" (RSV).

27 I use the designation apocalypse following the definition in *Apocalypse: The Morphology of a Genre* (ed. J. J. Collins; *Semeia* 14; Missoula, MT: Scholars Press, 1979).

28 Considering the ubiquity of scales in the ancient world, it is unsurprising that the idea of a post-mortem weighing of good and bad deeds was fairly common. It is often suggested that the idea originated in Egypt. See Dale C. Allison, Jr., *Testament of Abraham* (CEJL; Berlin/New York: Walter de Gruyter, 2003), 272. See also Job 31:6 and Dan 5:27.

29 Cf., also 38:1−2; 41:1−2; 45:3. Commenting on treasure in heaven in 1 Enoch, Klaus Koch notes "Wie in den Synoptikern hängt also das eschatologische Erscheinen der Werke mit der Verwirklichung des Reiches Gottes zusammen" ("Der Schatz im Himmel" in *Leben Angesichts des Todes: Beiträge zum theologischen Problem des Todes: Helmut Thielicke zum 60. Geburtstag* [eds. Berhard Lohse and H. P. Schmidt; Tübingen: Mohr Siebeck, 1968), 54.

that is notoriously difficult to date, but which some would place before
the destruction of the temple, the day of judgment is compared to a
marketplace:

> Happy is the person who does not direct his heart with malice toward any
> person, but who helps the offended and the condemned, and lifts up those
> who have been crushed, and shows compassion on the needy. Because on
> the day of the great judgment every weight and every measure and every
> set of scales will be just as they are in the market. That is to say, each will be
> weighed in the balance, and each will stand in the market, and each will
> find out his own measure and in accordance with that measurement each
> shall receive his own reward. (44:4–5)[30]

Those who help the needy tip the scales in their own favor and earn a
reward for the day of judgment.

In chapters 12–14 of *Testament of Abraham*, parts of which were arguably written around the end of the first century, Abraham is given a
vision of the judgment of souls by Abel, which is a preliminary judgment to be followed by judgment by the twelve tribes of Israel
(13:3), and finally by God (13:7–8).[31] A person's deeds and sins are
weighed in a balance and also tested with fire, and the souls are then
given their "repayment" (ἀνταπόδοσις):

> And a marvelous man, resembling the sun, like unto a son of God, sat upon
> [the terrifying throne]. Before him stood a table with the appearance of
> crystal, wholly made of gold and silk. On the table lay a book; its thickness
> was three cubits and its width was six cubits. On the right and on the left
> stood two angels who were holding a papyrus roll and ink and a reed-pen.
> In front of the table sat a glorious angel holding a scale (ζυγόν) in his hand.
> On his left sat a fiery angel, altogether merciless and relentless, holding in
> his hand a trumpet, which contained an all-consuming fire that tests sin-
> ners. And the marvelous man, sitting on his throne, judged and declared
> a verdict upon the souls. The two angels on the right and the left were
> making a written register (ἀπεγράφοντο). The one on the right recorded
> righteous deeds (τὰς δικαιοσύνας) and the one on the left recorded sins.
> And the one in front of the table, the one holding the scale, weighed
> the souls. And the fiery angel, the one holding the fire, tested the souls
> with fire. And Abraham asked the Commander-in-chief, "What are
> these things that we see?" And the Commander-in-chief said, "These

---

30 F. I. Anderson, *OTP*, 1:170–71. Andrei A. Orlov argues that 2 Enoch's un-
    abashed concern for temple and priesthood are strong evidence for a pre-70
    date. *The Enoch-Metatron Tradition* (TSAJ 107; Tübingen: Mohr Siebeck,
    2005), 330–33.

31 Allison, *Testament of Abraham*, 34–40.

things that you see, pious Abraham, are the judgment and repaying (ἡ κρίσις καὶ ἀνταπόδοσις). (12:5 – 15)[32]

Those whose righteous deeds outweigh their sins enter into paradise and are said to be among those who are "being saved" (τοῖς σωζομένοις) (12:18), but those whose sins are heavier are handed over to the torturers (τοῖς βασανισταῖς ἐξέδωκεν).[33] If a soul's sins and righteous deeds are equally balanced "He neither gave it over to the torturers nor (did he set it) among the saved, but he placed it in the middle" (12:18). When Abraham asks what this soul needs to be saved the Commander-in-chief says, "If it could get one righteous deed more than (the number of its) sins, it will come to salvation" because the scales will be tipped in favor of the righteous deeds (14:4).

Interestingly, the righteous deed that tips the scale comes not from the soul itself, but from Abraham, who intercedes for the soul:

> "Come, Michael, Commander-in-chief, let us pray for the soul, and let us see if God will hear us." And the Commander-in-chief said, "Amen, so be it." And they made petition and prayer to God for the soul. And God heard their prayer; and rising from their prayer they did not see the soul standing there. And Abraham said to the angel, "Where is the soul?" The Commander-in-chief said, "It was saved by your righteous prayer (Σέσωται διὰ τῆς εὐχῆς σου τῆς δικαίας). And behold! A glorious angel took it and carried it into paradise." (14:5 – 8)[34]

As in 2 Maccabees 12, the prayers of the living are able to atone for the dead, here gaining "paradise" for the soul with an equal number of righteous deeds and sins on the scale.

Having achieved success in praying for this middling soul, Abraham goes on to beg for mercy for "the souls of the sinners whom I [Abraham], once despising, destroyed…" (14:11), as well as for his own sins. After Abraham and Michael pray for these souls "for a long while" a voice from heaven calls,

> "Abraham, Abraham, the Lord has heard your prayer and your sins are forgiven. And those (persons) you earlier thought I had destroyed, I have recalled them and brought them unto eternal life on account of my utter

---

32 Allison, *Testament of Abraham*, 253 – 54. Slightly altered. All further citations of *T. Ab.* also from Allison.

33 Cf. Matt 18:34. The similarity could be due to the influence of Christian scribes.

34 Allison (*Testament of Abraham*, 296) argues that chapter 14, which has no parallel in the short recension of *T. Ab.*, contains "several phrases likely to be Christian" though "its basic content is presumably ancient."

goodness. For a time I repaid them with judgment (πρὸς καιρὸν εἰς κρίσιν αὐτοὺς ἀνταπέδωκα), but those I requite while they live on the earth, I will not requite in death." (14:14–15)

God answers Abraham's prayers and brings these sinners into eternal life, saving them from the fate of being "repaid in death," that is, being denied eternal life. Yet, this mercy is based not only on Abraham's prayers and God's mercy, but also on the fact that God has already "repaid" these sinners the debt of their sin by allowing them to die a violent death.[35] Moreover, since these sinners had been handed over to the torturers, it is also possible that the repayment for their debt includes the time the sinners spent suffering at the hands of the torturers.

The fact that God heeds Abraham's prayers and shows mercy to sinners illustrates an important point: belief that treasure in heaven determines one's fate on the day of judgment did not require the concomitant belief that God is rigidly mechanistic in meting out judgment. This can be seen even more clearly in *2 Baruch*, a text commonly dated to some point between 70–100 C.E. Here again good works are stored up in treasuries and may acquit one on the day of judgment:

> For the righteous justly have good hope for the end and go away from this habitation without fear because they possess with you a store of good works which is preserved in treasuries. Therefore, they leave this world without fear and are confident of the world which you have promised to them with an expectation full of joy. (14:12–13)[36]

Nevertheless, God will show mercy to those without heavenly treasure:

> For behold, the days are coming, and the books will be opened in which are written the sins of all those who have sinned, and moreover, also the treasuries in which are brought together the righteousness of all those who have proven themselves to be righteous. And it will happen at that time that you shall see, and many with you, the long-suffering of the Most High, which lasts from generation to generation, who has been long-suffering toward all who are born, both those who sinned and those who proved themselves to be righteous. (24:1–2)[37]

Once again, a coming day of judgment is predicted when God will examine both the heavenly treasure and the sins of humanity. Despite

---

35 Allison, *Testament of Abraham*, 306.

36 A. F. J. Klijn, *OTP*, 1:626.

37 Ibid., 1:629. Since the sins are said to be written in books and these books are the antithetical parallel to the treasuries of the righteous, it is possible that a record of indebtedness is in view. Cf. *Apoc. Zeph.* 3:9; *Apoc. Paul* 17; Col 2:14.

viewing the last judgment as the time when humanity will quite literally be called to account, however, the author sees the coming revelation of heavenly treasuries and debts as an opportunity for God to demonstrate his patience with sinners.[38]

A similar sentiment appears in *4 Ezra*, a text which is thought to have a literary relationship with *2 Baruch* and to have been written around the same time. Ezra is assured that, unlike those destined for perdition, he has a "treasure of works laid up with the Most High (*thesaurus operum repositus apud Altissimum*)" that he will not see until the last times (7:77).[39] Then a little later on Ezra prays for mercy for those without a treasury of works:

> For we and our fathers have passed our lives in ways that bring death, but you, because of us sinners, are called merciful. For if you have desired to have pity on us, who have no works of righteousness, then you will be called merciful. For the righteous, who have many works laid up with you, shall receive their wage in consequence of their own deeds (*Iusti enim, quibus sunt operae multae repositae apud te, ex propriis operibus recipient mercedem*). But what is man, that you are angry with him; or what is a mortal race, that you are so bitter against it? For in truth there is no one among those who have been born who has not acted wickedly, and among those who have existed there is no one who has not transgressed. For in this, O Lord, your righteousness and goodness will be declared, when you are merciful to those who have no store of good works (*In hoc enim adnuntiabitur iusticia tua et bonitas tua, Domine, cum misertus fueris eis qui non habent substantiam operum bonorum*). (8:31–36)[40]

Again, though heavenly treasure will save the righteous in the judgment, those without a store of good works present an opportunity for

---

38   Cf. Philo's *Sacr.* 118–126, where he reads Num 3:12–13 LXX to show that "every wise man is a ransom-price (λύτρον) for the fool." As an illustration of this principle, Philo points to the destruction of Sodom: "For thusly also Sodom is destroyed, when no good could balance the unspeakable multitude of evil that weighed down the scale." Conversely, if good people can be found in a place, God shares his riches with everyone for the sake of the good: "For my own part, when I see a good man living in a house or city, I hold that house or city happy and believe that their enjoyment of their present blessings will endure, and that their hopes for those as yet lacking will be realized. For God for the sake of the worthy dispenses to the unworthy also his boundless and illimitable wealth (τὸν ἀπεριόριστον καὶ ἀπερίγραφον πλοῦτον αὐτοῦ)." (Colson and Whitaker, LCL). See also *Praem.* XVI, 104.

39   B. M. Metzger, *OTP*, 1:539. Latin text in A. F. J. Klijn, *Der Lateinische text der Apokalypse des Esra* (TUGAL 131; Berlin: Akademie-Verlag, 1983).

40   Ibid., alt. *OTP*, 1:543.

God to show forth his clemency. Interestingly, however, other charac-
ters in 4 Ezra do not agree with Ezra's prayer for mercy.[41]

1.4 Rabbinic literature

The language of sin and forgiveness in rabbinic Hebrew and Aramaic is
drawn almost exclusively from the world of commerce. As Eliezer Diamond puts it,

> A marketplace model was…used by the sages to portray the calculation of
> one's spiritual merits and debts…The word generally used by the sages for
> reward, *sākhār*, has the primary meaning of wages or payment. *Pûr'ānût*, a
> common rabbinic term for punishment (literally: retribution), derives from
> the root *pr'*, "to pay off a debt." The notion of *pûr'ānût* is connected to
> viewing one who sins as having incurred a *hôbâ*, an obligation towards
> God. As George Foot Moore puts it, 'Man *owes* God obedience, and
> every sin, whether of commission or of omission, is a defaulted obligation,
> a debt.' That obligation is satisfied through God's retribution; God allows
> one to pay off one's debt by undergoing punishment. One significance of
> this imagery is that there is assumed to be some degree of proportionality
> between righteousness and sinfulness on the one hand and reward and pun-
> ishment on the other. Although God is not obligated a priori to reward the
> righteous nor does God need for his own sake to punish the wicked, God
> has created a system of debts, credits, rewards and punishments and he op-
> erates within its confines.[42]

Unsurprisingly, there are many passages in rabbinic literature relevant to
this study. For the sake of brevity – and in light of the difficulty of dating much of this material – I shall with a few exceptions discuss examples only from the Mishnah and the Tosephta.

---

41 E. P. Sanders points out that the angel's response to Ezra seems not to affirm his
    view of things and eventually the angel tells Ezra to stop asking about those
    who will perish (8:55), *Paul and Palestinian Judaism: A Comparison of Patters of
    Religion* (Philadelphia: Fortress Press, 1977), 415. Karina Martin Hogan (*Theol-
    ogies in Conflict in 4 Ezra: Wisdom, Debate, and Apocalyptic Solution* [Supplements
    to the Journal for the Study of Judaism; Leiden: Brill, 2008]) argues that 4 Ezra
    presents a theological debate between Ezra (covenantal wisdom) and Uriel (es-
    chatological wisdom) which is finally resolved by a third, apocalyptic form of
    theology.
42 *Holy Men and Hunger Artists: Fasting and Asceticism in Rabbinic Culture* (New
    York: Oxford University Press, 2004), 67.

Like Matthew, the Mishnah warns that everyone will "settle accounts" with God. According to *m. 'Avot* 3:1 Akabya b. Mahalaleel said,

> Consider three things and thou wilt not fall into the hands of transgression. Know whence thou art come and whither thou art going and before whom thou art about to give account and reckoning (ולפני מי אתה עתיד ליתן דין וחשבון). 'Whence thou art come' – from a putrid drop; 'and whither thou art going' – to the place of dust, worm, and maggot; 'and before whom thou art about to give account and reckoning'- before the King of kings, the Holy One, blessed is he.[43]

Also like Matthew, this settling of accounts is sometimes compared to an employer who will repay his workers at the appointed time. *Mishnah Avot* 2 contains the following example:

> R. Eleazar said: Be alert to study the Law and know how to make answer to an unbeliever; and know before whom though toilest and who is thy taskmaster (בעל מלאכתך) who shall pay thee the wage (שישלם-לך שכר) of thy labor.
>
> R. Tarfon said: The day is short and the task is great and the labourers are idle and the wage is abundant (והשכר הרבה) and the master of the house (ובעל הבית) is urgent.
>
> He [also] used to say: It is not thy part to finish the task, yet thou art not free to desist from it. If thou hast studied much in the Law much will be given thee, and faithful is thy taskmaster (בעל מלאכתך) who shall pay thee the wage (שישלם-לך שכר) of thy labor. And know that the recompense of the wage of the righteous is for the time to come. (*m. 'Avot* 2:14–16)[44]

God is likened to a master of the house who will pay his workers their wages at the end of the "day", that is, in the life to come.[45] Workers are

---

43   All translations of the Mishnah are from Herbert Danby, *The Mishnah: Translated from the Hebrew with Introduction and Brief Explanatory Notes* (Oxford: Oxford University Press, 1933; repr., 1983). Cf. *m. 'Avot* 4:22; Matt 18:23; 25:19.

44   When Danby translates שכר as "reward" I have changed it to "wage". In contemporary English "reward" suggests something that is given for work occurring outside the confines of an employee/employer or creditor/debtor relationship, and it is precisely the image of an employer that is envisioned here. For a fuller defense of this translation see the closely analogous discussion of μισθός and ἀποδίδωμι in Matthew below.

45   The description of God as a בעל הבית resonates with Matthew, where God or Jesus is described as οἰκοδεσπότης six times, two of which deal with God's payment of workers (10:25; 13:27; 52; 20:1, 11; 21:33). Cf. zero such uses of οἰκοδεσπότης in Mark and two in Luke (13:25; 14:21). See also Matt 9:37–38; 25:14–30.

not obliged to finish the task, but they must keep their noses to the grindstone, as it were.[46]

The coming settling of accounts is also described as the time when God, like a shopkeeper who gives out loans, collects from his debtors (cf. Matt 18:23–35). A well-known passage in the Mishnah states that R. Akiba used to say:

> All is given against a pledge (הכל נתון בערבון), and the net is cast over all living; the shop stands open and the shopkeeper gives credit and the account-book lies open and the hand writes and every one that wishes to borrow let him come and borrow; but the collectors go their round continually every day and exact payment of men with their consent or without their consent, for they have that on which they can rely [i.e., the record of indebtedness]; and the judgement is a judgement of truth; and all is made ready for the banquet. (*m. 'Avot* 3:16)

All people are portrayed as God's debtors. Everything people have is from God and must be returned to him. Though the mention of "the banquet" gives this saying an eschatological hue, the collectors collect debts from people not only at the end but "continually every day." It is not clear in this passage what it means for these debts to be collected continuously, but according to *Sifre Deut.* 307 God punishes the righteous for sins in the present life so they will not build up a debt, but waits to repay them for obeying a *mitzvah* until the world to come.[47] Along similar lines, *t. Pe'ah* 1:2–3 explains that some sins incur a debt the interest of which must be paid in this life, while the principal (קרן) of the loan – that is, punishment in Gehenna – remains for the world to come. The same idea appears in the parallel text in the Mishnah but in reference to good deeds rather than sins. Those who honor father and moth-

---

46 The fact that God will faithfully repay wages in the life to come is used to encourage faithful behavior in the face of present discomfort. As *'Avot* 6:5 puts it, "Seek not greatness for thyself and covet not honour... and crave not after the tables of kings, for thy table is greater than their table and thy crown than their crown; and faithful is thy taskmaster who shall pay thee the wage of thy labor (ונאמן הוא בעל מלאכתך שישלם לך שכר פעלתך)." Danby translates the *waw* in ונאמן as "and", but it could also be rendered as "because": the crown and table of those who work for God is greater than those of kings because God will faithfully repay them in the life to come. Crowns are a common image of eschatological recompense in the NT. See, e.g., 1 Cor 9:25; 2 Tim 4:8; Jas 1:12; 1 Pet 5:4; Rev 2:10; 3:11.

47 The wicked, on the other hand, are paid for their good deeds now and are punished for their misdeeds in the world to come. The theodical utility of this way of understanding God's bookkeeping is obvious. Cf. 2 Macc 6.

er, give charity, make peace between others, and study the Torah store up the principal for the world to come, but the interest is enjoyed in the present life.

Similar to *Testament of Abraham*, judgment is sometimes described in rabbinic literature as the weighing of debts and credits. One of the clearest examples of this may be *t. Qiddushin* 1:13–14:

> A. *Whoever does a single commandment – they do well for him and lengthen his days and his years and he inherits the Land.*
> B. And whoever commits a single transgression – they do ill to him and cut off his days, and he does not inherit the Land.
> C. And concerning such a person it is said, *One sinner destroys much good* (Qoh. 9:18).
> D. By a single sin this one destroys many good things.
> E. A person should always see himself as if he is half meritorious and half guilty.
> F. [If] he did a single commandment, happy is he, for he has inclined the balance for himself to the side of merit.
> G. [If] he committed a single transgression, woe is he, for he has inclined the balance to the side of guilt....
> A. R. Simeon b. Eleazar says in the name of R. Meir, "Because the individual is judged by the majority [of deeds], the world is judged by its majority.
> B. "And [if] one did one commandment, happy is he, for he has inclined the balance for himself and for the world to the side of merit.
> C. "[If] he committed one transgression, woe is he, for he has inclined the balance for himself and for the world to the side of guilt.

E. P. Sanders rightly points out that the advice here is to regard oneself as if one is half meritorious and half guilty.[48] It does not necessarily follow, then, that someone whose deeds are 51 % bad goes to Gehenna, but only that "one should *always* try to obey and should act *as if* each deed were decisive."[49] Nevertheless, the mere fact that this exhortation is framed in terms of the weighing of debts and merits shows that this way of imagining judgment had some purchase. As in *2 Baruch*, the be-

---

48 *Paul and Palestinian Judaism*, 130.
49 Ibid. The editor of the Tosephta follows this tradition with one that seems to exclude the idea that a person is judged strictly according to the majority of his deeds: "A. R. Simeon says, '[If] a man was righteous his entire life but at the end he rebelled, he loses the whole, since it is said, *The righteousness of the righteous shall not deliver him when he transgresses* (Ezek 33:12)...[If] a man was evil his entire life but at the end he repented, the Omnipresent accepts him" *t. Qidd.* 1:15–16.

lief that God judges according to the merits one has stored up need not require one to imagine judgment as strictly according to desert.

A similar point is illustrated in a saying attributed to R. Akiva: "with goodness is the world judged, and all is according to the majority of the work" (ובטוב העולם נדון והכל לפי רוב המעשה) (m. 'Avot 3:15).[50] The waw in והכל is usually taken to be adversative; God judges the world in goodness – that is, he judges charitably – but he also judges according to people's deeds.[51] Sanders finds this saying "enigmatic." He writes, "The only clear meaning is that grace and judgment of one's deeds are held in tension."[52] There is another possibility, however. The idea that God judges according to the amount of work a person has done is not necessarily "in tension" with judgment "in goodness." Psalm 62:13 illustrates the point: "To you, O Lord, belongs covenant faithfulness (חסד), for (כי) you will repay each according to his deeds." Here God's grace is not held in tension with the axiom that he will repay everyone. Rather, his repayment of deeds is an expression of his חסד. Similarly, the sense of m. 'Avot 3:15 may be that God's repayment according to the amount of work done is an expression of his goodness.

As seen above in 2 Maccabees and *Testament of Abraham*, debts and credits with God were not always seen as a purely individualistic matter. The entire people could be in debt with God, just as the righteous deeds of a few could benefit others. The same is true in early rabbinic Judaism, as the following saying illustrates:

> Rabban Gamaliel the son of R. Judah the Patriarch said: Excellent is study of the Law together with worldly occupation, for toil in them both puts sin out of mind. But all study of the Law without [worldly] labour comes to naught at the last and brings sin in its train. And let them that labour with the congregation labour with them in the name of heaven (לשם שמים), for the merit of their fathers (שזכות אבותם) supports them and their righteousness endures for ever. And as for you, [will God say,] I will count you worthy of great wages (שכר הרבה) as if you yourselves had wrought [it all] (m. 'Avot 2:2).[53]

This saying promises that those who labor in some worldly occupation "in the name of heaven" (i. e., because of heaven) will receive the support of the merit of their fathers and that their righteousness (וצדקתם)

---

will endure forever. At first glance it is not clear what it means for the merits of the fathers to "support" such work or for this righteousness to endure forever, but the meaning of this promise would seem to be clarified by the final sentence: "And as for you, [will God say,] I will count you worthy of great wages as if you yourselves had wrought [it all]." In other words, God will generously repay those who labor in the name of heaven not only the wages they themselves earned, but also the wages earned by their fathers.[54]

In sum, Tannaitic literature contains a rich variety of economic language in contexts dealing with divine recompense. God is portrayed variously as an employer who pays his workers, or as a creditor who will be sure to collect the loans given to humans. Repayment for deeds shows God's goodness and goes beyond what is strictly deserved. In *m. 'Avot* 2:2 repayment for worldly labor done for God's sake include not only a just wage but the merits of the fathers.[55]

1.5 Earliest Christian literature

The richest source of information about heavenly treasure in earliest Christianity is probably the Synoptic Gospels. I shall discuss the relevant passages in Mark and Luke later, while dealing with their Matthean parallels. In this section I shall very briefly examine discussions of heavenly treasure outside of the Synoptic Gospels.

---

54 For a discussion of זכות אבות in Talmudic thought see Solomon Schechter, *Aspects of Rabbinic Theology* (New York: Macmillan, 1909; repr., New York, Schocken Books, 1961), 170–98. See also Sanders, *Paul and Palestinian Judaism*, 183–98.

55 It should be noted that while Tannaitic sages display a lively interest in describing divine recompense as wages and in describing God variously as an employer or someone as gives out loans he is sure to collect, the traditions discussed here do not represent a universally held rabbinic doctrine. Indeed, the Mishnah contains a number of sayings that would warm the heart of any Kantian New Testament scholar were they found in the New Testament. E.g., *m. 'Avot* 1:3: "Antigonus of Soko received [the Law] from Simeon the Just. He used to say: Be not like slaves that minister to the master for the sake of receiving a bounty, but be like slaves that minister to the master not for the sake of receiving a bounty; and let the fear of Heaven be upon you."

The Didache's relationship to Matthew is a subject of ongoing dispute.[56] Regardless of whether they have a direct literary relationship, they share many traditions and probably come from a similar Jewish-Christian milieu. In 4:5−7 there is a passage that echoes Sirach 4:31 and Daniel 4:24:

> Do not be the sort of person who holds out his hands to receive but draws them back when it comes to giving. If you have [something] through the work of your hands, you shall give [it as] ransom of your sins (λύτρωσιν ἁμαρτιῶν σου). You shall not hesitate to give, and when you give you shall not grumble, for you will know who the good Repayer of wages (ὁ τοῦ μισθοῦ καλὸς ἀνταποδότης) is.[57]

Money which is given away on earth earns a wage from God, and this wage is the ransom of the debt of sin. In other words, by giving alms one is able to invest one's money in heaven, thereby paying down one's debt. As with Daniel 4, one may object that λύτρωσις need not refer to the actual payment of a debt, but only to "redemption" in a less specific sense. The context, however, draws attention to the economic connotation of λύτρωσις; one is to give money away and so receive a wage from God to ransom one's sins. Moreover, the author explicitly refers to sin as debt (ἄφες ἡμῖν τὴν ὀφειλὴν ἡμῶν ὡς καὶ ἡμεῖς ἀφίεμεν τοῖς ὀφειλέταις ἡμῶν) (8:2) as well as the "wages of righteousness" (μισθὸν δικαιοσύνης) (5:2).[58]

Another text closely related to Matthew is the Epistle of James.[59] In 1:12 and 2:5 the author says suffering and faithfulness in this life merit

---

56 *Did.* is usually dated anywhere from 50 to 150 C.E. Scholarly attention has focused on the question of whether or not it is dependent on Matt, but A.J.P. Garrow has argued that Matthew is dependent on *Did.*, *The Gospel of Matthew's Dependence on the Didache* (London/New York: T&T Clark, 2004).

57 Cf. the parallel passage in *Barn.* 19:9−11: "Remember the day of judgment night and day, and you shall seek out on a daily basis the presence of the saints, either laboring in word and going out to encourage, and endeavoring to save a soul by the word, or work with your hands for the a ransom-price for your sins (διὰ τῶν χειρῶν σου ἐργάσῃ εἰς λύτρον ἁμαρτιῶν σου). You shall not hesitate to give, nor shall you grumble when giving, but you will know who is the good Repayer of wages (ὁ τοῦ μισθοῦ καλὸς ἀνταποδότης)." Translation from *The Apostolic Fathers: Greek Texts and English Translations* (3rd ed; edited and translated by Michael W. Holmes; Grand Rapids, MI: Baker Academic, 1992; repr., 2007). See also *Apos. Con.* 7.12.

58 See below on the Matthean version of "cancel for us our debts."

59 For recent discussions of the overlaps between the three see *Matthew, James, and Didache: Three Related Documents in Their Jewish and Christian Settings* (ed. Huub

the crown of life (τὸν στέφανον τῆς ζωῆς) and the kingdom. In chapter 5 James warns the rich about the recompense they will receive in the last days:

> Come now, you rich people, weep and wail for the miseries that are coming to you. Your riches have rotted, and your clothes are moth-eaten. Your gold and silver have rusted, and their rust will be evidence against you, and it will eat your flesh like fire. You have laid up treasure for the last days (ἐθησαυρίσατε ἐν ἐσχάταις ἡμέραις). Listen! The wages (ὁ μισθὸς) of the laborers who mowed your fields, which you kept back by fraud, cry out, and the cries of the harvesters have reached the ears of the Lord of hosts. You have lived on the earth in luxury and in pleasure; you have fattened your hearts in a day of slaughter. (5:1–5 NRSV)

Note the underlying image of the eschatological law court.[60] The rusty gold and silver of the rich offer a damning testimony (ὁ ἰὸς αὐτῶν εἰς μαρτύριον ὑμῖν ἔσται) of their ill-gotten opulence. Here the author tweaks the common image of heavenly treasure which acquits on the day of wrath; the rich store up treasure for the last days, although not heavenly treasure that acquits one on the day of judgment, but earthly treasure, which proclaims guilt.[61] Both the rich and the poor, therefore, have a treasure laid up for the last days.[62] The poor will receive the kingdom. The rich, on the other hand, will be condemned in the last judgment by the witness of their treasures on earth.

The image of evil-doers treasuring up a punishment for themselves to be revealed in the last days also appears in Romans. In chapter 2 Paul addresses the unrepentant sinner who despises the "riches of God's kindness and forbearance and patience" (2:4):

> By your hard and unrepentant heart you are treasuring up (θησαυρίζεις) for yourself wrath on the day of wrath, the day of the revelation of the righteous judgment of God. For 'he will repay to each according to his deeds' [Ps 62:13; Prov 24:12]. To those who by patiently doing good seek for glory and honor and immortality, he will give eternal life; to those who out of ambition obey not the truth but wickedness there will be wrath and fury" (2:5–8).

---

van de Sandt and Jürgen K. Zangenberg; SBLSymS 45; Atlanta: Society of Biblical Literature, 2008).

60 Patrick J. Hartin, *James* (SP 14; Collegeville, Minnesota: Liturgical Press, 2003), 228.

61 Cf., *Pss. Sol.* 9:5, discussed above.

62 On the eschatological valence of "last days" in the passage see Hartin, *James*, 228.

Paul fills out the logic of the dictum from Psalm 62:12/Proverbs 24:12: if God will repay each according to his deeds, then those who are doing evil are treasuring up wrath for themselves, just as those who do good are storing up immortality. Or, as Paul puts it in 6:23, "the wages of sin is death" (τὰ γὰρ ὀψώνια τῆς ἁμαρτίας θάνατος).[63]

Colossians describes heavenly treasure as the ground of action in the present. In 1:5 the author speaks of the "hope which is laid up for you in the heavens (τὴν ἐλπίδα τὴν ἀποκειμένην ὑμῖν ἐν τοῖς οὐρανοῖς)" as the basis of the love the Colossian Christians have for all the saints.[64] This accords with what the author says in 3:1–11:

> So if you have been raised with Christ, seek the things that are above, where Christ is, seated at the right hand of God (τὰ ἄνω ζητεῖτε, οὗ ὁ Χριστός ἐστιν ἐν δεξιᾷ τοῦ θεοῦ καθήμενος). Set your minds on things that are above, not on things that are on earth, for you have died, and your life is hidden with Christ in God (τὰ ἄνω φρονεῖτε, μὴ τὰ ἐπὶ τῆς γῆς. ἀπεθάνετε γὰρ καὶ ἡ ζωὴ ὑμῶν κέκρυπται σὺν τῷ Χριστῷ ἐν τῷ θεῷ). When Christ who is your life is revealed, then you also will be revealed with him in glory.
>
> Put to death, therefore, whatever in you is earthly: fornication, impurity, passion, evil desire, and greed (which is idolatry). On account of these the wrath of God is coming on those who are disobedient. These are the ways you also once followed, when you were living that life. But now you must get rid of all such things – anger, wrath, malice, slander, and abusive language from your mouth. Do not lie to one another, seeing that you have stripped off the old self with its practices and have clothed yourselves with the new self, which is being renewed in knowledge according to the image of its creator, where there is no longer Greek and Jew, circumcised and un-

---

63 See also Peter Arzt-Grabner's argument that Paul uses economic language, especially ἀρραβών, to depict God as a reliable buyer, "Gott als verlässlicher Käufer: Einige Papyrologische Anmerkungen und bibeltheologische Schlussfolgerungen zum Gottesbild der Paulusbriefe," *NTS* 57 (2011): 392–414. See also Kent L. Yinger, *Paul, Judaism, and Judgment According to Deeds* (SNTMS 105; Cambridge: Cambridge University Press, 1999); Simon J. Gathercole, *Where Is Boasting? Early Jewish Soteriology and Paul's Response in Romans 1–5* (Grand Rapids: Eerdmans, 2002).

64 I understand διὰ τὴν ἐλπίδα τὴν ἀποκειμένην ὑμῖν ἐν τοῖς οὐρανοῖς to refer to verse 4 not 3. The reason will become clear in the following discussing of 3:1–5. Cf., also Barth and Blanke: "Serious consideration has been given to the question whether 'because of hope' refers to *eucharistoumen* (we thank)....The counter-argument is that Paul refers to the conditions of the communities or specifically to those addressed in all his expressions of thanksgiving. In addition, it seems forced to consider v 4 as an insert which does not indicate the cause of thanksgiving." *Colossians: A New Translation with Introduction and Commentary* (trans. A. B. Beck; AB 34B; New York, New York: Doubleday, 1994), 154.

circumcised, barbarian, Scythian, slave and free; but Christ is all and in all! (NRSV)

The author strikingly refers to "the things that are above" rather than "the One who is above" or the like. I would suggest that these heavenly objects are the life that is hidden with God, stored up to be revealed when Christ is revealed.[65] Like 2 Maccabees 12:45, then, the author speaks of the coming resurrection as something that is laid up in heaven (1:5), but with a twist; the Colossians already participate in the resurrection through their union with Christ. Heavenly treasure becomes not just the goal to which one strains – though it is that too – but also the basis of life in the present. Both reward and punishment loom, but the heavenly reward is already tasted and, paradoxically, enables one to attain the reward.[66]

Colossians also contains one of the New Testament's most striking descriptions of sin as debt:

> And while you were dead in trespasses and in the uncircumcision of your flesh, he made you alive together with him, forgiving (χαρισάμενος) us all the trespasses. Erasing the bond of indebtedness with its ordinances that was against us (ἐξαλείψας τὸ καθ᾽ ἡμῶν χειρόγραφον τοῖς δόγμασιν ὃ ἦν ὑπεναντίον ἡμῖν), he took it away, nailing it to the cross. (2:13–14)

As the papyri show, the word χειρόγραφον commonly referred to bonds of indebtedness.[67] For instance, a χειρόγραφον written on a papyrus fragment from first or second century Palestine details the responsibilities of a debtor to his creditor. The surviving portion concludes with these words:

ἐὰν δὲ μὴ ἀποδῶ
τῇ ὡρισμέν[η] προθεσμίᾳ τελέσω σοι τὸν ἐγ διατάγ-

---

65 Charles H. Talbert (*Ephesians and Colossians* [Paideia; Grand Rapids, MI: Baker Academic, 2007], 226–27). See also 1 Pet 1:3–4: "Blessed be the God and Father of our Lord Jesus Christ, who by his great mercy has given us a new birth into a living hope through the resurrection of Jesus Christ from the dead, and into an inheritance that is imperishable, undefiled, and unfading, kept in heaven for you (εἰς κληρονομίαν ἄφθαρτον καὶ ἀμίαντον καὶ ἀμάραντον, τετηρημένην ἐν οὐρανοῖς εἰς ὑμᾶς)" (NRSV alt.).

66 See also 3:24: ἀπὸ κυρίου ἀπολήμψεσθε τὴν ἀνταπόδοσιν τῆς κληρονομίας.

67 E.g., Tob 5:3. In *Apoc. Zeph.* 3:9–9 and *Apoc. Paul* 17 χειρόγραφον refers to the heavenly books that record the good and bad deeds of humans. See also Gustav A. Deissmann, *Light from the Ancient East: The New Testament Illustrated by Recently Discovered Texts of the Graeco-Roman World* (trans. Lionel R. M. Strachan; New York: George H. Doran, 1927), 329–34; Anderson, *Sin*, 113–18.

ματος τόκ[ον] μέχρι οὗ ἂν ἀποδῶ ἢ εἰσπραχθῶ τὸ
πᾶν δά[νει]ον ἐκ πλήρους τῆ[ς] πράξεώς σοι οὔσης
καὶ ἄλ[λῳ π]αντὶ τῶν διά σου ἢ ὑπέρ σου κυρίως προ-
φερ[όντων τόδε τὸ χ]ειρόγραφον ἔκ τε ἐμοῦ καὶ ἐκ τ-
ῶν ὑ[παρχόντων μοι] π[ά]ντων...[68]

But if I do not repay in the period stipulated I will pay you the established
interest until I repay or be forced to pay the entire loan, completely; the
right of execution [i.e., the right to exact the money from the debtor] belongs to you and to anyone who through you or on your behalf validly
presents this bond of indebtedness both from me and from all my possessions ...

Should the debtor fail to repay the loan, the creditor or his agent only
has to produce this very χειρόγραφον to gain the legal right to seize both
the debtor and all his possessions.[69] The χειρόγραφον contains a number
of δόγματα (ordinances, requirements) – though the word δόγμα is not
used – detailing how the debtor must pay and what will happen if he
does not. The image in Colossians would seem to be that through
the cross God has done away with the χειρόγραφον that recorded the un-
paid debt of sin along with its stipulations, thereby freeing humanity
from death that was its lot.[70]

1 Timothy 6:18–19 says that the rich are to be generous and ready
to share, thereby "treasuring up for themselves a good foundation for
what is coming, in order to take hold of true life." This passage is remarkably similar to Tobit 4:

...ἀποθησαυρίζοντας ἑαυτοῖς θεμέλιον καλὸν εἰς τὸ μέλλον,
ἵνα ἐπιλάβωνται τῆς ὄντως ζωῆς. (1 Tim 6:19)

θέμα γὰρ ἀγαθὸν θησαυρίζεις σεαυτῷ εἰς ἡμέραν ἀνάγκης
διότι ἐλεημοσύνη ἐκ θανάτου ῥύεται καὶ οὐκ ἐᾷ εἰσελθεῖν εἰς τὸ σκότος (Tob
4:9–10)

In both texts those with money are to "treasure up" (ἀπο/θησαυρίζω) for
themselves (ἑαυτοῖς / σεαυτῷ) a good foundation or treasure (θεμέλιον
καλὸν/ θέμα ἀγαθὸν) for the future (εἰς τὸ μέλλον/εἰς ἡμέραν ἀνάγκης). 1

---

68 Greek text from P. Benoît et. al., *Les grottes de Murabba'ât* (DJD II; Oxford:
    Clarendon, 1961), 241.
69 Πρᾶξις refers to the right to exact money (LSJ), i. e., the right of "execution,"
    which frequently included imprisonment intended to compel the debtor or his
    family to find a way to repay the debt.
70 Joram Luttenberger ("Der gekreuzigte Schuldschein: Ein Aspekt der Deutung
    des Todes Jesu im Kolosserbrief," *NTS* 51 [2005]: 80–95) argues that Christ
    himself is the χειρόγραφον (92–93).

Timothy says that this treasuring up will allow the wealthy to "take hold of true life." Similarly, Tobit explains that almsgiving delivers from death.[71] The principal difference is that 1 Timothy has an eschatological future in view.[72]

1.6 Summary

We are now in a position to state some of the broad agreements or recurring motifs about heavenly treasures and debts in the Hebrew Bible, Septuagint, and early Jewish and Christian texts.

1. *The widespread conception of sin as debt and of righteous deeds as earning wages or treasure generated a rich variety of economic tropes in texts dealing with divine recompense.* For example, the recompense of righteousness is depicted variously as God's repayment of a loan made to him, as the wage due a worker, or as the ransom-price for sins. In addition to the many texts where heavenly treasure is necessary to gain entrance to eternal life, there are places where it appears that heavenly treasure is enjoyed as a sign of honor or achievement in the life to come. For instance, heavenly treasure is not always described as "wages"; frequently the recompense stored up for good deeds is a crown (e.g., *m. 'Avot* 6:5; 1 Cor 9:25; 2 Tim 4:8; Jas 1:12; Rev 2:10; 3:11). In *m. 'Avot* 6:5 the crown is a sign of royalty. In 1 Corinthians 9:25 and 2 Timothy 4:8 the crown is the wreath of the tri-

---

71 Both texts are classic cases of redemptive almsgiving, contra Roman Garrison, *Redemptive Almsgiving in Early Christianity* (JSNTSup 77; Sheffield: Sheffield Academic Press, 1993), 71, who claims that "While [1 Tim 6:17–19] still falls short of an unequivocal endorsement of redemptive almsgiving, the text is clearly consistent with such a doctrine." One wonders what Garrison would consider an unequivocal endorsement. The rich are to give money away, thereby treasuring up a foundation in order to take hold of true life.

72 In my article on 1 Tim 6 ("Almsgiving is 'The Commandment': A Note on 1 Timothy 6.6–19," *NTS* 58 [2012]: 144–50) I argue that "the commandment" in 6:14 refers to almsgiving – an idiom that is common in rabbinic literature and may go back to the second temple period. If this is correct then the whole of 1 Tim 6:6–19 deals with the proper use of money and the need to give alms to "take hold" of eternal life. See also 2 Tim 4:6–8, where Paul says that because he has kept the faith there is "stored up for me the crown of righteousness (ἀπόκειταί μοι ὁ τῆς δικαιοσύνης στέφανος), which the Lord, the righteous judge, will pay (ἀποδώσει) on that day, and not only to me but also to all who have longed for his appearing. (NRSV alt.)

umphant athlete. This sort of treasure is not placed on scales in the marketplace, but is a sign of achievement.

2. *Almsgiving is the quintessential, but not the only, act that earns heavenly treasure.*

3. *Heavenly treasure is frequently described as being "stored up" in treasuries though it is not always clear what sort of cosmology or ouranology this presupposes.* As we shall see below, Matthew is unusually clear in this regard.

4. *Heavenly treasure delivers from death and punishment.* As Tobit tells his son, quoting Proverbs, by giving alms you can treasure up "a good treasure for yourself against the day of necessity, for almsgiving delivers from death and keeps you from going into the darkness" (4:9–10). In texts without a clear sense of an afterlife, such as Tobit and Proverbs, the death and punishment in question appears to be earthly.

5. *In eschatological contexts heavenly treasure acquits one on the day of judgment.* This is a natural development of the conviction that almsgiving delivers from death into contexts where recompense for good and evil deeds is deferred until the afterlife. First Timothy's interpretation of Tobit is a good example of an eschatological reinterpretation of heavenly treasure; by storing up treasure in heaven one is able to take hold of true, eternal life.[73] Conversely, one could also treasure up punishment for oneself.

6. *Heavenly treasure redeems from the debt of sin.* This point is closely connected to the previous two. Though the underlying logic is not always made explicit, heavenly treasure rescues one from punishment by paying a ransom for sins (e. g., *Did.* 4:5–7). Given the ubiquity of scales in the ancient world, it is not surprising that treasure in heaven is sometimes found being weighed against the debt of sin (e. g., *1 En.* 61:1–5; *T. Ab.* 12:5–15; *t. Qidd.* 1:13–14).

7. *Treasure in heaven was closely associated with resurrection.* In 2 Maccabees, Colossians, and 1 Peter the recompense laid up in heaven for those who sleep in godliness *is* resurrection. In 1 Timothy heavenly treasure is the foundation that allows one to take hold of eternal life. Similarly, Wisdom of Solomon describes the afterlife of the godly as the "wages of holiness."

8. *Despite the axiomatic belief that God will "repay to each according to his deeds," the meting out of heavenly treasure is not rigidly mechanistic.* As

---

73 Cf. the interpretation of Prov 19:17 and 10:2 in *Sib. Or.* 2.78–82

Sanders recognized, the belief that God repays everyone according
to their deeds is based on a belief that God is just.[74] This point is illustrated well in Psalm 62:13: "to you O Lord belongs covenant
faithfulness (חסד), for you repay each according to his deeds." Belief
that God "repays" everyone according to their deeds was not based
in the conviction that God is like a strict bank manager who only
gives people exactly what they deserve, but in the conviction that
God is good. Frequently one finds frank admissions that the repayment one can expect goes far beyond what one actually deserves. As
Sirach puts it, "Give to the Most High as he has given to you, and as
generously as you can afford. For the Lord is the one who repays,
and he will repay you sevenfold" (35:12–13). Similarly, *2 Baruch*
notes that it is precisely in showing mercy to those without heavenly
treasure that God shows his patience.[75]

9. *Heavenly treasures are sometimes said to benefit people other than those who
earned them.* In 2 Maccabees 12, for example, Judas and his men pray
and collect money to offer sacrifices so that their comrades who had
died while committing idolatry would receive "the splendid reward
that is stored up for those who sleep in godliness" (see also *T.
Ab.* 14; Philo's *Sacr.* 118–126; *m.'Avot* 2:2).

---

74 *Paul and Palestinian Judaism*, 127–28.
75 To invoke the typology of reciprocity of Marshall Sahlins (*Stone Age Economics*
[2nd ed.; London/New York: Routledge, 2004], esp. 185–230), many of the
tropes in the literature surveyed here are drawn from the realm of "balanced
reciprocity," i.e., reciprocity which aims for strict *quid pro quo* accuracy, especially when it comes to market exchange. Yet, these texts describe God as forgiving and faithful etc. and the language of balanced reciprocity frequently gives
way to "generalized reciprocity," i.e., the open and less defined exchange
found in families and between close friends.

2 Heavenly Treasures and Debts in Matthew

Having traced the broad contours of heavenly debts and treasures in other early Jewish and Christian texts, we turn now to a thematic study of Matthew's treasure and debt language.

2.1 Debts

2.1.1 "Cancel our Debts for us" (6:9−15) and the Parable of the Unforgiving Servant (18:23−35)

As noted in the introduction, the most famous example of debt language in the New Testament may be the Matthean version of the Lord's Prayer, usually translated: "Forgive us our debts as we also forgive our debtors" (ἄφες ἡμῖν τὰ ὀφειλήματα ἡμῶν, ὡς καὶ ἡμεῖς ἀφήκαμεν τοῖς ὀφειλέταις ἡμῶν) (6:12). Matthew's restatement of the petition in verses 14−15 ("For if you forgive people their trespasses (παραπτώματα), your heavenly Father will also forgive") shows that "debt" is used here to mean sin. The familiarity of these words can obscure the fact that, if judged by non-Jewish and Christian Greek, this petition is rather odd. As Raymond Brown noted, "The Matthean use of 'debts' has a Semitic flavor; for, while in secular Greek "debt" has no religious coloring, in Aramaic *ḥôbâ* is a financial and commercial term that has been caught up into the religious vocabulary… The idea of remitting (*aphienai*) debts which appears in our petition is also more Semitic than Greek, for 'remission' has a religious sense only in the Greek of the LXX, which is under Hebrew influence."[1] In other words, ἀφίημι and ὀφείλημα were not ordinarily used in contemporary Greek to refer to the forgiveness of sins, but if ret-

---

1   "The Pater Noster as an Eschatological Prayer," *TS* 22 (1961): 175−208, 200. Some copyists of Luke 23:34a ("Father forgive [ἄφες] them, for they do not know what they are doing") took advantage of the idiomatic Jewish-Christian use of ἀφίημι, replacing it with the synonym συγχωρέω, apparently in an attempt to avoid portraying Jesus praying for the forgiveness of the Jews. See Nathan Eubank, "A Disconcerting Prayer: On the Originality of Luke 23:34a," *JBL* 129 (2010): 521−36, esp. 531−32.

rojected into a Semitic idiom the prayer is not unusual at all.[2] Indeed, the Lukan version, "Forgive us our sins (τὰς ἁμαρτίας)" (11:4), may be an attempt to translate the prayer into more idiomatic Greek.[3]

The standard translation of ἀφίημι in the Lord's Prayer as "forgive" obscures the fact that the petition uses the language of commerce. Though the English word "forgive" can be used in economic contexts (e. g., "debt forgiveness"), among Anglophones it is also the generic, all-purpose word for overlooking or eliminating wrongdoing. It does not evoke any particular understanding of sin and its absolution. It is, in other words, the most non-metaphorical word of its kind in English. Therein lies its inadequacy; the petition in Matthew 6:12 does not use generic language of forgiveness but the unmistakable language of commerce.[4] Greek speakers who encountered the prayer presumably would have heard it first as a request for debt-cancellation. One possible alternative would be "remit," a word with stronger financial connotations.[5] Like ἀφίημι, "remit" suggests release or sending forward; debts are "released" or let go. Yet, "remit" is admittedly somewhat obscure. A clearer translation would perhaps be "cancel," a word which, along with its cognates, is the commonest way to refer to the elimination of debts in English. The petition in 6:12 would therefore be rendered something like "Cancel our debts for us, as we too cancel for those in debt to us."[6] In contexts where "debts" are clearly the object of ἀφίημι, both "remit" and "cancel" are preferable to forgive.

In the parable of the ungrateful servant (18:23–35) Matthew clarifies the meaning of Jesus' command to pray that our debts would be

---

2   See LSJ; MM. The use of ἀφίημι as "forgive" is not unheard of in non-Jewish and non-Christian sources. See Herodotus' *Hist.* 8.140 (using the object τὰς ἁμαρτάδας).

3   Davies and Allison, *A Critical and Exegetical Commentary on the Gospel according to Saint Matthew* (3 vols; ICC; Edinburgh: T&T Clark, 1988–1997), 1.611, et al. Note also the retention of ὀφείλοντι in Luke 11:4b, which suggests Luke was working with a version of the prayer that preserved the Semitic expression.

4   For a discussion of the pairing of ἀφίημι and ὀφείλημα/ὀφειλέτης in documentary papyri noting similarities between the Lord's Prayer and Ptolemaic amnesty decrees, see Giovanni Battista Bazzana, "*Basileia* and Debt Relief: The Forgiveness of Debts in the Lord's Prayer in the Light of Documentary Papyri," *CBQ* 73 (2011): 511–25.

5   Cf. the Jerusalem Bible: "Remets-nous nos dettes comme nous-mêmes avons remis à nos débiteurs."

6   This is very similar to Bazzana's translation of the petition, "*Basileia* and Debt Relief," 512.

cancelled just as we cancel the debts of others. After telling Peter that he must forgive one who sins against him, not seven times, but seventy-seven times (ἑβδομηκοντάκις ἑπτά[7]), Jesus says,

> For this reason the kingdom of the heavens may be compared to a king who desired to settle accounts (συνᾶραι λόγον) with his slaves. When he began the settling, a debtor who owed him ten thousand talents (εἷς ὀφει-λέτης μυρίων ταλάντων) was brought to him; and, as he could not pay (μὴ ἔχοντος δὲ αὐτοῦ ἀποδοῦναι), his lord ordered him to be sold (πραθῆναι), along with his wife and children and all his possessions (καὶ τὴν γυναῖκα καὶ τὰ τέκνα καὶ πάντα ὅσα ἔχει), and payment to be made (ἀποδοθῆναι). So the slave fell prostrate before him, saying, "Have patience with me, and I will pay you everything (πάντα ἀποδώσω σοι)." And out of pity for him, the lord of that slave released him and canceled the debt for him (τὸ δάνειον ἀφῆκεν αὐτῷ). But that same slave, as he went out, came upon one of his fellow slaves who owed him a hundred denarii; and seizing him he began to choke him saying, "Pay what you owe (ἀπόδος εἴ τι ὀφεί-λεις)." Then falling down his fellow slave pleaded with him, "Have patience with me, and I will pay you (ἀποδώσω σοι)." But he refused; then he went and threw him into prison until he would pay what he owes (ἕως ἀποδῷ τὸ ὀφειλόμενον). When his fellow slaves saw what happened, they were greatly distressed, and they went and reported to their lord all that happened. Then his lord summoned him and said to him, "You wicked slave! I forgave you all that debt (πᾶσαν τὴν ὀφειλὴν ἐκείνην ἀφῆκά σοι) because you pleaded with me. Should you not have had mercy on your fellow slave, as I had mercy on you?" And in anger his lord handed him over to the torturers until he would pay all that he owes (ἕως οὗ ἀποδῷ πᾶν τὸ ὀφειλόμενον). So my heavenly Father will also do to every one of you, if you do not cancel (ἐὰν μὴ ἀφῆτε) for your brother from your hearts.

The parable is reminiscent of the χειρόγραφον (note of indebtedness) discussed above in connection with Colossians 2:13−14.[8] The servant who

---

7 The phrase ἑβδομηκοντάκις ἑπτά is also found in Gen 4:24 where it refers to the limitless vengeance of Lamech. Here it refers to limitless forgiveness. See Davies and Allison, *Matthew*, 2.792−94. Though a direct allusion is unlikely, one is also reminded of the *shemittah* year described in Deut 15: every seven years there is to be שמטה (LXX: ἄφεσις) of debts. The Year of Jubilee, which, according to Lev 25, was to occur after seven sevens of years, is called τὸ ἔτος τῆς ἀφέσεως in the LXX. In 11QMelch the "release" of Jubilee is reinterpreted as a release from sins. See John Sietze Bergsma, *The Jubilee from Leviticus to Qumran: A History of Interpretation* (VTSup 115; Leiden: Brill, 2007), 277−91.

8 Cf. the line in the χειρόγραφον discussed above: "But if I do not repay in the period stipulated I will pay you the established interest until I repay or be forced to pay the entire loan, completely; the right of execution [i.e., the right to exact the money from the debtor] belongs to you and to anyone who through you or

defaults on his loan is liable to be sold along with all his possessions so that payment can be made. The parable expands on the petition in 6:12 and 14. Sin puts one in danger of becoming a debt-slave, but God will cancel the debts of those who ask him, provided that they in turn cancel the debts of their fellow servants.[9]

2.1.2 Pay back all you owe (18:34–35; 5:21–26)

Another detail in the parable of the unforgiving servant is worth noting. At the conclusion in 18:34–35 the master hands the servant over to the torturers "until he pays all that he owes (ἕως οὗ ἀποδῷ πᾶν τὸ ὀφειλόμε-νον)." This raises the question of how the servant could repay all that he owes if he is in prison. Most commentators assume that the servant can-not pay back what he owes, and that Jesus' words refer here in a round-about way to eternal punishment. For instance, Davies and Allison say that "As the parable now stands, with the debt amounting to 10,000 tal-ents, the punishment must be perpetual, for a debt so immense could never be repaid. Thus the situation is a transparent symbol of eschato-logical judgment."[10] It is true that 10,000 talents was a fantastically high sum. One might object, however, that the point in making the first servant's debt so great is not to illustrate the impossibility of repay-ment so much as to contrast it with the relatively paltry debt (100 de-narii) that his fellow servant owed him. The hortatory force of the con-trast is similar to the earlier image of someone with a plank in his eye who attempts to remove a speck from someone else's (7:3–5). The in-congruity emphasizes the folly of refusing to cancel the debt of one's brother – chances are the person who refuses to forgive has already

---

on your behalf validly presents this bond of indebtedness both from me and from all my possessions (ἔκ τε ἐμοῦ καὶ ἐκ τῶν ὑ[παρχόντων μοι] π[ά]ντων)."

9 Gary Anderson, *Sin: A History* (New Haven: Yale University Press, 2009), 32–3.

10 *Matthew*, 2.803. cf. Craig Keener, "The magnitude of the debt was simply un-payable by any means, and the man would *never* escape the torturers," (*A Com-mentary on the Gospel of Matthew* [Grand Rapids, MI.: Eerdmans, 1999], 461; Marie-Joseph Lagrange, *Évangile selon Saint Matthieu* (EBib;Paris: Gabalda, 1927), 363. Luz is a bit more cautious: "Jedenfalls ist im Gefälle der Erzählung deutlich, daß der 'Große' mit seiner Riesenschuld, die er nun ganz abzahlen muß, kaum mehr eine Chance hat, wieder aus dem Gefängnis herauszukom-men, obwohl die Parabel auch das nicht explizit sagt," (*Das Evangelium nach Matthäus* [4 vols.; EKK 1/1–4; Düsseldort: Benziger, 1990–2002], 3.73.

been forgiven an even greater debt. It is worth exploring, therefore, whether the parable does envision some means of paying back the debt while in prison. After all, in light of the words ἕως οὗ ἀποδῷ πᾶν τὸ ὀφειλόμενον it would seem prima facie likely that the parable does not envision never-ending confinement.

Matthew 5:21–26, the first so-called antithesis in the Sermon on the Mount, may help to clarify matters. In 5:22 Jesus says that it is not enough simply to refrain from murder; mere anger against a brother makes one guilty: "But I say to you that whoever is angry with his brother is liable to judgment. And whoever says to his brother 'Idiot,' will be liable to the council. And whoever says 'Fool,' will be liable to the Gehenna of fire." This claim is given further elaboration in the next two verses, which explain that one's ability to bring an offering to God is impeded if there is unresolved sin between the person bringing the offering and his brother. In other words, sins again one's brother damage one's relationship with God: "Therefore, when you bring your gift to the altar and there remember that your brother has something against you (ἔχει τι κατὰ σοῦ), leave your gift there before the altar and go first and be reconciled with your brother and then go and offer your gift" (5:23–24). Like verse 22, this continues the intensification of the command "you will not murder," by claiming that even the most minor sins against one's brother – note the indefinite ὁ ἀδελφός σου ἔχει τι κατὰ σοῦ – should be dealt with before bringing an offering. The section ends with verses 25–26: "Make friends with your enemy quickly, while you are with him on the way (ἕως ὅτου εἶ μετ' αὐτοῦ ἐν τῇ ὁδῷ), lest your enemy hand you over to the judge, and the judge to the guard and you will be thrown into prison. Truly I say to you, you will certainly not go out from there until you repay the last penny (οὐ μὴ ἐξέλθῃς ἐκεῖθεν, ἕως ἂν ἀποδῷς τὸν ἔσχατον κοδράντην)." Most commentators see this as a close parallel of the parable of the ungrateful servant rather than just a bit of advice on how to avoid being thrown into debtor's prison. In verse 22 and again in verses 23–24 Jesus emphasizes that any sin against another person is an issue not just between people but between the sinner and God. Indeed, the earthly judgment in verse 22 (ἔνοχος ἔσται τῷ συνεδρίῳ) is restated to culminate in divine judgment (ἔνοχος ἔσται εἰς τὴν γέενναν τοῦ πυρός). Furthermore, as Luz notes, the introduction ἀμήν almost always introduces some sort of eschatological

saying, oftentimes dealing with divine recompense.[11] Thus, it would go
against the grain of both the Matthean idiom and the flow of 5:21–26 if
verses 25–26 have only earthly debts in view. Davies and Allison would
seem to be largely justified, then, if a bit overconfident, in concluding
"No doubt Matthew thought of this clause [ἕως ἂν ἀποδῷς τὸν ἔσχατον
κοδράντην] as alluding to punishment in Gehenna (cf. 5.22)."[12] Just as
the earlier verses indicate, then, unresolved debts (i. e., sins) against another person are in fact sins against God, who will certainly collect what
is due.

Jesus' warning "Truly I say to you, you will certainly not go out
from there until you repay the last penny" is an illuminating parallel
of 18:34.[13] There is no question here of a debt that is too large to
repay, only that one's entire debt must be repaid before "you go out
from there." In spite of this, however, commentators still almost universally assume that verses 25–26 refer to never-ending punishment. Gundry, for instance, writes that "failure to make things right with a brother
in the church falsifies profession of discipleship and lands a person in
hell, the prison of eternally hopeless debtors…"[14] Yet, both here and
in 18:34 Jesus' warning seems to indicate that imprisonment will last
until the debt is paid. It is worth exploring the possibility that Matthew
is saying that it is possible to repay debts from prison, that is, from Gehenna.[15]

---

11   "So wird hinter der Oberfläche eines Klugheitsrates die Perspektive des letzten
     Gerichts sichtbar. Matthäus signalisiert sie durch sein fast immer auf eine escha-
     tologisch-endgerichtliche Aussage weisendes Lieblingswort ἀμήν und das an
     vielen Stellen ähnlich gebrauchte λέγω…" *Matthäus*, 1.346.
12   *Matthew*, 1.521. cf. also Keener, *Matthew*, 185; John Nolland, *The Gospel of
     Matthew: A Commentary on the Greek Text* (NIGTC; Grand Rapids, MI: Eerd-
     mans, 2005), 234; Robert Horton Gundry, *Matthew: A Commentary on his
     Handbook for a Mixed Church under Persecution* (2d ed; Grand Rapids, MI: Eerd-
     mans, 1994), 87. Hans Dieter Betz argues to the contrary, *The Sermon on the
     Mount: A Commentary on the Sermon on the Mount* (Minneapolis; Fortress
     Press, 1995), 227.
13   A κοδράντης, from the Latin *quadrans*, is worth one sixty-fourth of a denarius.
14   *Handbook*, 87. Cf. Keener, "Through a variety of terrible, graphic images, Jesus
     indicates that when one damages one's relationship with others one damages
     one's relationship with God, leading to eternal punishment (cf. 18:21–35),"
     Matthew, 185.
15   It is also possible that Matthew is simply sustaining the metaphor of debt-bond-
     age to the end of the saying. I shall return to this point momentarily.

According to both Greek and Roman sources, debt was the commonest reason for imprisonment in antiquity, including first-century Palestine.[16] The purpose of such imprisonment was not purely punitive but coercive. That is, incarceration was intended to compel debtors to produce any hidden funds they might have, and, should that fail, to incite friends or family to pay the ransom – that is, to pay the debt.[17] Physical torments added further incentive.[18] When the debt was paid prisoners were released. For modern biblical scholars the image of someone being confined until he "repays the last penny" may evoke images of everlasting damnation, but Matthew's audience would have thought first of prisons which were for the most part "temporary holding cells in which offenders, and these mainly debtors, endured brief stays."[19]

Just as debtor's prison was intended to be a temporary means of facilitating the repayment of a debt, Gehenna was sometimes thought of as a temporary place of chastisement. Scholars tend to equate Gehenna with eternal perdition or "hell," but the concept was in fact more fluid than that. According to t. *Sanhedrin* 13:3 the House of Shammai taught that Gehenna was a place where some go temporarily to atone for sin, while others are punished there eternally:

> A. The House of Shammai says, "There are three groups, one for eternal life, one *for shame and everlasting contempt* (Dan. 12:2) – these are those who are completely evil.
> B. "An intermediate group go down to Gehenna and scream and come up again and are healed,
> C. "as it is said, *I will bring the third part through fire and will refine them as silver is refined and will test them as gold is tested, and they shall call on my name and I will be their God* (Zech. 13:9).
> D. "And concerning them did Hannah say, *The Lord kills and brings to life, brings down to Sheol and brings up* (I Sam. 2:6)."[20]

This passage indicates that Gehenna was sometimes viewed as a place where redemptive suffering takes place, a process of purification

---

16   Ramon Sugranyes de Franch, *Études sur le droit palestinien à l'époque évangélique* (Fribourg: Librairie de l'Université, 1946), 60–3; John Bauschatz, "Ptolemaic Prisons Reconsidered," *The Classical Bulletin* 83 (2007): 3–47, esp. 4–5.
17   Sugranyes de Franch, *Études*, 60; Hans G. Kippenberg, *Religion und Klassenbildung im antiken Judäa* (SUNT 14; Göttingen: Vandenhoeck und Ruprecht, 1978), 142–44; Bauschatz, "Ptolemaic Prisons Reconsidered," 4–5.
18   Sugranyes de Franch, *Études*, 62–3.
19   Bauschatz, "Ptolemaic Prisons," 5. Ptolemaic prisons, in contrast, were more likely to hold offenders for a longer period of time.
20   Cf., *m. 'Ed.* 2:10.

which is compared to refining metal in fire (Zech 13:9). Similarly, according to the Mishnah, rabbi Akiva said that the unrighteous will suffer in Gehenna for only twelve months (*m. 'Ed.* 2.10). Second Maccabees 12 shows that there existed the belief that some kind of atonement could take place after death and prior to the resurrection well before the late first century C.E when Matthew was written. *Testament of Abraham* (c. late first century) describes God weighing the debt of sin against righteous deeds and temporarily "repaying" (ἀνταπόδοσις) sinners with punishment at the hand of torturers (τοῖς βασανισταῖς ἐξέδωκεν) but then answering Abraham's prayer for mercy by letting them go.

It may be that something closely analogous to these texts forms a part of Matthew's view of the repayment of the debt of sin. In some instances Matthew does speak of eschatological punishment in a way that gives no indication that it is anything but permanent (e.g., 25:41). In 5:25–26 and 18:23–35, however, Matthew uses the image of debtor's bondage, stating that the debtor would not get out until he "repays the last penny/all that he owes." I would suggest that there is little reason other than theological prejudice to assume that this must refer to eternal damnation.[21] The point of debtor's prison was to secure the missing funds, not to lock debtors away indefinitely. In light of this and the fact that belief in the post-mortem atonement of sins is fairly well-attested, it seems reasonable to suppose that when Matthew speaks of debt-bondage that lasts "until" the debt is repaid it means that the debt-bondage will in fact come to an end.[22] This is not to suggest that Matthew features a well-developed understanding of purgato-

---

21   One could appeal to the fact that the overall emphasis in Matthew is decidedly on the last judgment when some will be sent into "eternal" (αἰώνιος) punishment (e.g., 25:46) or the "outer darkness where there will be weeping and gnashing of teeth" (22:13). Yet, belief in a final judgment is not mutually exclusive with the belief that some sort of judgment takes place prior to the eschaton. *T.Ab.* 13, for instance, speaks of an initial judgment of souls which is followed by a final and irrevocable judgment by God. Luke appears to maintain belief in recompense at the return of the Son of Man (9:26; 12:35–48; Acts 17:30–31), but is also able to entertain the idea of immediate post-mortem judgment (16:19–31), albeit in a parable with a folkloric quality. Matthew's main concern is obviously the Parousia, but this does not preclude the additional possibility of judgment prior to that time.

22   While it is true that ἕως does not require a change of circumstances (e.g., Matt 28:20; 1 Cor 15:25), it is difficult to see how ἕως could be understood in any other way here in light of the coercive nature of debt-bondage.

ry, but only that 5:25–26 and 18:23–35 may assume that it is possible to pay one's debts after death.[23]

This raises the question of what sort of payment one could generate while in prison. As already noted, debtor's prison was used to compel family and friends to pool resources to free the debtor. It is possible, therefore, that these passages would have evoked something like the scenes in 2 Maccabees 12 or *Testament of Abraham*, where the comrades of those who died in sin pray on their behalf. According to this line of thinking, a person would be in Gehenna until his friends generate enough treasure in heaven to free him. There is another possibility which may be closer to Matthew's own concerns. In 18:34 the unforgiving servant is not simply confined but handed over to "the torturers" (τοῖς βασανισταῖς). It may be that the suffering endured generates heavenly capital. A number of OT and early Jewish texts describe suffering as something that repays the debt of sin, and Matthew states that suffering on behalf of Jesus earns a heavenly wage (e. g., 5:11–12).[24] Both 5:25–

---

23 Cf. Tertullian (c. 160–220), who identifies the accuser in 5:25 with the devil. Those who default on the obligation to renounce the devil and follow the requirements of the faith are incarcerated in the prison below (*in carcerem infernum*), where they remain in the time before the resurrection until they have repaid even their smallest sins (*An.* 35). Cyprian (d. 258) argues that Christian penitential practices do not destroy the "vigor of continence" because "it is one thing to stand for pardon, another to arrive at glory. *It is one thing, having been cast into prison, not to go out from there until one has paid the very last* quadrans, *another, to receive immediately the wages of faith and virtue.* It is one thing, having been tortured for sins by long suffering, to be cleansed and long purged by fire; another to purge all sins by suffering. In short, it is one thing to pay out until the sentence of the Lord at the day of judgment, another to be crowned immediately by the Lord (*Epistle 55*)." Commenting on Rom 5, Origen (c. 184–253) says that righteousness will be effective in all people when they are able "not only to hear and understand the word of God but to do it. For although it is promised one to go out of prison at some point, nevertheless it is ordained that it is not possible to go out from there unless each person pays back even the last penny. But if even the punishment of a penny – which is that of the least sin – is not remitted unless it is paid back in prison through suffering, how could someone be released in hope of impunity or think that the gift of grace is a license to sin?" (*Comm. Rom.* 5.2). On Luke 12:57–59//Matt 5:25–26 Origen says "It is not possible to say clearly how long we are shut up in the prison while we pay the debt. For if one who owes a little does not come out until he pays the last penny, then surely for one who owed a great debt boundless ages will be numbered for paying what is owed" (*Hom. Luc.* 35.15).

24 Isaiah 40:1–2. See Anderson, *Sin*, 44–54.

26 and 18:23–35 may, therefore, envision suffering that allows one to repay to the last penny one's debt of sin. This would be similar to *t. Sanhedrin* 13:3 except for the fact that the Tosefta says that suffering in Gehenna heals the sufferer, as fire cleanses impurities from metal, whereas Matthew uses the language of repayment.[25]

One might object that when Jesus says, "You will never go out from there until you repay the last penny," he is simply sustaining the metaphor of debt bondage until the end of the saying. Not every detail of a parable – or, in 5:21–26, parabolic discourse – is significant. It is possible that Jesus speaks of release from prison only because this language followed naturally from the image of debt bondage. I would suggest, however, that the flow of 5:21–26 as a whole tips the scales against this reading. The emphasis in this passage is on the punishment of small offenses. In 5:22 Jesus says that those who call someone a "fool" are liable to punishment in Gehenna. There is an apparent increase in severity in 5:22 in the movement from the generic κρίσις to συνέδριον and then to γέεννα τοῦ πυρός.[26] Many interpreters have sought to find a corresponding increase in severity in the progression from being angry to saying ῥακά and then μωρέ, but none of these is clearly

---

25 Another Matthean oddity is worth considering in light of 5:25–26 and 18:23– 35. In the Beelzebub controversy Jesus claims that "Whoever speaks a word against the Son of Man, it will be forgiven him; but whoever speaks a word against the Holy Spirit, it will not be forgiven him in this world nor in the world to come (12:32)." This is a notoriously difficult verse. Augustine and others after him argued that this verse shows that some sins are forgiven in the world to come (*De civ. Dei* 21.24; cf. also Gregory the Great, *Dial.* 4.39). This is by no means a necessary conclusion. Indeed, a more obvious reading of this verse taken in isolation would be to take οὔτε ἐν τῷ μέλλοντι as roughly equivalent to saying this sin will never be forgiven. Yet, the hints in 5:21–26 and 18:23–35 that payment of sins is possible after death lend a new plausibility to Augustine's interpretation. In the Markan version Jesus simply says that the one who blasphemes the Holy Spirit οὐκ ἔχει ἄφεσιν εἰς τὸν αἰῶνα, ἀλλὰ ἔνοχός ἐστιν αἰωνίου ἁμαρτήματος. Luke more tersely states that such blasphemy οὐκ ἀφεθήσεται. Matthew, however, stresses that this blasphemy will be forgiven neither in the present age nor in the coming age. This special Matthean emphasis is suggestive in combination with Matthew's image of debt-bondage; whereas Mark simply states that blasphemy against the Holy Spirit is an unforgiveable sin, Matthew may be indicating that this sin is the one sin that cannot be repaid in Gehenna.

26 Keener, *Matthew*, 183–84, argues that there is no increase in severity because κρίσις refers to God's judgment and συνέδριον refers to God's heavenly court.

more severe than another.[27] Luz's analysis is more satisfying: "V 22a ist allgemeiner Obersatz, V 22b.c sind zuspitzende Konkretionen. Sie machen klar, wie ernst V 22a gemeint ist, und lassen 'Zorn' schon bei den banalsten Schimpfworten beginnen."[28] Even the commonest insults, as expressions of anger, make one liable to be punished by the council and by the fires of Gehenna. This would seem to be an impossibily harsh saying; even the least expression of anger makes a person subject to punishment in "hell" (as γέεννα is usually translated here). Indeed, though much has been written on Matthew's high ethical demands and his emphasis on divine judgment, commentators do not often directly confront the fact that in this verse Jesus appears to say that anyone who calls his brother a moderately rude name will be eternally damned. Even if the saying is read as hyperbole, as Davies and Allison plausibly suggest, it gestures toward an astonishingly strict understanding of divine judgment.

Verses 25–26 may clarify what verse 22 is saying; even the last penny of debt must be paid. It is not only obvious sins such as murder which will be punished. Rather, the law applies to one's inner life and motivations, and to one's everyday dealings with others. Thus, even if a person refrains from murder, he will be thrown into "prison" and will not go out until he has paid the last penny if he does not settle the debt with his brother. It is possible that this means everlasting punishment, but another possibility emerges in light of verses 21–26 taken as a whole. Even the smallest sins against a "brother" obstruct one's relationship with God. Thus, it is necessary to deal with such sin before bringing a gift before the altar (23–24) or before facing God's judgment (25–26). Similarly, verses 21–22 show that even the smallest sins against a brother are, like murder, punishable offenses. Those who simply call someone "fool" will pay for it in Gehenna, not with everlasting torment, but "until they repay the last penny."

2.1.3 Fill up the measure (23:32; 7:1–2)

After Jesus enters Jerusalem the conflict with the chief priests and elders of the people as well as the scribes and Pharisees reaches a fever pitch. In chapter 23 Jesus denounces the scribes and Pharisees at length, claiming

---

27   Davies and Allison, *Matthew*, 1.515.
28   *Matthäus*, I. 337–38. Also Nolland, *Matthew*, 231.

that eschatological judgment is about to come on them. At one point
Jesus ironically tells them to "fill up the measure of your fathers":

> Woe to you, scribes and Pharisees, hypocrites, because you build the tombs
> of the prophets and decorate the graves of the righteous, and say, "If we
> had lived in the days of our fathers, we would not have participated with
> them in the blood of the prophets. Thus you witness against yourselves
> that you are the sons of those who murdered the prophets. *Fill up the meas-
> ure of your fathers!* Snakes, brood of vipers, how can you escape the judg-
> ment of Gehenna? Therefore, behold, I send you prophets and wise
> men and scribes; you will kill and crucify some of them and you will
> whip some of them in your synagogues and pursue them from city to
> city, so that all the righteous blood shed on earth may come on you,
> from the blood of Abel the righteous to the blood of Zechariah son of Bar-
> achiah, whom you murdered between the sanctuary and the altar. Truly I
> say to you, all these things will come on this generation. (23:29–36)

Scholars agree that the words ὑμεῖς πληρώσατε τὸ μέτρον τῶν πατέρων
ὑμῶν envision a preordained amount of evil that will be tolerated before
God steps in to punish the offenders.[29] The guilt for all the blood which
has been shed since Abel will come on this generation because the
scribes and Pharisees finally "fill up" the measure that has been filling
throughout the history of the world. The guilt reaches a certain tipping
point and so God will step in and punish them.

What sort of filling up is in view here? Keener imagines a cup of
suffering: "Jesus tells his adversaries to fill to the brim the role of proph-
et-murderers they had inherited, and that the judgment collecting for
generations would finally be poured out in their generation."[30] Matthew does describe this filling up as leading to the suffering of "this generation" and he does speak of a cup of suffering on a number of occasions (20:22–23; 26:39). Yet, none of the parallels cited by Keener, nor
any others of which I am aware, describe a cup of suffering as gradually
filling up because of sin before it is poured out or drunk. Moreover,
Jesus says "fill up the measure (τὸ μέτρον) of your fathers," not "fill
up the cup of your fathers." Though it is not impossible that a cup is
implied (i. e., "Fill up the limit [of the cup] of your fathers"), a less
strained interpretation would be worth considering.[31]

Matthew himself provides a clue to another possibility. In 7:1–2
Jesus says Μὴ κρίνετε, ἵνα μὴ κριθῆτε· ἐν ᾧ γὰρ κρίματι κρίνετε κριθήσεσθε,

---

29 E.g., Davies and Allison, *Matthew*, 3.306.
30 *Matthew*, 554.
31 See LSJ μέτρον 3.b for μέτρον as "limit".

καὶ ἐν ᾧ μέτρῳ μετρεῖτε μετρηθήσεται ὑμῖν. The basic sense of this statement is clear: the harshness or leniency with which one judges others will determine the harshness or leniency by which one will be judged by God. As Luz puts it, "Da wir alle vor Gottes Gericht stehen werden, werden diejenigen Maßstäbe, die wir an andere anlegen, einst an uns angelegt werden."[32] The synonymous parallel of verse 2 moves from a generic claim that people will be judged according to the way they have judged others (ἐν ᾧ γὰρ κρίματι κρίνετε κριθήσεσθε) to the vivid image of a "measure" (καὶ ἐν ᾧ μέτρῳ μετρεῖτε μετρηθήσεται ὑμῖν). The saying "by the measure you use it will be measured to you" is a common one in rabbinic literature, where it frequently expresses the principle of *lex talionis*; punishments are given which fit the crime.[33] In Matthew 7, however, the expression is used in a more specific sense; it is not only that everyone will receive a punishment fitting their crimes, but that God will judge a person using the same standard of judgment that that person used in judging others.[34]

Bernard Couroyer's 1970 article, "De la mesure dont vous mesurez il vous sera mesuré," may shed light on what sort of measure is in view.[35] Demotic and Greek loan contracts from Egypt frequently include the proviso that when grain is repaid it must be measured with the same measure that was used to measure the grain that was loaned. For example, a contract from the year 113 B.C.E. states that the loan must be repaid "in wheat, new, pure, paid at the house [of the lender],

---

32 *Matthäus*, I.491. Note the very different use of the saying in Mark 4:24 which Joel Marcus summarizes as "people will receive insight according to the measure of their attentiveness." *Mark*, 1.320.

33 E.g., *t. Soṭa* 3.1–5 where it is said that an adulteress receives punishments fitting her crimes, such as having her hair untied since she had braided it for her co-adulterer.

34 Cf. Theodor Zahn, who notes that in rabbinic literature "'Mit dem Maß, womit der Mensch mißt, mißt man ihm' ist die Kongruenz zwischen Sünde und Strafe, nicht wie hier [Matt 7:2] zwischen der Strafzumessung des richtenden Menschen und der Strafzumessung Gottes oder anderer Menschen ausgedrückt." *Das Evangelium des Matthäus* (Kommentar zum Neuen Testament; 1927; repr., Wuppertal: R. Brockhaus, 1984), 303n22.

35 *RB* 77 (1970): 366–70. The papyrological evidence supporting Couroyer's argument has been greatly augmented in the last forty years. See John S. Kloppenborg, "Agrarian Discourse and the Sayings of Jesus: 'Measure for Measure' in Gospel Traditions and Agricultural Practices," in *Engaging Economics: New Testament Scenarios and Early Christian Reception* (ed. Bruce W. Longenecker and Kelly D. Liebengood; Grand Rapids, MI: Eerdmans, 2009), 104–28.

at his own cost, [measured] with the measure with which he took it (μέτρῳ ὦι καὶ παρείληφεν)."[36] The same and similar formulae are repeated in numerous papyri dating from the third century B.C.E. into the third century C.E.[37] It is not hard to imagine why this was a common practice. Weights and sack sizes would have varied, even when no fraud was intended. The best way to ensure that someone pays exactly what is owed is to require him to repay his debt with the same measure that he used to measure out the loan in the first place. Something similar appears to be imagined in Matthew 7:2. When assessing the debt of someone else's sin, the sort of measure one uses makes all the difference. One could endeavor to be unwaveringly accurate, using weights or sacks that ensure the debt is recorded perfectly. On the other hand, one might be tempted to use a dishonest measure that exaggerates the debt of sin. Another option – the one implicitly recommended in 7:2 – is to be less than exacting with one's measure. God will use the same measure to assess a person's sin that that person used in assessing others. It would be wise, therefore, to use a very generous measure, lest one's own debts be recorded with exacting precision, or worse – dishonest exaggeration.[38]

This warning to assess the debts of others generously is closely related to the preceding petition in the Lord's Prayer (ἄφες ἡμῖν τὰ ὀφειλήματα ἡμῶν, ὡς καὶ ἡμεῖς ἀφήκαμεν τοῖς ὀφειλέταις ἡμῶν). Both the parable of the unforgiving servant and 7:1–2 appear to be illustrations of this idea. In the parable, it is not a question of how to record the debts. It is simply stated that the servant owed his master ten thousand talents and another servant owed the first servant a much lower sum, a hundred denarii. The warning in 7:2 approaches the issue from a different angle. Just as it is necessary to cancel the debts of others, care must be taken in recording those debts in the first place. A person who uses a measure that exaggerates the debts of others or that records them exactly will have his debt assessed with the very same measure. It would be wiser to "cancel for our debtors" by not recording their debts at all.

I would suggest that the measure in 23:32 is, like the measure in 7:2, a measure that records the amount that is owed. Jesus describes the scribes and Pharisees as the sons of those who murdered the prophets. Guilt has been piling up for centuries but the breaking point is near.

---

36 *P.Amh.* II 46.
37 See Kloppenborg, "Agrarian Discourse and the Sayings of Jesus," 111–12.
38 Cf. 1 Cor 13:5.

When Jesus tells them to "fill up the measure of your fathers," he would be ironically telling them to bring the debt of their fathers to its limit, the point at which the creditor can tolerate it no more and steps in to collect what is due. The underlying conception of sin as debt is identical to 7:2. The difference is that 7:2 is a warning to be generous when measuring the debts of others, whereas 23:32 is a prophetic declaration that the debt is about to reach its full measure, the time when the creditor comes to settle accounts.[39]

In sum: for Matthew sin is debt. Those who sin against God or against another person are in danger of being thrown into debtor's prison (i.e., Gehenna) where they will remain until they pay back all they owe. God, however, will cancel the debts of those who ask him provided that they in turn cancel the debts of those who have sinned against them. Similarly, God will evaluate the indebtedness of a person using the same measure (i.e., probably a sack size) that he uses to measure the indebtedness of others. As in texts such as 2 Maccabees, the debt of sin is not only an individual matter but a corporate one as well. This can be seen clearly when Jesus tells the scribes and Pharisees to "fill up the measure of [their] fathers," thereby bringing the punishment stored up by generations of sin on their heads. In the following chapter I shall argue that the prologue of the Gospel (1:1–4:22) portrays Jesus' people as in exile due to the debt of sin.

---

39 This interpretation of 23:32 finds corroboration in Gary Anderson's (*Sin*, 75–94) argument that the idiom found in the Hebrew Bible, Dead Sea Scrolls, and elsewhere "to complete the sin" refers either to the moment when a debt reaches the point where the creditor must step in and collect, or, depending on context, to the time when the debtor has fulfilled his obligation by repaying the debt. Cf. Gen 15:16; Dan 8:23; 9:24; 4Q388 col. 2 frag. 9:4–6; 1 Thess 2:15–16; L.A.B. 26:13; 36:1; 41:1. *Diogn.* 9 contains another interesting instance of this. The epistle sets out to answer why "the new race" of the Christians did not come into the world at an earlier time (1:1). The answer is that God allowed unrighteousness to fill up (πεπλήρωτο) so that it would clear that humankind is powerless to escape paying the wages (ὁ μισθός) of unrighteousness – punishment and death.

2.2 Treasures

2.2.1 Key terms (μισθός, ἀποδίδωμι, κληρονομέω)

For English speakers Matthew's frequent descriptions of God's recompense for righteous deeds are obscured by imprecise translations of some of the key terms, in particular ὁ μισθός (5:12; 5:46; 6:1–2; 6:5; 6:16; 10:41–42; 20:8) and ἀποδίδωμι (6:4; 6:6; 6:18; 12:36; 16:27; 18:25–26; 18:28–29; 18:30; 18:34; 20:8; 21:41; 22:21). English Bibles since the King James Version have generally translated both the noun ὁ μισθός and the verb ἀποδίδωμι in Matthew as "reward" (e.g., NRSV, NIV, NASB). In contemporary English "reward" suggests something that is given for work occurring outside the confines of an ordinary employee/employer or creditor/debtor relationship, such as a thank-you for finding a lost dog. One offers a reward for information leading to the arrest of a felon, but one would pay wages – not a reward – to the person who mows the lawn every week. Similarly, one who is in debt "repays" one's creditor; one does not "reward" a creditor. In other words, if recompense is given in response to the duties one is expected to perform, it is misleading to call such a thing a "reward" (cf. Rom 4:4).[40]

In Matthew divine recompense is given in response to the work demanded of those who would follow Jesus; it is a wage, not a reward. For instance, in 16:24–28 Jesus explains the necessity of cross-bearing in terms of the eschatological repayment:

> Then [after rebuking Peter] he said to his disciples, "If anyone wants to follow behind me, let him deny himself and take up his cross and follow me. For whoever desires to save his life will lose it; but whoever loses his life on my account will find it. For what will it profit a person if he gains the whole world but forfeits his life? Or what will a person give in exchange for his life? *For the Son of Man is about to come in the glory of his Father with his angels, and then he will repay* (ἀποδώσει) *to each according to his deeds*

---

40 According to BDAG both μισθός and ἀποδίδωμι can refer to the payment of wages or to a reward. BDAG defines μισθός first as "remuneration for work done, pay, wages" and secondly in an extended sense as "recognition (mostly by God) for the moral quality of an action, recompense" or "affirmation of laudable conduct." Similarly, BDAG says that ἀποδίδωμι can mean "pay back" or "render to someone wages" but can also be translated "reward." BDAG's evidence for μισθός/ἀποδίδωμι as "reward" should arouse suspicion in the reader of Matthew; most of the examples cited are from Matthew itself as well as synoptic parallels.

(Cf. Ps 62:13; Prov 24:12). Truly I say to you that some are standing here who will not taste death before they see the Son of Man coming in his kingdom.

Like the Markan parallel (8:34–9:1), this pericope explains that following Jesus entails giving one's life to gain it back – that is, to follow Jesus who will be killed and then raised from the dead (see 16:21). Matthew, however, explicitly frames this "losing in order to regain" in terms of eschatological repayment; those who lose their life following Jesus will regain it because the Son of Man is about to repay to each according to his deeds. The crucial point here is that Jesus is not calling the disciples to perform some supererogatory deed that will earn them a "reward." Rather, all who follow Jesus are expected to take up their cross, lose their lives, and be repaid in the resurrection. Similarly, in the Sermon on the Mount Jesus explains the "greater righteousness" that is necessary to enter into the kingdom (5:20). It is necessary to love one's enemies to receive a μισθός (5:46). Those who do righteousness and receive credit from people will not have a μισθός from their Father (6:1), but God will repay (ἀποδώσει) those who do their righteousness in secret (6:4, 6, 18). The recompense described here is not a mere token of God's gratitude for those who go the extra mile. It is, rather, the recompense for obligatory behavior. Matthew's parables provide further illumination. The parable of the workers in the vineyard (20:1–16) compares the kingdom to a master hiring (μισθώσασθαι) workers and at the end of the day paying them their wage (ἀπόδος αὐτοῖς τὸν μισθόν). Of course, the master is fantastically generous to those who had not been working for long (20:9–10), but these workers receive a generous *wage*, not a reward. Matthew also compares divine recompense to the settling of accounts. Though the parable of the unforgiving servant (18:23–35) and the parable of the talents (25:14–30) do not use the words μισθός and ἀποδίδωμι, they describe divine recompense as a settling of accounts, the time when God's workers repay to him the money he entrusted to them. It is not that "reward" is utterly misleading in every context. For instance, the μισθός given to those who shelter missionaries in 10:41–42 might be considered a reward – though 25:31–46 would seem to suggest that such aid is actually one of the necessary duties for those who wish to enter the kingdom. The main thrust of these words in Matthew is clear: μισθός and ἀποδίδωμι describe the repayment that God gives for the work that he demands, work that is described as necessary to enter the kingdom.

This raises the question of why English translations have settled on "reward" with such uniformity.[41] The solution may lie with the evolution of the meaning of the word "reward." When the King James Version was written "reward" was a perfectly accurate translation of μισθός and ἀποδίδωμι because it was still used to refer to pay or wages for work done, a use which is now "rare" according to the Oxford English Dictionary.[42] The meaning of "reward" gradually shifted, and by the time English speakers had ceased to speak of the "reward" due a worker, this translation was ensconced as the standard translation of much of the wage language in the Gospels, thereby obscuring its significance.

A similar problem obtains with the word κληρονομέω, a word which occurs in several important passages in Matthew (5:5; 19:29; 25:34). Κληρονομέω is almost universally translated in these passages as "inherit," a word which usually means that someone (an "heir") acquires something (an "inheritance") when the former possessor dies. To be sure, κληρονομέω can mean inherit (e.g., Gen 15; cognates in Matt 21:38). But, like the Hebrew ירש, κληρονομέω is frequently used to mean "possess" or "acquire" in contexts where someone acquires something not because he is an heir but for some other reason. Consider 1 Maccabees 2:57: "David, because he was merciful, inherited (ἐκληρονόμησεν) the throne of the kingdom forever" (NRSV). The context is the last words of Mattathias, who enjoins his sons to "Remember the deeds of the ancestors, which they did in their generations; and you will receive great honor and an everlasting name" (2:51 NRSV). This is followed by a list of how God repaid the good deeds of Abraham, Joseph, and others. David is said to "acquire" the throne because of his mercy. To translate ἐκληρονόμησεν as "inherited" confuses the sense of the verse. Or consider Genesis 24:60 LXX: "And [Rebekka's kinsmen] blessed their sister Rebekka and said to her, 'You are our sister. Become thousands of myriads, and let your offspring gain possession (κληρονομησάτω) of the cities of their adversaries'" (NETS). Obviously the sense here is not that Rebekka's offspring will "inherit" the cities of their adversaries.

---

41   The Vulgate and Luther's translation typically render μισθός and ἀποδίδωμι more satisfactorily with (merces/reddo) and (Lohn/vergelten), respectively.

42   "Reward" 6a. The OED cites inter alia Adam Smith's Wealth of Nations, "A little school, where children may be taught for a reward so moderate, that even a common labourer may afford it." (II. v. i. 370).

Many other examples of κληρονομέω being used to mean acquisition by means other than inheritance could be adduced (cf., BDAG).[43]

What, then, is the proper translation of κληρονομέω in Matthew? The three instances closely resemble each other:

μακάριοι οἱ πραεῖς, ὅτι αὐτοὶ κληρονομήσουσιν τὴν γῆν. (5:5)

καὶ πᾶς ὅστις ἀφῆκεν οἰκίας ἢ ἀδελφοὺς ἢ ἀδελφὰς ἢ πατέρα ἢ μητέρα ἢ τέκνα ἢ ἀγροὺς ἕνεκεν τοῦ ὀνόματός μου, ἑκατονταπλασίονα λήμψεται καὶ ζωὴν αἰώνιον κληρονομήσει. (19:29)

τότε ἐρεῖ ὁ βασιλεὺς τοῖς ἐκ δεξιῶν αὐτοῦ· δεῦτε οἱ εὐλογημένοι τοῦ πατρός μου, κληρονομήσατε τὴν ἡτοιμασμένην ὑμῖν βασιλείαν ἀπὸ καταβολῆς κόσμου. (25:34)

None of these verses deals with an inheritance, and in the latter two instances Jesus is clearly speaking of the recompense due for acts of righteousness. A more suitable translation will illuminate the logic of these passages; those who leave all their possessions for Jesus and those who do the works of mercy will acquire eternal life or the kingdom, not as an inheritance, but as recompense for their deeds (cf. the Vulgate *possidebit*). One could argue that "inherit" is a good translation insofar as becoming "sons of your Father in heaven" (5:45) is intrinsic to Matthean soteriology. Yet, no English word is a perfect equivalent to the Greek, and the emphasis in Matthew is not on "inheritance" but on recompense for righteousness.[44]

2.2.2 Treasures "in" the Heavens

Throughout 6:1−24, and in a number of other passages as well, Matthew repeatedly contrasts possessions on earth with possessions "in the heavens with God." This raises a number of questions: Does Matthew

---

43 The OED notes that "inherit" can mean "To come into possession of, as one's right or divinely assigned portion; to receive, obtain, have, or hold as one's portion." but that this use is found "Chiefly in biblical and derived uses." In other words, to use the word "inherit" when one means "come to possess" is to speak Christianese and to obscure the logic of how exactly the inheritance is seized, by merit, fiat, or whatever.

44 Admittedly, it would be easier to discuss the correct translation of these words at the end of this chapter, after having investigated Matthew's understanding of heavenly wages. Yet, constant references to "rewarding" and "inheriting" would have diluted that analysis of Matthew's descriptions of divine repayment for righteous deeds.

describe heaven as an actual space that can be contrasted with earth? Is heavenly treasure "stored up" in an actual place? How literal are Matthew's admonitions to earn wages to be kept "with your Father in the heavens" (6:1, 20)?

It was observed in chapter 1 that spatial descriptions of divine recompense were common. Tobit 4:9 says that those who give alms "store up" a good deposit for themselves (θέμα... ἀγαθὸν θησαυρίζεις) for the day of necessity (cf. 1 Tim 6:19). Sirach 29:12 speaks of shutting up almsgiving in one's storeroom (σύγκλεισον ἐλεημοσύνην ἐν τοῖς ταμιείοις σου). Second Baruch 14:12–13 mentions good works "preserved in treasuries" that acquit one after death (cf. 4 Ezra 7:77). In 2 Maccabees 12:45 there is said to be a splendid reward "laid up" (ἀποκείμενον) for those who have died (cf. 2 Tim 4:8). Many texts describe good works being weighed in the balance against sins (1 En. 61:1–5; 2 En. 44:4–5; T. Ab. 12–14; t. Qidd. 1:13–14). It is clear, therefore, that Matthew is not unusual in describing divine recompense both as something that is paid back after death or at the eschaton and also as something that exists in the present somewhere.[45]

A recent study by Jonathan Pennington, however, has shown the particular importance of "heaven" as a space distinct from earth in the Gospel.[46] The standard explanation for Matthew's predilection for the word οὐρανός, which goes back to Gustaf Dalman, is that Matthew uses οὐρανός as a reverent circumlocution for God.[47] In other words, Matthew uses the expression ἡ βασιλεία τῶν οὐρανῶν rather than ἡ βασιλεία τοῦ θεός in order to avoid using the word θεός. Pennington dismantles this thesis, noting that Matthew himself uses the word θεός in excess of fifty times and exposing the lack of evidence for any such reverential periphrasis prior to or during the first century C.E.[48] Pennington then convincingly shows that Matthew's use of οὐρανός consistently follows an idiosyncratic pattern that illuminates a number of central Matthean concerns. In Greek texts prior to Matthew singular forms of οὐρανός were by far the most common, being used to refer both to visible sky

---

45 Cf. also Dale Allison's excursus on the spatial reality of the kingdom of God/the world to come in the early Jesus traditions, *Constructing Jesus: Memory, Imagination, and History* (Grand Rapids, MI.: Baker, 2010), 164–204.

46 Jonathan T. Pennington, *Heaven and Earth in the Gospel of Matthew* (NovTSup 126; Leiden: Brill, 2007; repr. Grand Rapids: Baker Academic, 2009).

47 Dalman, *The Words of Jesus* (trans. D. M. Kay; Edinburgh: T&T Clark, 1902), 91–95.

48 *Heaven and Earth in the Gospel of Matthew*, 13–39.

above and the invisible, divine realm. Yet, in the Gospel the singular οὐρανός always refers to the visible sky above, except for instances where it appears in pairings of "heaven and earth." The plural οὐρανοί, on the other hand, invariably refers to the invisible realm where God is, such as the many references to God "who is in the heavens" (ὁ ἐν τοῖς οὐρανοῖς).[49] Out of the eighty-two occurrences of οὐρανός in Matthew, there are only a handful of instances that do not fit neatly into this pattern, but Pennington produces plausible explanations for even these four aberrations.[50]

Pennington argues that Matthew's idiosyncratic use of the plural οὐρανοί as well as his preference for ἡ βασιλεία τῶν οὐρανῶν over ἡ βασιλεία τοῦ θεοῦ serves to draw attention to the tension between heaven and earth and the coming eschatological resolution of this tension. The heavens – the invisible realm of God's kingdom – is where God's will is done. Jesus tells his followers to pray that God's will be done on earth as well (6:10). For example, children have no status on earth, but Jesus warns his followers, "See that you do not despise one of these little ones; for I tell you that in the heavens (ἐν οὐρανοῖς) their angels always behold the face of my Father who is in the heavens (τὸ πρόσωπον τοῦ πατρός μου τοῦ ἐν οὐρανοῖς)" (18:10). This fleshes out what it means to say that God's will is done in heaven; on earth children

---

49 E.g., the singular referring to the visible sky, 6:26; 8:20; 13:32; 16:2–3; the singular heaven and earth pair, 5:18; 6:10; 6:20; 11:25; 24:35. Most of the instances of οὐρανός are plural. E.g., 3:2; 4:17; 5:3; 5:10; 5:12; 5:16.

50 The only glaring exception to the pattern discovered by Pennington is in 16:19 where Jesus gives Peter the keys to the kingdom of the heavens and tells him "whatever you bind on earth will be bound in the heavens (ἐν τοῖς οὐρανοῖς), and whatever you loose on earth will be loosed in heavens (ἐν τοῖς οὐρανοῖς)." Because this is a heaven and earth pairing, one would expect οὐρανός to be singular as it is in every other such case in the Gospel, including the related words in 18:18: "whatever you bind on earth will be bound in heaven (ἐν οὐρανῷ), and whatever you loose on earth will be loosed in heaven (ἐν οὐρανῷ)." Pennington suggests that this exception is due to the fact that the plural is used in the preceding sentence: "If Matthew were to follow ἡ βασιλεία τῶν οὐρανῶν (plural) with the statement about binding and loosing ἐν τῷ οὐρανῷ (singular), this could misleadingly suggest a contrast between the terms and confuse the teaching. Thus, in this direct juxtaposition of kingdom of heaven with heaven and earth – the only occurrence of such in Matthew – the normal form of the heaven and earthpair [sic] is overridden" (148–49). Yet, as Pennington notes, in the parallel in chapter 18 the plural heaven appears in the following sentence. Moreover, there are other examples of the heaven and earth pair occurring in close proximity to the plural, e. g., 6:9–10.

are despised, but "in the heavens" their angelic representatives behold the face of God. Jesus' followers are to live according to the heavenly reality and become like a child "or you will never enter into the kingdom of the heavens" (18:3).[51]

There are two important implications here for understanding what Matthew says about heavenly treasure. First, perhaps the most prominent way that Matthew contrasts heaven with earth is in the discussions of treasure. For Matthew, it is vital that one give away earthly treasures in order to store up treasure in heaven. Pennington's analysis thus situates Matthew's repeated admonitions to this effect against the backdrop of his larger heaven/earth contrast. Second, for Matthew, as for many early Jews and Christians, heaven (or "the heavens") is an actual place, a realm where God's will is done. Though this belief may be unpalatable to modern interpreters, it illuminates a number of difficult passages. To take one example among the passages to be discussed, in 6:1 most translations render μισθὸν οὐκ ἔχετε παρὰ τῷ πατρὶ ὑμῶν ἐν τοῖς οὐρανοῖς as "you will have no reward *from* your Father in heaven." This odd rendering of παρά plus the dative and the present tense ἔχετε ignores Matthew's conception of the heavens as a place where wages for good deeds are stored up and kept "with" the Father to be repaid at the Parousia (16:27).

2.2.3 Sermon on the Mount

2.2.3.1 Beatitudes (5:3–12)

Though Matthean scholarship has tended to focus on the question of whether the Beatitudes make an ethical demand or offer a word of consolation, this dichotomy does not illuminate the text.[52] It is true that there are no explicit imperatives in 5:3–12 apart from the command to rejoice and be glad in verse 12. Certain people are simply pronounced blessed, a fact which could suggest that Jesus' words are not in-

---

51   The Matthean phrase ἡ βασιλεία τῶν οὐρανῶν thus denotes the same reality as ἡ βασιλεία τοῦ θεοῦ but has different connotations. For other examples of the way the heaven/earth contrast plays out in the Gospel see Pennington.

52   Hans Windisch (*Der Sinn der Bergpredigt: Ein Beitrag zum Problem der richtigen Exegese* [Leipzig: J. C. Hinrichs'she, 1929]) famously argued that the Beatitudes were entrance requirements. Davies and Allison (*Matthew*, 1.439–40) et al. have argued to the contrary. For a helpful summary – though not limited to the Beatitudes – see Luomanen, *Entering the Kingdom of Heaven*, 7–34.

tended to make a demand so much as comfort the afflicted. What is less often observed, however, is that most of the Beatitudes correspond to ethical demands made subsequently in the narrative. The mention of the poor in spirit and the meek (5:3, 5) foreshadows Jesus' claim that it is necessary to become like a child to enter the kingdom of the heavens (18:1−4), as well as the call to renunciation of possessions (19:16−30).[53] The blessedness of those who hunger and thirst for righteousness (5:6) corresponds to the command to "Seek first the kingdom of God and his righteousness, and all these things will be added to you" (6:33).[54] The fifth beatitude says the merciful (οἱ ἐλεήμονες) are blessed because they will be shown mercy (ἐλεηθήσονται) (5:7), an idea which is repeated in the Lord's Prayer (6:12, 14) and in the parable of the unforgiving servant (18:23−35).[55] The sixth Beatitude (purity of heart which allows one to see God) is similar to the call to have a single or generous eye which allows one to serve God rather than money (6:19−24).[56] Peacemakers are said to be blessed because they will be called sons (υἱοί) of God (5:9), which foreshadows Jesus' command to "Love your enemies and pray for those who persecute you so that you may become sons (υἱοί) of your Father in the heavens" (5:44−45). The last two Beatitudes declare the blessedness of those who endure persecution and insults for the sake of righteousness and Jesus (5:10−11), which is repeated in Jesus' call to take up one's cross (10:38;

---

53 The phrase οἱ πτωχοὶ τῷ πνεύματι is not exclusive of material poverty, though its valence is wider. I am convinced by Mark Goodacre's argument for the secondary nature of the Lukan version (μακάριοι οἱ πτωχοί), *The Case Against Q: Studies in Markan Priority and the Synoptic Problem* (Harrisburg, PA: Trinity Press International, 2002), 133−151. Even if one should regard τῷ πνεύματι as Matthean redaction, however, Matthew's concern for almsgiving (6:2−4; 25:31−46) and renunciation of possessions (8:19−20; 19:16−30) casts serious doubts on the claim that Matthew "spiritualizes" the Lukan beatitude.

54 Benno Przybylski (*Righteousness in Matthew and His World of Thought* [SNTSMS 41; Cambridge: Cambridge University Press, 1980]) has managed to convince most scholars that every instance of δικαιοσύνη in Matthew refers to right behavior rather than a (Pauline) saving righteousness. Donald A. Hagner ("Law, Righteousness, and Discipleship in Matthew," *WW* 18 [1998]: 364−71) has objected, arguing that 3:15 and 5:6 are examples to the contrary. The similarity of 5:6 to 6:33, however, suggests that Przybylski is correct in this instance as well. I shall deal with 3:15 in the next chapter.

55 See esp. 18:33: "Was it not necessary for you to show mercy (ἐλεῆσαι) on your fellow slave just as I had mercy (ἠλέησα) on you?"

56 See the discussion of this text below.

16:24–28). The Beatitudes, therefore, while not paraenetic in form, proclaim the blessedness of those who follow Jesus' teaching.[57]

Rather than describing the Beatitudes as either a word of consolation or an ethical demand, I would suggest reading them through the lens of the summary of Jesus' preaching given in 4:17: "From then on Jesus began to proclaim and say: 'Repent, for the kingdom of the heavens has come near!'" In other words, the Beatitudes describe the way of life that is necessary in light of the nearness of the kingdom. This way of life is "blessed" because God is about to repay those who live this way. The shape of the Beatitudes illustrates the point: in each case a certain group is pronounced blessed because (ὅτι) of what they will receive. In five cases (5:4, 6, 7, 9, 11) a future divine passive is used. Those who mourn are blessed because God will comfort them. The merciful are blessed because God is about to show them mercy. Thus, in spite of the obvious influence of wisdom literature on 5:3–11 (e.g., Ps 1), the Beatitudes quiver with apocalyptic expectation. Righteousness is about to be recompensed; God's will is about to be done on earth as it is in heaven. There are elements of consolation here insofar as God appears to be about to effect a great reversal, but the Beatitudes also declare in programmatic fashion what Jesus demands from his followers in light of the nearness of the kingdom.[58]

This contrast between the present earthly suffering and the coming consolation illuminates the concluding promise of "great wages" for those who endure persecution on behalf of Jesus: "Blessed are you when they insult and persecute you and say all kinds of evil against you falsely on my account. Rejoice and be glad, because your wage is great in the heavens (ὁ μισθὸς ὑμῶν πολὺς ἐν τοῖς οὐρανοῖς), for thus they persecuted the prophets who were before you" (5:11–12).

---

57 As the narrative progresses it becomes clear that the way of life commended in the Beatitudes is also that of Jesus himself, who is meek and lowly in heart (πραΰς εἰμι καὶ ταπεινὸς τῇ καρδίᾳ) (11:29) with no place to lay his head (8:20), who had filled up all righteousness (3:15), showed mercy (9:2, 27; 17:15; 20:30–31), and who endured insults and persecution (20:19; 26:67–68; 27:27–44).

58 A common sub-species of the view that the Beatitudes are a message of consolation is the view that they formulate a distinctively Christian way of life in contrast to pharisaic Judaism. The Beatitudes function, according to this view, as identity description for the community. See, e.g., W. D. Davies, *The Setting of the Sermon on the* Mount (BJS 186; Atlanta: Scholar's Press, 1989), 256–315. It is possible to offer partial corroboration to this view: the Beatitudes proclaim the blessedness of those who follow Jesus' teaching and example.

Those who, like Jesus (20:19; 26:67–68; 27:27–44), endure insults and persecution possess wages in the heavens that are about to be repaid by God.[59]

2.2.3.2 "Antitheses" (5:21–48) and Doing Righteousness (6:1–18)

Matthew prefaces the so-called "antitheses" with verses 17–20, thereby precluding any attempt to read what follows as an abolishment of the Law or the prophets.[60] Jesus "fulfills" (πληρῶσαι) the Law, which could indicate that Jesus "does" or "performs" the Law, but it is more likely that πληρόω is used here with the same meaning as in the fulfillment quotations – the Law points to and is brought to fruition by Jesus.[61] In any case, this preface to the "antitheses" indicates that what follows is in continuity with the Law. The medieval *Glossa Ordinaria* captures this dynamic perfectly: *Mandatum Christi non est contrarium legi, sed latius legem in se continens.*[62] There is an intensification and inte-riorization, but not a rejection of the commandments. This intensifica-tion is described as going beyond what is normally expected. This can be seen in verse 20 when Jesus says, "I say to you that unless your right-eousness abounds (περισσεύσῃ) more than that of the scribes and Phar-isees, you will certainly not enter the kingdom of the heavens." Similar-ly, in verse 47 Jesus asks rhetorically, "And if you greet only your brothers, what extraordinary thing (περισσόν) do you do? Do not even the Gentiles do the same?" Just as 5:21–30 focuses on the neces-sity of the greater righteousness for avoiding punishment in Gehenna, 5:43–48 describes the greater righteousness as that which earns divine recompense:

---

59 Cf. Wis 1:12–3:19, esp. 2:22.
60 Betz (*Commentary on the Sermon on the Mount*, 200) notes that it was Marcion who first called 5:21–48 "antitheses". The key passage was an emended version of 5:17, which proclaimed that Jesus did in fact come to abolish the law and the prophets. Marcion was correct to identify the contrasting statements in 5:21–48 as an example of the rhetorical device *antitheton*, yet the un-emended text of Matthew shows that "antithesis" is a misleading description of 5:21–48.
61 Πληρόω was not often used in other literature to mean "to do what is required." In the dozens of instances where Matt speaks unambiguously of doing that which is required ποιέω or τηρέω is always used.
62 Cf. Davies and Allison who claim that 5:21–48 shows both "what sort of at-titude and behavior Jesus requires" and "how his demands surpass those of the Torah without contradicting the Torah" (*Matthew*, 1.509); Stanton, *Gospel for a New People*, 302.

> You heard that it was said, "You will love your neighbor and hate your enemy." But I say to you, love your enemies and pray for those who persecute you so that you may become sons of your Father in the heavens, because he makes his sun rise on evil people and good people and sends rain on the righteous and unrighteous. For if you love those who love you, what wage do you have (τίνα μισθὸν ἔχετε)? Do not even the tax collectors do the same? And if you greet only your brothers, what remarkable thing are you doing? Do not even the Gentiles do the same? You must be perfect, therefore, as your Father in heaven is perfect.

The NAB renders the present tense ἔχετε with "what recompense will you have," presumably imagining the eschatological payment of wages, but this is unnecessary. Matthew repeatedly speaks of the wages which are to be paid in the eschaton as stored up in the heavens in the present (see below on 6:1, 19–21). This wage cannot be earned by simply loving one's neighbors. One must attain the greater righteousness to earn treasure in heaven.[63]

In 6:1–18 the Sermon on the Mount turns from the so-called antitheses to the question of how to "do righteousness," an issue announced in verse 1: "Take care not to do your righteousness before people in order to be seen by them. Otherwise, you have no wage with your Father who is in the heavens" (Προσέχετε τὴν δικαιοσύνην ὑμῶν μὴ ποιεῖν ἔμπροσθεν τῶν ἀνθρώπων πρὸς τὸ θεαθῆναι αὐτοῖς· εἰ δὲ μή γε, μισθὸν οὐκ ἔχετε παρὰ τῷ πατρὶ ὑμῶν τῷ ἐν τοῖς οὐρανοῖς). While this section departs from the formula in 5:21–48 of quoting a biblical prohibition and then reinterpreting it (Ἠκούσατε ὅτι ἐρρέθη... ἐγὼ δὲ λέγω ὑμῖν), it remains formally quite similar to 5:21–48. In both cases a piece of traditional piety is named, a biblical injunction in 5:21–48 and, in 6:1–21, almsgiving, fasting, and prayer.[64] Jesus does not reject the traditional piety but explains that the righteousness demanded by God must permeate one's motives and inner life. As Stanton puts it, the "greater righteousness" of 5:20 is here, as it is in 5:21–48, "purity of motive, rather than mere outward observance."[65]

The NRSV, NAB, and NIV translate μισθὸν οὐκ ἔχετε παρὰ τῷ πατρὶ ὑμῶν ἐν τοῖς οὐρανοῖς in 6:1 "you will have no reward from

---

63   Note that wages (μισθός) from God are juxtaposed with becoming "sons of your Father in heaven" as in the Beatitudes.

64   This trio appears in Tob 12:8, prayer and alms in Sir 7:10.

65   Stanton, *Gospel for a New People*, 303. Perhaps a less theologically-loaded way of putting this claim would be "purity of motive, rather than outward observance alone."

your Father in the heavens."[66] As noted above, this is an odd and unnecessary translation of παρά with the dative. A more natural translation
would be "you have no wage with your Father in the heavens."[67] The
usual sense of παρά with the dative fits perfectly with Matthew's understanding of treasure laid up in heaven to be paid back in the last judgment. The present tense ἔχετε underscores the point. Matthew is not
saying that a person who does righteousness already has wages "from"
the Father, but that such a person has wages "with" the Father, laid
up in heaven.[68] The concluding verses of this section emphasize this
very point: "Do not store up treasure for yourselves on earth where
moth and rust destroy and where thieves break in and steal. Rather,
store up for yourselves treasure in heaven, where neither moth nor
rust destroys and where thieves do not break in and steal. For where
your treasure is, there will be your heart also" (6:19–21). The question
in verses 2–19 is whether one receives wages or "credit" from people
now, or whether one receives a wage that is stored up in heaven.[69]

Matthew moves from δικαιοσύνη in general to three specific examples, beginning with almsgiving:

> So when you give alms (ποιῇς ἐλεημοσύνην) do not sound a trumpet before
> you as the hypocrites do in the synagogues and in the streets so that they
> may be glorified by people. Truly I say to you, they receive their wage
> (ἀπέχουσιν τὸν μισθὸν αὐτῶν). Rather, when giving alms, let not your left
> hand know what your right hand is doing, so that your almsgiving may
> be in secret, and your Father who sees in secret will repay you (ἀποδώσει
> σοι). (6:2–4)

Those who draw attention to their almsgiving and receive glory from
people do not receive a wage from God because they have already received one. As Deissmann noted, ἀπέχω is a technical term used with

---

66 The NAB has "recompense" instead of "reward". The NRSV lacks "will."
67 Cf. *Pss. Sol.* 9:5: "The one who does righteousness treasures up life for himself
    with the Lord (ὁ ποιῶν δικαιοσύνην θησαυρίζει ζωὴν αὑτῷ [sic] παρὰ κυρίῳ)."
68 cf. Matt 19:29 and the absence of the claim in Mark 10:30 that wages are also
    enjoyed νῦν ἐν τῷ καιρῷ τούτῳ.
69 Cf. Ambrose (*Sacr.* 1.2): "You contend in the world, but you are crowned by
    Christ. And for the struggles of the world you are crowned; for, though the
    reward is in heaven, the merit of the reward is nevertheless established here."
    Latin: *Luctaris in saeculo, sed coronaris a Christo. Et pro certaminibus saeculi coronaris;
    nam etsi in caelo praemium, hic tamen meritum praemii conlocatur.*

great regularity on receipts (i. e., an ἀποχή).[70] Acknowledgment of payment was expressed by saying "I receive (ἀπέχω) payment, etc." For instance, a receipt from 44 c.e. Egypt reads καὶ ἀπέχω τὴν συνκεχωρημένην τιμὴν πᾶσαν ἐκ πλήρους (and I receive the entire agreed price in full).[71] The sense in 6:2 would seem to be that those who draw attention to their almsgiving are in so doing acknowledging receipt of their wages. They receive a wage when they receive glory from people and are renouncing any claim to future payment. The common translation of ἀπέχουσιν τὸν μισθὸν αὐτῶν as "they have received their reward" (NRSV, NAB, NIV) obscures this point. This translation treats ἀπέχουσιν as a perfective present ("they have received"), but it should probably be understood as a habitual or customary present in parallel with ποιοῦσιν in the preceding sentence. The hypocrites (habitually) make a show of their almsgiving (ποιοῦσιν). When they do this they acknowledge that they are receiving (ἀπέχουσιν) their wages and are therefore not due to be paid again when God repays (ἀποδώσει) righteous deeds. The same pattern is repeated with regard to prayer and fasting. Those who pray or fast ostentatiously acknowledge receipt of their wages (ἀπέχουσιν τὸν μισθὸν αὐτῶν), but "your Father who sees in secret will repay (ἀποδώσει)" those who pray or fast in secret (6:5−6).

2.2.2.3 Treasure in Heaven and the Sound Eye (6:19−24)

Following the three examples of righteous deeds comes a new section (6:19−24) that breaks down into three subunits in 19−21, 22−23, and 24. Whereas the preceding section (6:1−18) focused on how to earn a wage for righteous deeds from God rather than from people, this section approaches the question of heavenly treasure from a slightly different angle. The first part of the trio, verses 19−21, contrasts the ephemerality of earthly treasures with heavenly treasures:

> Do not treasure up for yourselves treasures on earth (Μὴ θησαυρίζετε ὑμῖν θησαυροὺς ἐπὶ τῆς γῆς), where moth and rust destroy and where thieves break in and steal. Rather, treasure up for yourselves treasures in heaven (θησαυρίζετε δὲ ὑμῖν θησαυροὺς ἐν οὐρανῷ), where neither moth nor rust destroys and where thieves do not break in nor steal. For where your treasure

---

70 *Bible Studies: Contributions Chiefly from Papyri and Inscriptions to the History of the Language, the Literature, and the Religion of Hellenistic Judaism and Primitive Christianity* (trans. Alexander Grieve; Edinburgh: T & T Clark, 1903), 229.

71 Cf. another from 57 c.e.: ἀπέχω παρ' ὑμῶν τὸν φόρον τοῦ ἐλα[ι]ουργίου, ὧν ἔχετέ [μο]υ ἐν μισθώσει.

is, there also will be your heart (ὅπου γάρ ἐστιν ὁ θησαυρός σου, ἐκεῖ ἔσται καὶ ἡ καρδία σου).

Earthly wages are here today and gone tomorrow. Pursuit of such wages is antithetical to the pursuit of heavenly wages.[72] The parables of the treasure hidden in a field and of the pearl of great price (13:44–45) make a similar point: the kingdom is like a treasure that compels a person to sell all her possessions in order to gain it.[73]

The next subunit in 22–23 is more difficult:

> The lamp of the body is the eye. If, therefore, your eye is undivided, your whole body will be radiant. But if your eye is evil, your whole body will be dark. If then the light in you is darkness, how great is the darkness.
>
> Ὁ λύχνος τοῦ σώματός ἐστιν ὁ ὀφθαλμός. ἐὰν οὖν ᾖ ὁ ὀφθαλμός σου ἁπλοῦς, ὅλον τὸ σῶμά σου φωτεινὸν ἔσται· ἐὰν δὲ ὁ ὀφθαλμός σου πονηρὸς ᾖ, ὅλον τὸ σῶμά σου σκοτεινὸν ἔσται. εἰ οὖν τὸ φῶς τὸ ἐν σοὶ σκότος ἐστίν, τὸ σκότος πόσον.

At first blush Jesus appears to be making a physiological claim about the role of the eye, but the saying is sandwiched between two sayings that set pursuit of money and pursuit of God in opposition to each other. Moreover, the word ἁπλοῦς was rarely used in physiological descriptions, but it was frequently used in an ethical sense.[74] Thus it would ap-

---

72 Cf. Luke's parable of the rich fool, which illustrates the same point. The rich man plans to build ever bigger barns to store his crops, but God says to him: "You fool! This very night your life is being demanded of you. And the things you have prepared, whose will they be?" Then Jesus adds "So it is with those who store up treasures for themselves but are not rich toward God." (12:20–21). This thought receives further elaboration a few verses later when Jesus says "Sell your possessions, and give alms. Make money-bags for yourselves that do not wear out, an unfailing treasure in heaven, where no thief comes near and no moth destroys. For where your treasure is, there also will be your heart" (12:33–34). Incorruptible money-bags are to be prized above earthly money bags because they can be counted on even after death.

73 Cf. Gos. Thom. 76, which combines a parallel of Matt 13:46 with a parallel of Matt 6:19–21: "Jesus said: The kingdom of the Father is like a merchant who had merchandise (and) who found a pearl. This merchant was prudent. He got rid of the merchandise and bought the one pearl for himself. You also must seek for the treasure which does not perish, which abides where no moth comes near to eat and (where) no worm destroys." See also J. Ramsey Michaels, "Almsgiving and the Kingdom Within: Tertullian on Luke 17:21," CBQ 60 (1998): 475–83.

74 Betz, Sermon on the Mount, 451. Candida R. Moss ("Blurred Vision and Ethical Confusion: The Rhetorical Function of Matthew 6:22–23," CBQ 73 [2011]:

pear that, as in 5:25–26, the humdrum imagery of the saying conceals a deeper theological claim.

Much has been written about this saying and its Lukan parallel (11:34–36).[75] There are two key exegetical questions. The first is the meaning of ὁ λύχνος τοῦ σώματός ἐστιν ὁ ὀφθαλμός. Allison notes that modern exegetes have incorrectly assumed that this refers to the eye acting as a window that allows light into the body.[76] Ancient Jews, however, thought that the eye contained its own light, hence the metaphor of a lamp, which is a source, not a channel, of light.[77] Allison goes on to read the conditionals in 6:22b–23 so that the apodosis entails the realization of the protasis, rather than the reverse as is usually the case. Ἐὰν οὖν ᾖ ὁ ὀφθαλμός σου ἁπλοῦς, ὅλον τὸ σῶμά σου φωτεινὸν ἔσται would therefore mean not that an undivided eye enlightens the body but that an undivided eye is evidence of an inner light.[78] While this construal is possible grammatically (see 12:28), it ironically contradicts his own observation that it is the eye itself, the lamp, which is the source of the light, rather than a mere conduit.[79] If the eye is the lamp of the body then it would seem that it is the eye that enlightens the body. To discover what this actually means in this passage it is necessary to turn to the second key question.

The second question is the meaning of ἁπλοῦς (single, undivided) eye in contradistinction to a πονηρός eye. In Jewish literature an "evil eye" can refer to a greedy or jealous eye.[80] Significantly, Matthew uses the phrase this way in the parable of the workers in the vineyard when the master asks one of those grumbling at the generous wage given to those who arrived late in the day, "Are you greedy because I am good (ὁ ὀφθαλμός σου πονηρός ἐστιν ὅτι ἐγὼ ἀγαθός εἰμι)" (20:15). The word ἁπλοῦς could refer to something perfect or complete, possibly as a translation of the Hebrew חם or Aramaic שלם. On the other hand,

---

760) cites Damascius (5th-6th cen. c.e.) for an example of a physiological use of the word (*Vita Isid.* 16).

75 E.g., Hans Dieter Betz, "Matthew 6:22–23 and Ancient Greek Theories of Vision," in *Essays on the Sermon on the Mount* (Philadelphia: Fortress: 1985), 71–87; cf. Dale C. Allison, "The Eye is the Lamp of the Body," *NTS* 33 (1987): 61–83.

76 *Matthew*, 1.635.

77 E.g., 2 Sam 12:11; Sir 23:19; Dan 10:6; *T. Job* 18:3.

78 *Matthew*, 1.637–8.

79 As Luz notes, *Matthäus*, 1.466n26.

80 E.g., Deut 15:9; Prov 23:6, 28:22; Sir 14:10.

ἁπλοῦς and its cognates ἁπλότης, ἁπλόω, and ἁπλῶς could refer to generosity or contentment. For instance, *Testament of Issachar* 4:2 says "The generous person (ὁ ἁπλοῦς) does not desire gold," and Romans 12:8 speaks of the giver (ὁ μεταδιδοὺς) who has a gift from God to give ἐν ἁπλότητι.[81] Counterpoised to "the evil eye" and set in a context dealing with money, ἁπλοῦς probably means "generous."[82]

It is now possible to unpack the dense reasoning of verses 22–23 by bringing together Allison's observation that the eye was viewed as a source of light with the economic valence of ἁπλοῦς and πονηρός. The question of whether one has an undivided or an evil eye, that is, whether one is generous or rapacious, determines whether one's entire being is filled with light or shrouded in darkness. Luz summarizes the point well: "Die Qualität des 'Auges' entscheidet über den 'ganzen Leib'. Im Klartext: Die Integrität und Gradlinigkeit des menschlichen Handelns, insbesondere des Umgangs mit seinem Besitz, entscheidet über das, was der Mensch als ganzer ist."[83] A generous person is filled with light, but a rapacious person is left in darkness.

While some scholars have argued that ἁπλοῦς must mean *either* generous *or* single in this passage, it is more likely to be an instance of clever wordplay.[84] Verses 19–24 deal with both the right use of money and placing one's focus on God rather than on possessions. For Matthew, these two issues are inextricable. The ἁπλοῦς eye is not only generous, it is also the "single" eye, focused on God rather than on money, as the very next verse suggests: "No one is able to serve two lords, for he will either hate one and love the other, or he will be devoted to one and despise the other. You cannot serve God and money" (6:24). Any attempt to divide one's affections between the two is doomed to failure, a claim which is given vivid expression in the subsequent refusal of the rich young man to give up his possessions and follow Jesus (19:16–29). The idea of the ἁπλοῦς eye, therefore, encapsulates the whole of verses 19–24, and arguably the remainder of chapter 6 as well. Verses 19–21 say that since the location of one's treasure determines the location of one's heart – meaning the source of the intellect, emotions, and will

---

81 See also 2 Cor 8:2; 9:11; Jas 1:5; Henry J. Cadbury, "The Single Eye," *HTR* 46 (1954): 69–74; Davies and Allison, *Matthew*, 1.638.

82 Cf. Susan R. Garrett's discussion of the Lukan parallel: "'Lest the Light in You Be Darkness': Luke 11:33–36 and the Question of Commitment," *JBL* 110 (1991): 93–105.

83 Ibid., 467.

84 Keener, *Matthew*, 232–33.

– in giving away one's possessions one places one's treasures and heart in heaven with God. Similarly, verse 24 claims that one must choose to serve either God or money. The clever wordplay of the ἁπλοῦς eye sums all this up; it is necessary to be generous, which is also to say single-mindedly focused on God rather than on possessions.

2.2.3.4 Summary

As noted in the introduction, many scholars have argued that, while the Sermon on the Mount does use the language of "reward", it does not use the promise of heavenly treasure to motivate people to good deeds.[85] Yet, as we have seen, the Sermon on the Mount is filled with Jesus' pronouncements on how to acquire heavenly treasure and avoid debts and punishments.[86] The Beatitudes announce the coming recompense of those who follow Jesus' teaching; Jesus teaches his followers the "greater righteousness" that earns a wage with the Father in the heavens (5:43–48), and how to avoid receiving payment for their righteous deeds from people rather than from God (6:1–18); Jesus' disciples are to store up treasure in the heavens with their generosity, rather than storing up treasure on earth (6:19–23).

Despite the flimsiness of the arguments of those wishing to exclude the promise of divine recompense from Jesus' teaching, the Sermon

---

85 A recent article by Florian Voss ("Der Lohn der guten Tat: Zur theologischen Bestimmung der Beziehung zwischen Matthäus und Paulus," *ZTK* 103 [2006], 319–43): expresses the main argument found in much of this literature. Voss argues that in the Sermon on the Mount heavenly wages "dient also nicht dazu, den Menschen zum gerechten Handeln zu motivieren, sie wird hier vielmehr mit der Frage verknüpft, von woher der Lohn, d. h. das dem Tun entsprechende "Ergehen", erwartet wird: von den Menschen oder von Gott" (333). This claim is overly subtle. It is true that 6:1–19 contrasts the wage one receives from God with the wage or credit one receives from people: righteous acts done to receive credit from people will not receive credit from God. Yet, it is not merely the question of whence one's wages are derived, but also of motivation. The contrast between wages from God and wages from people derives its hortatory force from the fact that deeds done in order to receive credit from people will not receive credit from God. Verse 1 could therefore be paraphrased: "If you want to receive credit from your Father in the heavens for your righteous deeds, do not attempt to receive credit from people." This may conflict with a Kantian understanding of virtue, but Jesus was not a proto-Kantian.

86 Not unlike the book of Deuteronomy, to which the Sermon is often compared.

provides two important clues that nuance what sort of exchange is in view here. First, God repays righteous deeds with treasure in heaven, but this exchange takes place within the context of a relationship which is described as familial. The God who repays is repeatedly called "Father" (5:16, 45, 48; 6:1, 4, 6, 8–9, 14–15, 18, 26, 32; 7:11, 21), and those who do his will are called "sons" (5:9; 5:45). Those who do what the Sermon teaches are imitating the very qualities of their heavenly Father (5:48), qualities which are exemplified by Jesus himself as the narrative progresses. The Sermon does not describe an anonymous market governed only by self-interest, then, but the eschatological recompense due to those who imitate their Father.[87] Second, it becomes particularly clear in 6:19–24 that the "focus" of those storing up treasure in heaven is not on the treasure itself but God, though it is preposterous to claim that the promise of heavenly treasure is not a vital part of the paraenesis. Tremendous faith in God's reliability is an unspoken assumption in the Sermon as a whole; one must "wager" one's life on the belief that God can and will repay what God has promised.[88] Indeed, as was noted in chapter 1, almsgiving was commonly seen as an act of worship.[89] It is not surprising, then, that the ἁπλοῦς eye (6:22) is in context both the generous eye, the eye that leads one to store up treasure in heaven by giving away one's money, but also the "single" eye which is trained on God.

2.2.3 The Missionary Discourse (10:1–42)

In the missionary discourse Jesus sends out the twelve apostles, giving them authority to cast out unclean spirits and to heal sicknesses (10:1). Jesus warns them that they will be persecuted as he was, but that if someone confesses him before people Jesus will return this confession by confessing that person before his Father. In 10:37–39 Jesus says

---

87 The importance of familial context of the divine economy will become clearer in the discussion of the Last Supper in chapter 5 below.

88 I owe this observation to Bradley C. Gregory.

89 E.g., in Acts 10 Cornelius is said to give many alms (ποιῶν ἐλεημοσύνας πολλὰ) and in his vision he is told that his "prayers and alms have gone up as a memorial offering before God (αἱ προσευχαί σου καὶ αἱ ἐλεημοσύναι σου ἀνέβησαν εἰς μνημόσυνον ἔμπροσθεν τοῦ θεοῦ) (10:2, 4). See also the examples in chapter 1.

> The one who loves father or mother more than me is not worthy of me, and the one who loves son or daughter more than me is not worthy of me. And whoever does not take his cross and follow behind me is not worthy of me. The one who finds his life will lose it, and the one who loses his life on my behalf will find it.

The image of taking up a cross appears suddenly and is not connected explicitly to Jesus' crucifixion until chapter 16. In chapter 16 Peter objects to the idea that Jesus will be crucified, but here the image is for the disciples a mere symbol and there is no objection, though Matthew's audience cannot fail to miss the foreshadowing. Like the promise that those who confess Jesus before hostile authorities will be confessed by Jesus before God, the idea of losing one's life in order to find it smacks of eschatological recompense; those who give their lives will regain their lives in the resurrection.[90]

The discourse concludes by turning from the apostles to the recompense of those who receive them:

> The one who receives you receives me, and the one who receives me receives the one who sent me. The one who receives a prophet in the name of a prophet (εἰς ὄνομα προφήτου) will receive the wage of a prophet (μισθὸν προφήτου λήμψεται), and the one who receives a righteous person in the name of a righteous person (εἰς ὄνομα δικαίου) will receive the wage of a righteous person (μισθὸν δικαίου λήμψεται). And whoever gives one of these little ones only a cold drink in the name of a disciple (εἰς ὄνομα μαθητοῦ), truly I tell you, he will certainly not lose his wage (οὐ μὴ ἀπολέσῃ τὸν μισθὸν αὐτοῦ).(10:40–42)

Here, at the end of the discourse, Jesus turns from the apostle-missionaries themselves and addresses those who remain at home. Those who receive "you," that is the apostles, receive Jesus as well as God, who sent him. Jesus then moves from discussing those who receive the apostles to those who receive a prophet, then a righteous person, and finally "one of these little ones." Two relevant debates swirl around this passage. First, does this list refer to different groups within the church (apostle, prophet, righteous person, little one), perhaps even a descending gradation of offices, or is it simply "parallel designations of the dis-

---

90   Cf. Davies and Allison: "Matthew probably saw in 10.39 a pronouncement about eschatology: he who loses his life in this world – because he looks only to God (6.25–34) – will win it for the world to come; and he who wins his life for this world – that is, seeks to secure his earthly existence…will lose it in the world to come" (*Matthew*, 2.224).

ciple community as a whole"?[91] Second, is the promised wage eschatological or not, and if so does this passage imply gradations of heavenly
wages?

Goulder sees in 10:40−42 a descending list of offices, moving from
apostle, to prophet, to saint to lay Christian.[92] In favor of this view is the
fact that the list begins with the twelve apostles and ends with "one of
the least of these." Some have argued that the list does not actually begin
with apostles, since the word itself does not appear in verse 40, but the
"you" (ὑμᾶς) here refers to "the twelve apostles" whom Jesus is sending
out and who were named in 10:2−4.[93] As for prophets, 23:34 shows
that it is possible that this refers to a distinct Christian office.[94] It is
less likely that this is the case for "a righteous person," however, because
Matthew seems to use the word δίκαιος to describe any righteous person.[95] Similarly, Matthew uses μικρός to refer to any socially insignificant
person, including children.[96] It would be a stretch, then, to see in
10:40−42 a list of specific offices.

Yet, even if Matthew does not list four ecclesial offices, this does not
mean that apostle, prophet, righteous person, and little one are merely
alternating descriptions of the community as a whole, or even of its itinerant members. Apostles are not synonymous with prophets in Matthew, as the promise of twelve thrones for the apostles (19:28) and
the list of the twelve apostles (10:2−4) indicate. Similarly, "the righteous" includes any righteous person, and would therefore seem to be
a much broader category than apostle or prophet. And in verse 42
there is special emphasis on the insignificance of the little ones, presumably in contrast to those mentioned previously. This descent in ostensible prestige is the raison d'être of verse 42: whoever helps even the little

---

91 France, *The Gospel of Matthew* (NICNT; Grand Rapids: Eerdmans, 2007), 415.
    See also Davies and Allison, *Matthew*, 2.227−28.
92 *Midrash and Lection in Matthew* (London: SPCK, 1974), 352.
93 France, *Matthew*, 415.
94 Keener, citing 5:11−12, 11:9, and 13:17, claims that "Matthew repeatedly em-
    phasizes that disciples as Jesus' agents are his prophets, even greater than the
    prophets of old," *Matthew*, 332. Yet, none of the passages cited by Keener
    call the disciples prophets; 5:11−12 compares the suffering of the "blessed"
    to the suffering of the prophets of old, 11:9 refers to John the Baptist, and
    13:17 only refers to the prophets who preceded Jesus' disciples.
95 *Pace* Gundry, *Matthew*, 203 and David Hill, *Greek Words and Hebrew Meanings:
    Studies in the Semantics of Soteriological Terms* (SNTSMS 5; Cambridge University
    Press, 1967), 135−38. See 1:19; 5:45; 9:13; 13:43, 49; 25:37, 46; 27:19.
96 E.g., 11:11; 18:6, 10, 14.

ones with a mere cup of cold water will certainly not lose his wage (οὐ μὴ ἀπολέσῃ τὸν μισθὸν αὐτοῦ).

What sort of wage is in view? The phrase εἰς ὄνομα προφήτου/ δικαίου/μαθητοῦ appears to be equivalent to the rabbinic לשׁם, meaning "for the sake of" or "with reference to."[97] Hill argues that the genitives in the phrases μισθὸν προφήτου and μισθὸν δικαίου are genitives of origin, indicating that those who receive a prophet or a righteous person will be recompensed by the prophet or righteous person himself, presumably by hearing his words.[98] Matthew's typical use of wage language weighs against this proposal; in every other instance of wages received for some good deed it is clear that the wage is from God and will not be paid until the Parousia.[99] It is more likely, therefore, that the sense of 10:41–42 is that those who welcome a missionary will receive the sort of wage that that missionary will receive. By giving safe haven and comfort to itinerant evangelists, it is possible to earn a wage that is equal to the wages that they themselves earn. Verse 42 emphasizes that the missionary who is welcomed does not need to be of great stature, just as the aid given may be as humble as a cup of cold water.

This passage indicates two important things about the way wages from God work. First, God's economy is not a zero-sum economy. Those who take up their crosses by leaving all their possessions behind and enduring persecution will be repaid a hundred times as much (19:29). It may appear that there is nothing left for those who do not follow this course, but 10:40–42 makes it clear that those who give succor to itinerant evangelists receive a heavenly wage as if they themselves had left everything behind. One is reminded of *m. 'Avot* 2:2 where Rabban Gamaliel is reported to have said that those who labor in a worldly occupation "in the name of heaven" (לשׁם שׁמים) will be supported by "the merits of the fathers" and will be repaid not only the wage they themselves have earned but also the wages earned by their fathers. In both texts lowly deeds done "in the name of" something greater earn a fantastically disproportionate wage from God.[100]

---

97 Jastrow שׁם. BDAG ὄνομα.
98 David Hill, *The Gospel of Matthew* (New Century Bible Commentary; Grand Rapids, MI.; Eerdmans, 1972), 196.
99 Indeed, Matthew appears to omit Mark's promise of wages "now, in the present time" (10:30).
100 Though many have noted that εἰς ὄνομα + genitive is a semiticism, no one, to my knowledge, has noted that in both the Mishnah and Matthew action done

Second, this passage seems to indicate that there are degrees of heavenly wages. There is a "wage of a prophet" and a "wage of a righteous person." The phrase "wage of an apostle" does not appear, but 19:28 indicates that the apostles will be recompensed with a unique role in the coming rule of the Son of Man. Luz acknowledges that verse 41, which he takes to be pre-Matthean, assumes that there are different *Lohnklassen*, but argues that verse 42 undoes this by placing the little ones on the same level as the prophets and the righteous.[101] This is a non-sequitur. Verse 42 emphasizes that those who give even the humblest aid to any missionary will certainly be repaid for it. There is nothing here about the wage of the little ones being the same as every other wage. To be sure, the emphasis of the passage is on the generous wage that can be earned by helping an apostle or a righteous person and so on, but this presupposes that there is such a thing as "the wage of an apostle" and "the wage of a righteous person" that will be earned.

2.2.4 First Passion Prediction (16:13–28)

Much of the clearest material on heavenly wages in Matthew appears in chapters 16–25. This is not surprising; this section of the narrative contains the decisive turn to the cross and the recompense due those who follow Christ in cross-bearing, as well as descriptions of future judgment in 24–25.

Matthew seems to have had a particular concern to describe the Parousia as the time when debts are collected and deeds are "repaid." Though there are hints of this understanding of the Parousia in the Sermon on the Mount, this concern takes center stage in this pivotal passage.[102] After Peter's confession of Jesus as the Christ, Jesus begins to

---

"in the name of" something allows one to earn a wage that was, strictly speaking, earned by someone else.

101 *Matthäus*, 2.151–52.

102 Allison's division of the Gospel is largely convincing ("Structure, Biographical Impulse, and the *Imitatio Christi*," in *Studies in Matthew: Interpretation Past and Present* [Grand Rapids, MI: Baker Academic, 2005], 135–55). Nevertheless, no outline of the Gospel is perfect because of the complex way themes weave in and out of the narrative. One flaw in Allison's outline is that it marks chapter 19 as "the commencement of the passion." But of course the death of Jesus begins to take center stage from 16:13–28 because "from then Jesus began to show his disciples that it is necessary for him to go to Jer-

show the disciples that he must die and be raised (16:21). After Peter
rebukes Jesus for saying this, Jesus chastises him for thinking not "the
things of God but the things of people" (16:22−23). Then Jesus presses
the point further by explaining that losing one's life in order to find it is
not just his fate, but the fate of all who would follow him:

> Then Jesus said to his disciples, "If anyone wants to come behind me, let
> him deny himself and take up his cross and follow me. For whoever
> wants to save his life (ψυχήν) will lose it, and whoever loses his life for
> my sake will find it. For what will it profit (ὠφεληθήσεται) a person if he
> gains (κερδήσῃ) the whole world but forfeits (ζημιωθῇ) his life (ψυχήν)?
> Or what will a person give in exchange (ἀντάλλαγμα) for his life (ψυχῆς)?
> For the Son of Man is about to come in the glory of his Father with his
> angels, and then he will repay to each according to his deeds (ἀποδώσει
> ἐκάστῳ κατὰ τὴν πρᾶξιν αὐτοῦ). (16:24−27)

Verses 24−26 are nearly identical to the Markan parallel (8:34−37).
Matthew, however, goes on to make it explicit that cross-bearing is necessary because of the coming eschatological repayment of deeds: "For
the Son of Man is about to come in the glory of his Father with his angels, and then *he will repay to each according to his deeds.*" Only in Matthew's Gospel is cross-bearing necessary because of the coming "repayment." Moreover, by adding μέλλει Matthew emphasizes the nearness of
the Parousia more than Mark, and the imminence of the coming repayment has both a negative and a positive hortatory force. Those who
"gain the world" are warned that the Son of Man will come soon
and none of their wealth will suffice to purchase eternal life.[103] The passage as a whole, however, is a call to the disciples to follow Jesus in the
path of death and resurrection, losing life in order to find it. As noted in
chapter 1, heavenly treasure was frequently described as that which gains
one eternal life. Verse 27 makes it explicit that this line of thinking
stands behind Jesus' exhortation: the Son of Man will repay those
who give up their earthly lives with eternal life. Those who bear crosses
store up heavenly treasure that will avail them on the day of judgment,
unlike earthly treasure.[104]

---

usalem and to suffer much from the elders and chief priests and scribes and to be
killed and on the third day to be raised" (16:21; cf. 17:22−23).
103 Cf. the very similar warning in Luke 12:13−34.
104 This passage is treated more extensively in chapter 4.

2.2.5 The Rich Young Man and the Parable of the Workers in the Vineyard (19:16–20:16)

The parable of the workers in the vineyard has frequently been interpreted without regard for its narrative context. Matthew, however, presents the parable as the conclusion of Jesus' words to the disciples following the departure of the rich young man. Jesus concludes his response to Peter's question (19:27–30) with the words, πολλοὶ δὲ ἔσονται πρῶτοι ἔσχατοι καὶ ἔσχατοι πρῶτοι. Then the parable concludes οὕτως ἔσονται οἱ ἔσχατοι πρῶτοι καὶ οἱ πρῶτοι ἔσχατοι (20:16), with the οὕτως apparently indicating that the parable has just demonstrated what Jesus means when he tells the apostles that the first will be last and the last will be first.

The young man comes to Jesus seeking "eternal life," so Jesus tells him to obey the commandments and lists the second half of the Decalogue and Lev 19:18. The man says he has kept these but wants to know what he still lacks. Jesus responds: "If you want to be perfect (τέλειος), go sell your possessions and give to the poor, and you will have treasure in the heavens (ἕξεις θησαυρὸν ἐν οὐρανοῖς), then come, follow me.[105] When the young man heard this word he went away grieving, for he had many possessions" (19:21–22). What does "sell your possessions and give the money to the poor, and you will have treasure in the heavens" mean?[106] We have seen that many second temple and rabbinic texts describe treasure in heaven as that which gains one entrance into eternal life. We must ask, therefore, if Jesus is telling the young man that by giving up his possessions he will gain the heavenly treasure that one needs to enter into eternal life. Jesus' comments to the disciples after the man goes away suggest that this is the case:

> And Jesus said to his disciples, "Truly I say to you that a rich person will hardly enter into the kingdom of the heavens. Again I say to you, it is easier for a camel to pass through the eye of a needle than for a rich person to enter into the kingdom of God." And when the disciples heard this they

---

105 The Markan parallel (10:21) lacks the words εἰ θέλεις τέλειος εἶναι, which recall Matt 5:48.

106 Most commentators have been remarkably incurious about what Matthew is saying here. For instance, the excellent commentaries of Luz (*Matthäus*, 123–26), Daniel J. Harrington (*The Gospel of Matthew* [SP 1; Collegeville, MN.: Liturgical, 1991, 278–81), Senior (*Matthew* [ANTC; Nashville: Abingdon, 1998], 218–19), and Keener (*Matthew*, 475–76) simply pass over these words in silence.

were greatly astounded and said, "Then who is able to be saved?" Looking
at them Jesus said to them, "With people this is impossible, but with God
all things are possible." (19:23–26)

Note that Jesus does not say that the man's wealth prevents him from
joining an elite group that does more than what is required. Rather,
wealth makes it impossible for a person to enter into the kingdom of
God. In other words, though he obeys the commandments, the
young man's wealth prevents him from becoming τέλειος as he should
be (cf. 5:48). He has treasure on earth with which he is not willing to
part, illustrating Jesus' claim that no one can serve both God and
money (cf. 6:19–24). Eternal life is at stake in the accumulation of
heavenly treasure.

One may object that what was really at stake was trust in Jesus. It is
true that Jesus told the young man to sell his possessions, gain treasure in
heaven, and then follow him. Yet, the dichotomy between a decision to
follow Jesus and earning treasure in heaven is foreign to Matthew. A
parallel may illuminate the point. The author of 1 Timothy says that
the rich ought not "set their hopes on riches, but rather on God" and
to give their money away thereby "treasuring up a good foundation
for the future, in order that they might take hold of true life" (6:17–
19). In this text, as in Matthew, redemptive almsgiving and complete
trust in God are inseparable (cf. Matt 6:19–24; 25:31–46). A faith-ver-
sus-works paradigm does not illuminate Matthew's Gospel. One may
describe the young man's failure as a failure of both faith and works;
if he had sufficient faith in God, perhaps he would have been willing
to let go of his money and earn heavenly treasure.[107]

The following verses show that the offer to the young man to give
his possessions away and follow Jesus and so find eternal life is an offer
open to all:

> Then answering Peter said to him, "Behold, *we* have left everything and
> followed you. What then will there be for us?" Jesus said to them,
> "Truly I say to you that you who have followed me, in the new age
> when the Son of Man sits on his throne of glory, you yourselves also
> will sit on twelve thrones judging the twelve tribes of Israel. And whoever
> left houses or brothers or sisters or father or mother or children or fields on
> account of my name will receive a hundred times as much and will possess
> eternal life. (19:27–29)

---

107 Cf. Jas 2:14–26.

Peter asks whether Jesus' offer to the young man applies to the apostles as well. Jesus' reply is disarmingly straightforward; for forsaking everything the Twelve will receive not only treasure in heaven but thrones from which to rule alongside the Son of Man.[108] Jesus then goes on to specify that this is an open offer; anyone can renounce her possessions for his sake and come to possess eternal life in return.

A comparison with the Markan parallel (10:28–30) illuminates a number of typical Matthean emphases. First, in Mark Jesus simply tells Peter what anyone who renounces her possessions will receive. But in Matthew, this is preceded by Jesus' response to the Twelve in particular. This Matthean insertion connects the time when the apostles will receive their thrones with the scene of eschatological judgment running through the Gospel as a whole – when the Son of Man sits on his throne of glory (e.g., 25:31; 26:64). The apostles are therefore included in the scene drawn from Daniel 7 of the coming enthronement of the Son of Man. When that moment of vindication comes, the apostles will receive thrones for their efforts.[109] Second, unlike Mark, who claims that one can receive a hundred times as much "in the present time" as well as in the age to come, Matthew omits any mention of recompense in the present life. Matthew thereby heightens the contrast between the poverty of the present and the riches of the coming age.

Immediately following this promise of heavenly treasure, however, Jesus adds πολλοὶ δὲ ἔσονται πρῶτοι ἔσχατοι καὶ ἔσχατοι πρῶτοι (19:30) and tells the parable of the workers in the vineyard. As already noted, nearly all discussions of divine recompense in Matthew and in the teaching of Jesus as a whole have made the parable of the workers in the vineyard the interpretive key for unlocking the meaning of everything else. France represents the consensus when he claims that this parable is the passage in Matthew "which most directly addresses the issue" of recompense.[110] Similarly, Günther Bornkamm echoes the widespread hope

---

108 See Davies and Allison's refutation of the view that this judging consists of an end-time condemnation of Israel, *Matthew*, 3.55–6.
109 Luz argues that "Da für Matthäus aber die 'damaligen' Zwölf für die gegenwärtigen Jesusjünger/innen transparent sind, legt er vermutlich nicht darauf den Akzent, dass die zwölf Apostel einen Lohn erhalten werden, der sich vom Lohn aller anderen späteren Christ/innen unterscheidet, sondern er sieht V 28 und V 29 zusammen: Das Sitzen der Zwölf auf den Thronen ist für ihn eine besondere Gestalt des 'Hundertfältigen', das allen verheißen ist" (*Matthäus*, 3.128–9). See the Introduction for a critique of this reading.
110 E.g., France, *Matthew*, 258–59.

that this parable will solve the problem of apparent works-righteousness in the gospels, proclaiming that "dieses Gleichnis gerade auf dem Hintergrund menschlicher Begriffe von Gerechtigkeit, Lohn und Leistung das Wunder göttlicher Gerechtigkeit und Güte bezeugt und den Lohngedanken endgültig von dem Verdienstgedanken trennt."[111] At first blush, there is a certain plausibility in the sentiments represented by France and Bornkamm; this parable depicts all the workers in the vineyard receiving the same wage regardless of how long they had been working. It is no surprise, then, that some would read the parable as the undoing of the notion of *Verdienstgedanken*. Further complicating matters are the many allegorical interpretations of the parable which have been proposed. For instance, some take the workers hired last to be Gentiles and the workers who worked the whole day to be Jews. Others understand the workers who were hired last to represent those who begin following Jesus late in life. Numerous other readings have been offered.[112]

I would suggest that most interpretations of the parable have been hampered by a disregard for its context in Matthew – both the immediate context of 19:16–20:16 and the Gospel as a whole. The parable is introduced in 20:1 as Jesus' expansion of his answer to Peter in 19:28–29 (Ὁμοία γάρ ἐστιν ἡ βασιλεία τῶν οὐρανῶν...), and the parallels between the encounter with the young man and the parallel further underscore this unity. The parable describes a master who is good (ἐγὼ ἀγαθός εἰμι), recalling the description of God in the previous passage as "the good one" (εἷς ἐστιν ὁ ἀγαθός). The parable also describes workers who toil for varying amounts of time, just as the preceding passage discusses a man who follows the commandments but is unwilling to give up everything (19:18–22), contrasting him with those who do give up everything (19:27–29). Moreover, at the heart of both 19:16–26 and the parable is the question of how God will repay these different

---

111 Bornkamm, "Der Lohngedanke im Neuen Testament," in *Studien zu Antike und Urchristentum: Gesammelte Aufsätze* (2 vols.; Munich: Kaiser Verlag, 1963), 88. The original is in italics. See also Luz (*Matthäus*, 3.141–42) for a glowing catena of sentiments similar to Bornkamm's. Klyne R. Snodgrass (*Stories with Intent: A Comprehensive Guide to the Parables of Jesus* [Grand Rapids, MI: Eerdmans, 2008], 362) aptly summarizes the state of the question: "[M]ost interpreters want [the parable] to say more theologically than it does."

112 See Catherine Hezser (*Lohnmetaphorik und Arbeitswelt in Mt 20,1–16* [NTOA 15; Göttingen: Vandenhoeck & Ruprecht, 1990], 1–44) for a history of interpretation.

kinds of workers. The rich young man seeks eternal life but is unwilling to earn treasure in heaven. Jesus responds by saying that it is impossible for rich people to enter the kingdom, whereas those who leave possessions behind will receive a hundred times as much. Both the dramatis personae and the central theme (divine recompense for deeds) of 19:16−26 are therefore reproduced in the parable. A successful interpretation must take the unity of 19:16−20:16 into account.[113]

Warren Carter and Charles Talbert among others have argued that the disciples, who have no earthly status, are "the last" who came to work at the eleventh hour, whereas the rich young man and those like him are "the first", that is, those who have earthly status.[114] According to this proposal, the parable illustrates the reversal described in 19:16−26; those with status (the rich young man) become last and those without status (the disciples) become the first. Conversely, Davies and Allison suggest the parable warns the disciples not to think they are "the first" because they have left everything.[115] They should not boast in their achievements because everyone will receive the same wage. Both of these lines of interpretation offer a possible reading of the parable in its context. Nevertheless, there is a significant inconcinnity in Carter and Talbert's reading. In the parable "the first" seem to be those who have toiled all day in the master's vineyard, and "the last" are those who did less work. In other words, "the first" are those who have done more work for God. It seems unlikely, then, that the "status" of the first workers − status which is based on the fact that they toiled all day in the master's vineyard − corresponds to the "status" that the rich man has because of his many possessions. Rather, both 19:16−26 and the parable concern the recompense due those who have done

---

113 Though the Jew/Gentile reading must be judged secondary, an extension of the logic of the parable in this direction is in harmony with the Gospel as a whole, especially its conclusion. The Gentiles are called to work late in the day but they have been included just the same.

114 Carter, *Households and Discipleship: A Study of Matthew 19−20* (JSNTSup 103; Sheffield: JSOT Press, 1994), 127; Talbert, *Matthew* (Grand Rapids, MI.: Baker Academic, 2010), 238−39.

115 *Matthew*, 3.67−8. Sigurd Grindheim ("Ignorance is Bliss: Attitudinal Aspects of the Judgment according to Works in Matthew 25:31−46," *NovT* 50 [2008]: 313−31, 326) claims the parable "functions as a rejoinder to the question of eschatological reward." Hezser (*Lohnmetaphorik und Arbeitswelt in Mt 20, 1−16*, 251−89) reads the parable as a rebuke of the wandering missionaries of Matthew's day who thought they would receive a greater wage than other Christians.

less for God (the young man and the workers hired late in the day) and those who have done more (those who have renounced their possessions and the workers hired early in the day).

Davies and Allison would seem to be nearer the mark; the parable qualifies or nuances 19:16–26 rather than simply illustrating it. It is less certain, however, that the parable functions as a warning that "the promise of reward should not become ground upon which to stand,"[116] or that "It is all by grace."[117] In 19:27–29 the apostles are told that they and everyone else who gives up possessions will receive a hundred times as much and will possess eternal life. Far from squelching such hopes, the parable depicts those who worked all day receiving exactly what they were promised by the master. Indeed, the payment received by those who toiled all day confirms Jesus' answer to Peter; those who do much for the master will be repaid just as they expected to be. The point of the parable can hardly be that "everything depends on grace" since the early workers received exactly what they earned.

I would suggest, therefore, that the primary concern of the parable is to illustrate God's generous provision for those who have done less work and to warn those who have done more not to resent this generosity. The parable merely confirms what 19:27–29 said about those who *have* earned treasure in heaven, but it picks up and develops anew a question that was left dangling in 19:23–26: what is the fate of those who have not earned treasure in heaven? The rich man, like the workers who came later in the day, has done some work by keeping the commandments (19:20), but has failed to renounce his possessions.[118] In response to the man's failure to earn treasure in heaven Jesus says it is impossible for a rich person to enter the kingdom (19:23–24). But when the astonished disciples ask, "Who then can be saved?" Jesus gives the reply "With people this is impossible, but with God all things are possible" (19:26). The parable expands this point; God will faithfully repay those who have earned treasure in heaven, but those who have not done enough to enter the kingdom will receive a wage that is wildly disproportionate to what they have done.[119]

---

116 Davies and Allison, *Matthew*, 3.68.
117 France, *Matthew*, 752.
118 The text gives no support for the speculation that the man's claim to keep the commandments is disingenuous.
119 One notes that although Matthew addresses the question of God's repayment of those who have failed to practice radical renunciation, it is never stated that the rich young man himself will necessarily be saved.

Thus, the parable nuances but does not eliminate *Verdienstgedanken*; one may count on the fact that God will pay his workers what is just, but in his generosity he will also pay more than what is just – in this case paying all the workers the same wage. Indeed, 19:29 shows that even those who practice radical renunciation do not earn eternal life according to a strict accounting of deserts; rather, they will receive "a hundred times as much" in comparison to what they left behind.[120] As Heinemann put it in his excellent 1948 riposte to Strack and Billerbeck's interpretation of the parable, "It is the intention of the parable, then, to state that God will sometimes reward man in excess of what is his due, but certainly not to suggest that he will ever deny him his due reward."[121]

A similar passage in 2 Baruch may illuminate the point. As noted in chapter 1, 2 Baruch says that the righteous go to their deaths without fear because "they possess with [God] a store of good works which is preserved in treasures."[122] In the last judgment these treasuries and the books that record sins will be opened and God will repay what is just.[123] Yet, despite this confident assertion that the heavenly treasures will enable the righteous to enter the world to come, the author goes on to say that when the treasuries are opened "at that time you shall see, and many with you, the long-suffering of the Most High, which lasts from generation to generation, who has been long-suffering toward all who are born, both those who sinned and those who proved themselves to be righteous."[124] The author does not repudiate the notion that the righteous will receive their just recompense because just recompense is not necessarily opposed to mercy. As Psalm 61:13 LXX puts it, "To you, O Lord, belongs mercy (ἔλεος), for you repay a person according to

---

120 Thus the "the last will be first and the first will be last" is not a strict description of reversal wherein those who have worked are deprived of what they have, but something closer to a suggestive slogan indicating a relativization of status. See the attempt to nuance the meaning of "reversal" in Luke in Nathan Eubank, "Bakhtin and Lukan Politics: A Carnivalesque Reading of the Last Supper in the Third Gospel," *JGRChJ* 4 (2007): 32–54.

121 "The Conception of Reward in Mat. XX.1–16" *JJS* 1 (1948–49): 85–89, esp. 86. See also Daniel Marguerat: "Aucun des partenaires [scil. the master and the original workers] ne met en question le droit des ouvriers de la première heure à toucher leur salaire," *Le Jugement dans L'Évangile de Matthieu* (2nd ed.; *MdB* 6; Genève: Labor et Fides, 1995), 459.

122 A. F. J. Klijn, *OTP*, 1:626.

123 Ibid., 1:629.

124 Ibid.

his works."[125] While claiming that God repays deeds, 2 Baruch main-
tains that God shows himself to be long-suffering by showing mercy
to both sinners and the righteous.[126] These texts, like Matthew
19:16–20:16, do not set aside the belief that God faithfully repays
works, which would in any case be tantamount to claiming God is unjust or capricious.[127] Yet, God can be said to provide mercifully for those
without heavenly treasures just as he mercifully repays those who do
have heavenly treasures. From this angle one can see how misleading
it is to characterize the parable, as Jeremias did, as a setting aside of
merit and law in favor of grace and gospel.[128] Like 2 Baruch, the parable
affirms that God will indeed repay those who have stored up heavenly
treasure and will be merciful to those who have not. "Merit" and
"grace" exist here not as antitheses, but as varying expressions of
God's faithfulness.

In response to all this, one might still object that the equal wages received by all the workers subverts the idea that divine recompense is
based on obedience. If everyone receives the same payment then why
bother storing up treasure in heaven at all? There are two things to
say in response. First, there is no question that the parable sits somewhat
awkwardly alongside of passages in which there seem to be degrees of
recompense.[129] Yet, this tension becomes an outright contradiction
only if the parable is read in isolation from its context and turned
into a timeless depiction of how God always deals with humans.[130] A
second point builds on the first: while the parable addresses the question
of whether it is possible for someone who fails to practice radical renunciation to be saved, it does not discuss the fate of those who fail to do
any work for the kingdom. Unlike the wicked tenants (21:33–43), the
wedding guests who ignore the king's summons (22:1–14), or the

---

125 The MT makes the point with equal clarity: 'To you, O Lord, belongs covenant faithfulness (חסד), for you repay a person according to his works' (62.13).
126 See also *m. 'Avot* 3:15.
127 Sanders, *Paul and Palestinian Judaism: A Comparison of Patterns of Religion* (Philadelphia: Fortress Press, 1977), 127.
128 According to Jeremias, the parable shows the differences between two worlds:
   "Dort Verdienst, hier Gnade; dort Gesetz, hier Evangelium" (*Die Gleichnisse
   Jesu* [Göttingen: Vandenhoeck & Ruprecht, 1954], 138).
129 E.g., see the discussion of the parable of the talents (25:14–30) below.
130 The Son of Man will either "repay to each *according to his deeds*" (16:27) or he
   will give everyone the same payment. Both statements cannot be true *in abstrac-
   to*.

"goats" who do not feed the hungry etc. (25:31–46) – all of whom end up damned – the workers who came late in the day responded to the call of the master. Thus, while the parable warns against harboring resentment when God shows mercy to those who have done less work, it offers no comfort for those who would excuse themselves from working in the vineyard on the grounds that everyone will receive the same wage.

To sum up: in the parable of the workers in the vineyard (20:1–16) Jesus continues the discussion that ensued after the departure of the rich young man. In 19:16–29 two sorts of would-be disciples are discussed, those who leave possessions behind for Jesus and those rich who do not. The former sort earns treasure in heaven and eternal life, whereas it is impossible for the latter sort to enter the kingdom, though Jesus adds that "all things are possible with God." Jesus then nuances this picture by telling a parable about how a master pays workers who have done different amounts of work. Those who did much work receive the payment they expected, whereas those who did less surprisingly receive the same wage. The principal concern of the parable is unlikely to be a warning against looking forward to one's heavenly wages – after all, the workers hired early in the day receive what they expected. Rather, the parable expands on the hint in 19:26 that God would provide for those who have worked less (i.e., those who have not given away all their possessions); in his generosity God will pay them a wage that far exceeds what they deserve, though in so doing he will not treat the other workers unjustly (20:13).

2.2.6 Parable of the Just and Unjust Servants (24:45–51), the Parable of the Talents (25:14–30) and the Sheep and the Goats (25:31–46)

Matthew's last great block of teaching material contains a description of the coming days and the Parousia (24:1–41) and warnings to stay alert because the time of the return of the Son of Man is unknown (24:42–25:13). It concludes with two descriptions of the last judgment, the parable of the talents (25:14–30) and the sheep and the goats (25:31–46). As the conclusion to Matthew's fifth and final block of teaching, these pericopae are arguably of disproportionate weight.[131]

---

131 This section ends with the words καὶ ἐγένετο ὅτε ἐτέλεσεν ὁ Ἰησοῦς πάντας τοὺς λόγους τούτους. Cf. 7:28–29; 11:1; 13:53; 19:1.

The parable of the just and unjust servants, widely recognized to be a "transparent allegory,"[132] warns the servant whom the master appoints (κατέστησεν ὁ κύριος) to feed the household to do his duty in spite of the master's delay in returning. Leaders in the church – those given authority over their fellow servants (see 24:46, 49) – are probably the principal referent here.[133] The faithful and wise servant (ὁ πιστὸς δοῦλος καὶ φρόνιμος) who accomplishes this task will be richly repaid when the master returns – that is, at the Parousia of the Lord: "Blessed is that servant whom the master when he comes will find so doing. Amen I say to you that he will appoint him over all his possessions (ἐπὶ πᾶσιν τοῖς ὑπάρχουσιν αὐτοῦ καταστήσει αὐτόν)" (24:46–47). In other words, church leaders who perform their tasks faithfully will be repaid with greater authority at the Parousia.[134]

The parable of the talents is divided into three parts: first the master entrusts his possessions to his servants (14–15). The amount given to each varies according to their ability but they all receive a fantastically high sum. Then the servants go about their business (16–18), and, finally, after a long time (πολὺν χρόνον) the master returns to settle accounts (συναίρει λόγον) with them (19–30). Most commentators agree that this

---

132 Davies and Allison, *Matthew*, 3.386.

133 So Davies and Allison, *Matthew*, 3.386; Gundry, *Matthew*, 495. Καθίστημι is frequently used in the LXX to refer to the establishment of positions of authority over Israel (e.g., Exod 2:14; 18:2; Num 3:10, 32; 4:19; 31:48; Deut 1:13–15; 16:18; 17:14; 1 Sam 8:1; 10:19; 2 Sam 6:21; 1 Kings 4:5; 7:17; Ezra 7:25; 1 Macc 3:55; 2 Macc 3:4; Psalm 2:6; Jer 1:10) and over other peoples as well. See also in the NT Heb 5:1; 7:28; 8:3. Some commentators object to understanding "those appointed to feed the fellow-servants" as leaders, but none of which I am aware produce any evidence for this objection. E.g., Nolland (*Matthew*, 1000) simply says "A correlation between the serving role in the parable and the call to various forms of service in the church is appropriate, but any narrow focus on the role of church leaders is to be resisted." One wonders why this reading is "narrow" and "to be resisted." Luz (*Matthäus*, 3.464) claims that "Matthäus eine solche Unterscheidung von Amtsträger/innen und gewöhnlichen Christ/innen nicht zu machen scheint," noting that in 24:3 Jesus addresses all the disciples and that the parable of the talents applies to the whole community. This argument appears to be based on the rather odd assumption that if Jesus says something to the disciples (presumably just the twelve) it must apply with equal suitability to all Christians and that if one parable about servants applies to all Christians then all parables about servants must apply with equal suitability to all Christians – even a parable that describes those servants who have been appointed over their fellow servants.

134 Cf. LXX Genesis 39:4–5.

parable is an allegory wherein the master who leaves and then returns after a long time is Jesus, and the servants represent members of the church.[135] Like the immediately preceding material, the parable encourages Jesus' followers to be ready for his return, which may be delayed (cf. 24:48). Also, like the parable of the unforgiving servant (18:23–35) and the workers in the vineyard (20:1–16), the parable imagines a coming settling of accounts. Each of these uniquely Matthean parables describes this settling in a slightly different way. In 18:23–35 the master comes to collect on his servants' debt (i. e., their sin). In 20:1–16 the master repays his servants for the work they did during the day, answering the question of how someone like the rich young man will be repaid. In the parable of the talents, however, the money the master comes to collect is not a loan (i. e., the debt of sin) but money which he had entrusted to the servants with the expectation that they would invest it and so earn more.

The master gives the same response to the first two servants: εὖ, δοῦλε ἀγαθὲ καὶ πιστέ, ἐπὶ ὀλίγα ἦς πιστός, ἐπὶ πολλῶν σε καταστήσω· εἴσελθε εἰς τὴν χαρὰν τοῦ κυρίου σου. This has led some commentators to suggest that this parable, like the parable of the workers in the vineyard, shows that everyone receives the same wages regardless of the amount of work done.[136] This suggestion ignores two important details. First, both servants earn the same rate of return on their investment – one hundred percent.[137] It is not surprising that they receive similarly enthusiastic responses from their master. Second, despite telling both the first and second servant that he will place them in charge of "much," the master does not give them identical payment for their serv-

---

135 E.g., Davies and Allison, *Matthew*, 402; G. R. Beasley-Murray, *Jesus and the Kingdom of God* (Grand Rapids, MI: Eerdmans, 1986), 215–18. Others, such as C. H. Dodd (*The Parables of the Kingdom* [New York: Scribner, 1961], 151–52), have argued that Matthew allegorized a parable that was originally directed against the Jewish leaders to address the eschatological questions of his day. More recently, N. T. Wright (*Jesus and the Victory of God* [Minneapolis: Fortress Press, 1996], 632–39) has argued that this parable – and all the parables of Matt 25 – refer not to "the personal return of Jesus after a long interval" but to the coming sacking of Jerusalem (636). There are a number of problems with this proposal, not the least of which is found in 25:46.

136 E.g. Luz, *Matthäus*, 3.507, "Für beide Sklaven ist die Verheißung dieselbe; sie hängt nicht von der Höhe der Geldsumme ab, die sie erarbeitet haben. Die Leser-innen denken an den gleichen Lohn von 19,28–20,16." G. de Ru, "Conception of Reward," 218.

137 France, *Matthew*, 954.

ice. In verse 28 the third servant's one talent is taken from him and given to the servant with "the ten talents," showing that the first servant has been entrusted not only with his original five talents and the five additional talents he earned, but also this additional talent. By the end of the parable, then, the first servant has eleven talents and the second servant only four, making this parable an odd place to appeal to support the idea that all of God's workers receive the same recompense.[138]

This is confirmed by the final two verses of the parable which summarize its point: τῷ γὰρ ἔχοντι παντὶ δοθήσεται καὶ περισσευθήσεται, τοῦ δὲ μὴ ἔχοντος καὶ ὃ ἔχει ἀρθήσεται ἀπ' αὐτοῦ. καὶ τὸν ἀχρεῖον δοῦλον ἐκβάλετε εἰς τὸ σκότος τὸ ἐξώτερον· ἐκεῖ ἔσται ὁ κλαυθμὸς καὶ ὁ βρυγμὸς τῶν ὀδόντων. The voice of the master gives way to the voice of Jesus who is relating the parable and extracts a generalized statement from the events of the parable. Those who work, who earn more with the master's initial investment, will be repaid generously, but those who do not earn more will lose even what they do have and will be thrown into "the outer darkness." The fact that the "one who has" will be given an abundance (περισσευθήσεται) shows once again Matthew's insistence that heavenly wages go beyond what workers earn by strict desert, but it is equally clear that this generosity is a generous wage for work done rather than an unmerited gift. Indeed, the central concern of the final four verses of the parable is the unhappy fate of those who do not work. Verse 28 functions as a good summary of Matthew's *Lohngedanken*: it is necessary to earn heavenly wages to enter the kingdom, but this does not mean that salvation is by strict desert. Those who do not work are doomed, but those who do work are repaid far more than they have earned.[139]

The eschatological discourse beginning in 24:1 concludes in 25:31–46 with the depiction of the Son of Man judging the nations. Though it

---

138 Cf. Luke's version, where the bystanders balk at the master's command to give yet another mina to the servant who already had ten: "Master, he [already] has ten pounds!" (19:25).

139 See also the epistemological application of this maxim in 13:12. Luz (*Matthäus*, 3.508) says that 25:28 shows that "der Lohn im Jüngsten Gericht ein Geschenklohn ist, der das, was die Menschen durch ihre Taten verdienen, weit übersteigt." This is quite right, provided that *Geschenklohn* is understood as a generous wage, not an unmerited one. A Christian editor of *3 Bar.* inserted portions of this parable into a preexisting account of celestial judgment, offering a glimpse into the early reception history of Matthew that supports this reading. See esp. 15:1–16:2.

is said that the Son of Man will separate the nations "just as a shepherd separates the sheep from the goats" (25:32), this passage is not a parable. Rather, as Stanton has argued, it is an apocalyptic discourse similar to those found in texts such as 4 Ezra, 1 Enoch, 2 Baruch, and *Apocalypse of Abraham*.[140] Like the judgment scenes in those texts, judgment is rendered according to one's good works.

There is no explicit financial language in this pericope. The last judgment is likened instead to a shepherd separating sheep from goats. Yet, this passage recalls the notion found in many Jewish and Christian texts, that when one gives to the poor one is in fact giving to God.[141] Noting this passage's similarity to texts such as this, Bultmann argued that it is a reworking of a Jewish original which replaced the name of God with the title Son of Man.[142] Regardless of whether 25:31–46 is a reinterpretation of a Jewish original, it does seem to be a modification of the idea that deeds done to help the poor are in fact done for God. The remarkable thing is that Jesus is the unseen recipient of such deeds, rather than God.

Ancient Christian writers commonly saw a connection between the sheep and the goats and Proverbs 19:17.[143] This passage from Ireneaus' *Against Heresies* is particularly striking:

---

140 *Gospel for a New People*, 221–30. See the chart in Davies and Allison (*Matthew*, 3.419) comparing Matt 25:31–46 to Dan 7; *1 En* 62, 90; Rev 20; *2 Bar* 72; *T. Ab*.11; *Sib. Or.* 2.

141 E.g., Prov 19:17; Tob 4:5–11; Acts 10:4. I am persuaded by Davies and Allison's argument that ἑνὶ τούτων (τῶν ἀδελφῶν μου) τῶν ἐλαχίστων (25:40, 45) refers to anyone in need, whether they are Christian or not (*Matthew*, 3.428–29). Nevertheless, the view that Matt restricts "the least of these" to Christians only or Christian missionaries would not significantly alter the discussion here.

142 *History of the Synoptic Tradition* (trans. John Marsh; Oxford: Blackwell, 1972), 124.

143 See Sherman W. Gray, *The Least of My Brothers: Matthew 25:31–46: A History of Interpretation* (SBLDS 114; Atlanta: Scholars Press, 1989), 12–14, 16–17, 37–39, 56. Anderson notes that "The linkage of Prov 19:17 and Matt 25:31–46 becomes standard for almost all commentators after Ireneaus" (*Sin*, 227n6). Anderson cites Chrysostom, *On Repentance and Almsgiving*, trans. G. Christo (FC 96; Washington, D.C.: Catholic University Press, 1988), homily 7.24, 105; Gregory of Nazianzus, *Select Orations*, trans. M. Vinson (FC 107; Washington, D.C.: Catholic University Press, 2003), oration 14, 68–70; Clement of Alexandria, *Stromateis, Books One to Three* (FC; Washington, D.C.: Catholic University Press, 1991) 3.6, 290; *S. Ambrosii, De Tobia: A Commentary*, with an introduction and translation by L. Zucker (Patristic Studies 35; Washington, D.C.: Catholic University Press, 1933), 71–73.

Now we make offering to Him, not as though He stood in need of it, but rendering thanks for His gift, and thus sanctifying what has been created. For even as God does not need our possessions, so do we need to offer something to God; as Solomon says: "He that gives alms to the poor, loans to the Lord." (Prov 19:17). For God, who stands in need of nothing, takes our good works to Himself for this purpose, that He may grant us a recompense of His own good things, as our Lord says: "Come, ye blessed of My Father, receive the kingdom prepared for you. For I was hungry, and ye gave Me to eat: I was thirsty, and ye gave Me drink: I was a stranger, and ye took Me in: naked, and ye clothed Me; sick, and ye visited Me; in prison, and ye came to Me." As, therefore, He does not stand in need of these [services], yet does desire that we should render them for our own benefit, lest we be unfruitful; so did the Word give to the people that very precept as to the making of oblations, although He stood in no need of them, that they might learn to serve God: thus is it, therefore, also His will that we, too, should offer a gift at the altar, frequently and without intermission.[144]

The second half of Proverbs 19:17, which Irenaeus does not quote, is "...and he will repay him according to his gift (κατὰ δὲ τὸ δόμα αὐτοῦ ἀνταποδώσει αὐτῷ).[145] For Irenaeus, Matthew 25:31–46 clarifies how God will repay the loan or gift that he receives whenever someone gives to the poor; the Son of Man will give them the kingdom.[146] To be sure, Matthew itself does not describe the recompense of the righteous in this passage as the repayment of a loan, but Irenaeus' interpretation is deeply consonant with all that Matthew has said about recompense throughout the narrative.

2.3 Conclusion

Here are some of the basic contours of debts and wages in Matthew. A full account will only be possible after describing in the remaining chapters the role of wages and debts in the unfolding of the story.

1. *Matthew's depiction of heavenly debts and wages is in most respects not unusual in comparison to the texts discussed in chapter 1.* The understanding

---

144 4.18; translation altered from ANF 1:486.

145 κατὰ δὲ τὸ δόμα αὐτοῦ is missing from the MT. In the LXX δόμα regularly translates מנחה in cultic settings referring to gifts to YHWH, e.g., Exod 28:38. The LXX introduces a cultic element into the verse that is absent in the MT, following the general trend in Second Temple Judaism to associate almsgiving with cultic gifts to God.

146 As noted above, *Sib. Or.* interprets Prov 19:17 along similar lines.

of sin as debt and righteous deeds as earning wages is expressed in a wide variety of images. Almsgiving is the quintessential – but far from the only – act that earns heavenly treasure (see esp. 19:16–29). One's "account" with God determines one's fate in the judgment – that is, it determines whether one enters the kingdom (25:14–30), but heavenly treasure is also described as something enjoyed while already in the kingdom.[147] The possibility of post-mortem repayment of debts with temporary suffering seems to be presumed by Matthew. Heavenly wages can benefit people other than those who actually earned them (10:41–42). Finally, this economic language does not entail a description of God as coldly calculating in the meting out of justice, like some distant bank manager. God cancels the debts of those who ask him and repays righteous deeds far more than they are worth. All of these points are in deep continuity with the description of this theme in early Jewish and Christian literature at the end of chapter 1 above.[148]

2. *Despite the pervasive use of economic language, Matthew's discussions of recompense are not limited to it.* For instance, there is an important cluster of agrarian metaphors. John the Baptist tells the Pharisees and Sadducees to "bear fruit worthy of repentance" (3:8), warning them that every tree that does not bear good fruit will be cut down and thrown into the fire (3:10), and that Jesus will wield a winnowing fork to separate wheat from chaff (3:12). Jesus speaks in a similar manner in the Sermon on the Mount (7:16–20).[149] Matthew is a rich and complex text employing a wide variety of tropes drawn from Scripture and tradition. It would be a serious distortion to suggest that Matthew is limited to one set of metaphors, even one as foundational as that of debt and wages.

3. *The claims, surveyed especially in the Introduction, that the Matthean Jesus wanted the disciples to forsake any thought of recompense are entirely untenable.* Similarly untenable is the oft-made claim that the parable of the workers in the vineyard is the lens through which everything else Matthew says must be viewed – and that the parable eradicates the idea that the disciples should expect any heavenly wage. This

---

147 E.g., the thrones that will be given to the apostles (19:28).
148 There is also one other significant point of continuity that will be explained in the following chapters: heavenly wages repay the debt of sin.
149 Of course, Matthew lived in a largely agrarian economy; to bear fruit is to have more treasure.

reading fails to reckon with both the immediate context of the parable, where it develops the question left dangling by the preceding pericope of God's provision for those who fail to practice radical renunciation. It also ignores the arc of the narrative as a whole by ignoring the relationship of the parable to the programmatic Sermon on the Mount and the climactic final block of teaching material.

4. *If there is a single passage that best summarizes wages and debts in Matthew, it may be 25:29 ("For to all who have, it will be given and they will have an abundance, but from those who do not have, even what they have will be taken from them") along with 6:12 and 6:19–24.* God repays righteous deeds generously and cancels the debts of those who ask him. But those who refuse to earn wages or refuse to cancel the debts of others will be punished. To store up treasure in heaven is to be generous and in single-minded (or single "eyed") service to God, rather than clinging to ephemeral earthly possessions.

Three final points are of particular importance for the following chapters.

5. *For Matthew, wages from God are stored up "in the heavens with God" to be repaid at the Parousia.*

6. *Matthew uses the image of debt-bondage to describe the fate of insolvent sinners (5:21–26; 18:23–35).*[150]

7. *Matthew repeatedly describes the coming judgment as a settling of accounts.* There is the image in 16:27 of the Son of Man coming to "repay" everyone. In the parable of the unforgiving servant the kingdom is likened to a king who wanted to settle accounts with his servants (συνᾶραι λόγον μετὰ τῶν δούλων αὐτοῦ). Something similar appears in the parable of the talents (25:14–30). This parable is the penultimate pericope in the description of the last days that stretches throughout chapters 24–25. From 24:37 on the emphasis is on the necessity of preparing oneself for the unknown hour of the return of the Son of Man. The parable of the talents compares this to a man who entrusted his possessions to his servants before going on a journey. He returns after a long time (πολὺν χρόνον) to settle accounts with his servants (συναίρει λόγον). Because the parable of the ungrateful servant is about the necessity of forgiving others, it understandably frames the settling of accounts in terms of the repay-

---

150 The significance of this image beyond these two passages will be discussed in the next chapter.

ment of a loan (δάνειον) or debt (ὀφειλή). The parable of the talents, however, focuses on the necessity of earning more capital with the master's initial investment. Here it is not enough simply to give back what was entrusted. Rather, one must earn more money while the master is away. Those who do earn money will be given even more, whereas those who do not earn will lose even what they do have (25:28–29).[151] In 23:32 the scribes and Pharisees are said to push their debt to its limit, thereby tempting the creditor to step in and collect.

Having described the broad contours of heavenly debts and wages in Matthew, we are now in a position to turn to the way this language illuminates Matthew's story as a whole. Because the main focus of the narrative is the work of Jesus, it would be no less accurate to say that this also represents a turn from wages and debts as they function in Jesus' teaching to the question of how Jesus himself earns treasure in heaven. Dale Allison has noted that Matthew "hosts a multitude of obvious connections between Jesus' words and his deeds."[152] Again and again Jesus is depicted as doing what he enjoins others to do. It is not surprising, therefore, that, in addition to depicting Jesus as teaching others how to earn heavenly wages and as the one who will return to repay them, he is also depicted earning heavenly treasure. Those who endure insults and persecution have "great wages in the heavens" (5:11–12); Jesus endures insults and persecution (20:19; 26:67–68; 27:27–44). Those who confess Christ before authorities are rewarded with Christ's corresponding confession of them before the Father (10:32); Christ confesses his own identity before the Sanhedrin (26:64). Those who pray privately will receive a wage from their Father in the heavens (6:1, 5–6); Jesus withdraws to pray alone (14:23; 26:36). Those who do not store up their treasure on earth are able to store up treasure in heaven (6:19–21; 19:21) and those who leave their property behind will receive "a hundred times as much" (19:29); Jesus has no place to lay his head (8:20). Those who bear crosses, who lose their lives, will find their lives in the coming eschatological repayment of deeds (16:24–27); Jesus of course bears his cross and is raised from the

---

151 The master's multiplication of the investment of the servant who earned ten talents recalls Jesus' words to Peter, "And everyone who has left houses or brothers or sisters or father or mother or children or fields, for my name's sake, *will receive a hundredfold*, and will acquire eternal life" (19:29).

152 "Structure, Biographical Impulse, and the Imitatio Christi." 149.

dead. In return for forsaking everything and following Jesus the apostles will receive twelve thrones alongside the throne of the Son of Man (19:27–28); Jesus himself is enthroned as Son of Man from the time when he gives his life (26:64; 28:18). Would it be accurate, therefore, to describe Jesus as the earner of heavenly wages par excellence? The remaining chapters will seek to answer this question and describe the significance of Jesus as an earner of treasure in heaven.

3 Filling Up All Righteousness: Salvation from the Debt of Sin

The study turns now from a thematic investigation of heavenly wages and debts to an analysis of the light that this language sheds on the narrative, beginning with the prologue (1:1–4:22). Many have observed that Matthew's prologue foreshadows the main themes that are developed over the course of the story.[1] In this chapter I shall argue that Matthew begins by depicting Jesus as the one who will bring about the end of "exile" by paying the debt of sin with his superabundant righteousness.

3.1 Introducing Jesus (1:1–3:12)

The opening chapters of Matthew show that the end of Israel's exile is at hand with the advent of Jesus, the Davidic messiah.[2] The first line of the Gospel refers to Jesus as "Christ" and "son of David." The following genealogy divides Israel's history into fourteen generations stretching from Abraham to David, fourteen from David to the Babylonian

---

1   E.g., Graham Stanton: "In several important and impressive ways the infancy narratives foreshadow the main themes of the evangelist's story," (*Gospel for a New People: Studies in Matthew* [Louisville, Ky.: Westminster/John Knox Press, 1993], 279). Luz comments: "Der matthäische Prolog erzählt also nicht nur den Anfang der Geschichte Jesu, sondern er ist zugleich auch ihre *narrative Antizipation*. Er ist eine vorweggenommene Jesugeschichte in nuce ..." (*Das Evangelium nach Matthäus* [4 vols.; EKK 1/1–4; Düsseldort: Benziger, 1990–2002], 1.123). Though I am convinced by those who have argued that Matthew's prologue continues into the fourth chapter (e. g., Edgar Krentz, "The Extent of Matthew's Prologue: Toward the Structure of the First Gospel" *JBL* 83 [1964]: 409–14; Jack Dean Kingsbury, *Matthew: Structure, Christology, Kingdom* [Philadelphia, Fortress, 1975; repr., 1991], 7–17; Luz, *Matthäus*, 1:120–21), the present study will focus primarily on the introduction to Jesus in 1:1–3:12 and then his first words and deed in 3:13–17.
2   See Mervyn Eloff, "Exile, Restoration and Matthew's Genealogy of Jesus Ὁ ΧΡΙΣΤΟΣ," *Neot* 38 (2004): 75–87; Richard Hays, "The Gospel of Matthew: Reconfigured Torah" *HTS* 61 (2005): 166–90.

exile, and fourteen from the exile to "the Christ" (1:17), thereby suggesting that the renewal of the Davidic kingdom is at hand, a point which is reinforced by the number fourteen itself, which is of course the numeric value of דוד.[3] The implication, then, is that Jesus' birth signals the dawning of a new age in Israel's history, the coming of the messiah and the end of exile.[4]

---

3   See Davies and Allison (*A Critical and Exegetical Commentary on the Gospel according to Saint Matthew* [3 vols; ICC; Edinburgh: T&T Clark, 1988–1997], 1.161–65) on Matthew's use of gematria. Others, such as Daniel J. Harrington (*The Gospel of Matthew* [SP 1; Collegeville, MI.: Liturgical, 1991], 30), have found this suggestion unlikely, but there is no question that Matthew engages in Hebrew wordplay in 1:21. The Davidic motif is patent regardless.

4   A question that remains is what "exile" means in Matthew. As a working hypothesis, I would suggest that Matthew reads end of exile texts through his apocalyptic eschatology as prophecies of the coming Parousia of the Lord. The interpretation of Isaiah 40 in the Targum offers a helpful analogy, though the notorious complexities involved in dating this text preclude any attempt to read it as background to Matthew's interpretation:

> Prophets, prophesy consolations to my people. Speak to the heart of Jerusalem and prophesy to her that she is about to be filled with people of her exiles, that her debts have been remitted her, that she has taken a cup of consolations before the LORD as if she suffered two for one for all her sins. A voice of one who cries: "In the wilderness clear the way before the people of the LORD, level in the desert highways before the congregation of our God…And the glory of the LORD shall be revealed, and all the sons of flesh shall see it together, for by the Memra of the LORD it is so decreed."…Get you up to a high mountain, prophets who herald good news to Zion; lift up your voice with force, you who herald good tidings to Jerusalem, lift up, fear not; say to the cites of the house of Judah, "The kingdom of your God is revealed!" Behold, the LORD God is revealed with strength, and the strength of his mighty arm rules before him; behold, the wage of those who perform his Memra is with him, all those whose deeds are disclosed before him. Like the shepherd who feeds his flock, he gathers lambs in his arm, he carries tender ones in his bosom, and leads the nursing ewes gently. (Bruce D. Chilton, *The Isaiah Targum: Introduction, Translation, Apparatus and Notes* [ArBib 11; Wilmington, DE: Michael Glazier, 1987], 77–78 alt.)

The good tidings no longer concern Cyrus' decree that the Israelites could return home to Israel and rebuild the temple. Rather, the Targum reads Isaiah as a revelation of the "kingdom of God" and as a prophecy of the coming return of YHWH to Zion. I would suggest that Matthew reads passages dealing with the end of exile similarly as dealing with the coming moment of God's decisive intervention in history. See Craig A. Evans, "Aspects of Exile and Restoration in the Proclamation of Jesus and the Gospels," in *Exile: Old Testament,*

Matthew develops this suggestion in his account of what takes place before the adult Jesus appears by portraying the events surrounding Jesus as the fulfillment of a series of prophetic texts. There is good reason to believe that Matthew is evoking the larger context of these passages, and is crafting his account of Jesus in a way that depends on the readers to supply the missing information. The reason is twofold: (1) All the quotations come from passages that deal with the coming restoration of the Davidic monarchy or the end of exile (Isa 7:14; Micah 5:1–3; 2 Sam 5:2; Hos 11:1; Jer 31:15; Isa 40:3; Isa 8:23–9:1).[5] This is either an extraordinarily remarkable seven-fold coincidence or a deliberate attempt to evoke, not only the words explicitly cited, but the oracles and narratives of which they are a part. The cumulative effect of a series of passages that deal with these issues would be considerable to a reader familiar with them; alerted to the presence of Davidic and exilic themes, the reader would be that much more likely to hear them in the following citations. (2) These wider contexts all cohere perfectly with the emphasis on Jesus' Davidic messiahship and end of exile that was already established in 1:1–17. Thus, we may say with some confidence that the fulfillment of these passages involves not just the bare details mentioned in the quotations – birth from a virgin, the slaughter of infants, settling in Galilee and so on – but their wider contexts as well.[6] The net effect is a powerful reinforcement of what was already indicated in the genealogy.

This polyphony of allusions to Davidic messiahship and end of exile sheds light on the beginning of the narrative proper when an angel tells Joseph that Mary "will bear a son, and you will call his name Jesus, for he will save his people from their sins" (1:21). It is widely recognized that this is a key verse in the narrative, linking Jesus' name to his death, in which his blood is poured out for the forgiveness of sins

---

Jewish, and Christian Conceptions (ed. James M. Scott; Leiden/New York: Brill, 1997), 299–328.

5   This list skips over the seemingly irresolvable 2:23 ("He will be called a Nazorean"), but the fact that the other seven passages deal with either Davidic messiahship or end of exile strongly suggests that something similar was intended here. This would seem to tip the scales in favor of Isa 11:1, "A shoot will come forth from the stump of Jesse and a branch (נצר) from his roots will be fruitful." The wordplay only works in Hebrew, but Matthew has already resorted to folk etymology of the name יהושע in 1:21 and, perhaps, to Hebrew gematria in 1:17

6   See Hays's comments on Matthew's citation of Hosea 11:1 in "Reconfigured Torah," 173–76.

(26:28) as a ransom for many (20:28).[7] Less often noticed is the close link between salvation from sins and the exilic motif that dominates the birth narrative.[8] N. T. Wright correctly notes that

> the prophets of the time of the exile (in particular Jeremiah, Ezekiel, and Isaiah 40–55) saw Israel's exile precisely as the result of, or the punishment for, her sins. It should be clear from this that if the astonishing, unbelievable thing were to happen, and Israel were to be brought back from exile, this would *mean* that her sins were being punished no more; in other words, were forgiven.[9]

The logic is clear enough; if exile is the result of sin, end of exile must mean that sin has been dealt with in some way, and the passages cited by Wright show that this connection was frequently made explicit.[10]

For our purposes, however, it is necessary to probe more deeply into the relationship between forgiveness and exile. Given the fact that second temple Jews frequently described sin as debt, it would not be surprising if return from exile came to be described as the result of the debt of the people having been paid, or as the repayment of credits. This is in fact exactly the way return from exile is described in much of the literature. This link occurs in the later strata of the Hebrew bible and increases in prominence in the Second Temple period and in rabbinic literature. For instance, as already noted in chapter 1, the idiom "to complete/fulfill sin" can refer to the repayment of sin by enduring suffering that brings exile to an end.[11] Or consider Isaiah 50:1: "Thus says the LORD: Where is your mother's bill of divorce with which I put her away? Or which of my creditors is it to whom I have sold you? No, because of your sins you were sold, and for your transgressions your

---

7 E.g., Boris Repschinski, "For He Will Save His People from Their Sins (Matthew 1:21): A Christology for Christian Jews" *CBQ* 68 (2006): 248–67; Davies and Allison, *A Critical and Exegetical Commentary on the Gospel according to Saint Matthew* (3 vols; ICC; Edinburgh: T&T Clark, 1988–1997), 1.210;

8 Hays, "Reconfigured Torah," 171. See also Repschinski, "'For He Will Save His People from Their Sins.'"

9 *Jesus and the Victory of God* (Minneapolis: Fortress Press, (1996), 268. Emphasis original. On the same page Wright misleadingly offers a simple equation of the two concepts: "*Forgiveness of sins is another way of saying 'return from exile'.*" Emphasis original.

10 Wright discusses Lam 4:22; Jer 31:31–4; 33:4–11; Ezek 36:24–26, 33; 37:21–23; Isa 40:1–2; 43:25–44:3; 52:1–53:12; Dan 9:16–19; Bar 1:15–3:8.

11 E.g., Lam 4:22; Dan 9:24. See Gary Anderson, *Sin: A History* (New Haven: Yale University Press, 2009), 75–94.

mother was put away" (NRSV). Joseph Blenkinsopp argues that YHWH's rhetorical questions imply that the children (i. e., the Judeans) have accused their father (i. e., YHWH) of divorcing their mother and selling them into debt slavery.[12] God responds that their debt slavery − their exile in Babylon − was in fact the result of the debt of their own sin. For the indentured servitude to come to an end the debt must be paid off.[13]

In the Targumim, prophetic texts that relate the forgiveness of sins to end of exile without any explicit mention of debts are almost always reinterpreted to refer to debt. For instance, Jeremiah 33:4−11 describes how God will "restore the fortunes of Judah and the fortunes of Israel, and rebuild them as they were at first. I will cleanse them from all the guilt of their sin against me, and I will forgive all the guilt of their sin and rebellion against me" (33:7−8 NRSV). In the Targum, however, the language of cleansing is subordinated to debt forgiveness: "I will cleanse[14] them from all their debts (חוביהון) which they had incurred (דחבו) before me, and I will forgive (ואשבוק) all their debts (חוביהון) which they had incurred (דחבו) before me and in which they had rebelled against my Memra."[15] There are numerous other examples.[16] Though the targumic texts are notoriously difficult to date, the prevalence of debt language in early Judaism and Christianity suggests that this widespread shift in the Aramaic paraphrases is not likely to have emerged *de novo* in later centuries.

More important than all this, however, is the fact that two of the clearest examples of end of exile being linked with the repayment of debt in the Hebrew Bible are cited in short succession in Matthew: Jer-

---

12 *Isaiah 40−55: A New Translation with Introduction and Commentary* (AB 19 A; New York: Doubleday, 2002), 314; Anderson, *Sin*, 48−49.

13 See also Zech 9:11−12.

14 At first glance it appears that the Targum mixes the metaphors of cleansing and debt-forgiveness. In Aramaic as well as Greek, however, cleansing language is frequently used to refer to the clearing of debts. See Gary Anderson, "How Does Almsgiving Purge Sins," which will appear in *Hebrew in the Second Temple Period: The Hebrew of the Dead Sea Scrolls and of Other Contemporary Sources* (ed. S. E. Fassberg, M. Bar-Asher, and R. Clements; Studies on the Texts of the Desert of Judah; Leiden: Brill, 2012).

15 Robert Hayward, *The Targum of Jeremiah: Translated, with a Critical Introduction, Apparatus, and Notes* (ArBib 12; Wilmington, DE: Michael Glazier, 1987). Where Hayward translates חוב as "sin" I have changed it to "debt." See Jastrow חוב.

16 E.g., Ezek 36:24−6, 33; Isa 43.25−44.3; Jer 31:34.

emiah 31 and Isaiah 40. The mourning of Jeremiah 31:15, which is quoted in Matthew 2:18, is immediately followed by this word of comfort: "Let your voice stop weeping, and your eyes from tears, because there is a wage (שכר/μισθός) for your works and they shall come back from the land of enemies" (31:16). Similarly, a few verses later John the Baptist is described as the voice crying in the wilderness from Isaiah 40. The ground of this good news is stated in 40:2: "her humiliation has been fulfilled, her sin has been annulled, because she has received from the Lord's hand double that of her sins." The Lord comes to lead his people home with "his wages (שכרו/ὁ μισθὸς αὐτοῦ) with him, and his work before him" (40:10).[17]

To appreciate the significance of the quotation of Jeremiah and Isaiah here it is necessary to take a step back and discuss briefly Matthew's evocative use of Scripture in 1–3. By 1:21 Jesus has already been described as the Christ who will save his people from their sins. Then Matthew goes on to say that "all this happened to fulfill what was spoken by the Lord through the prophet: 'Behold, the virgin will conceive and will bear a son, and they shall call his name Immanuel.'"[18] This quotation of Isaiah 7:14 ties together birth from a virgin with the important Matthean theme of Jesus as the locus of God's presence (18:20; 28:20). But in Isaiah itself this prophecy occurs in the context of a promise of God's faithfulness to the "house of David" (Isa 7:13). Taken in isolation, Isaiah 7 would not necessarily evoke messianic themes. But when the birth of Jesus the messiah is read as the ultimate fulfillment of God's promise to Ahaz, this word spoken to the house of David is transformed from a prophecy for Ahaz himself to a prophecy for the entire Davidic dynasty.[19]

17　Matthew uses the same intertextual technique at the triumphal entry (21:5). See the discussion in chapter 5.

18　The claim that "*all* this happened (τοῦτο δὲ ὅλον γέγονεν)" to fulfill the prophecy – rather than the virgin birth alone – invites an interpretation of all of 1:18–21 through the lens of Isa 7:14.

19　Maria Theresia Ploner, *Die Schriften Israels als Auslegungshorizont der Jesusgeschichte: eine narrative und intertextuelle Analyse von Mt 1–2* (SBB 66; Stuttgart: Bibelwerk, 2011), 266–67; Rikki E. Watts, "Immanuel: Virgin Birth Proof Text or Programmatic Warning of Things to Come (Isa 7:14 in Matt 1:23)?" in *From Prophecy to Testament* (ed. by Craig Evans; Peabody, MA: Hendrickson, 2004), 92–113; Craig Keener, *A Commentary on the Gospel of Matthew* (Grand Rapids, MI.: Eerdmans, 1999), 87; See also James M. Hamilton Jr., "'The Virgin Will Conceive': Typological Fulfillment in Matthew 1:18–23," in *Built*

Then, when Herod asks the chief priests and scribes where the Christ would be born, they quote Micah 5:2: "And you Bethlehem, land of Judah, you are by no means least among the leaders of Judah, for from you will come out a leader who will shepherd my people Israel." In Micah this is a promise that, in spite of impending doom, a future Davidic ruler would emerge. The following verse indicates that this figure will bring about the end of exile when the messiah's "brothers return to the sons of Israel" (5:3).[20] Matthew increases the messianic overtones of this quotation by adding a line from 1 Chronicles 11:1–3//2 Samuel 5:1–3 ("who will shepherd my people Israel"). In this passage all Israel appears before David, declares fealty, and anoints him king:

> Then all Israel gathered together to David at Hebron and said, "See, we are your bone and flesh. For some time now, even while Saul was king, it was you who commanded the army of Israel. The LORD your God said to you: *It is you who shall be shepherd of my people Israel* (אתה תרעה את-עמי את-ישראל/σὺ ποιμανεῖς[21] τὸν λαόν μου τὸν Ἰσραηλ), you who shall be ruler over my people Israel." So all the elders of Israel came to the king at Hebron, and David made a covenant with them at Hebron before the LORD. And they anointed David king over Israel, according to the word of the LORD by Samuel. (NRSV)

This added quotation is all the more striking because Micah 5 alone would have been sufficient to connect the messiah to Bethlehem. That is, from the perspective of its immediate context in Matthew, the addition of 1 Chronicles/2 Samuel is gratuitous; it says nothing about where the messiah would be born. Yet, the addition of this line reads Jesus' birth through the lens of David's enthronement. Just as David was anointed king at Hebron, Jesus was from birth "the newborn king of the Jews" (ὁ τεχθεὶς βασιλεὺς τῶν Ἰουδαίων) (2:2). Moreover, the inclusion of this allusion to David's enthronement reinforces the sense that the wider contexts of the biblical passages cited are significant. Matthew's readers/auditors are rewarded for thinking of the original contexts of these initial biblical quotations and are therefore encour-

---

Upon the Rock: Studies in the Gospel of Matthew (ed. Daniel M. Gurtner and John Nolland; Grand Rapids, MI.: Eerdmans, 2008), 228–47.

20 Bruce K. Waltke, *A Commentary on Micah* (Grand Rapids, MI.: Eerdmans, 2007), 280, 293–305.

21 Matthew changes the second-person future (ποιμανεῖς) to a third-person future (ποιμανεῖ) to fit the context of Micah's prophecy.

aged to continue to seek out correspondences between them and the story of Jesus.

This pattern of richly allusive biblical quotations continues in the accounts of the flight into Egypt and the slaughter of the infants.[22] In 2:15 the return from Egypt is said to fulfill "that which was spoken by the Lord through the prophet: 'Out of Egypt I called my son.'" In Hosea 11, this line appears in the midst of God's declaration of undying affection for Israel despite Israel's perfidy. God remembers calling his "son" – which refers to the people as a whole – out of Egypt, and recoils at the thought of the punishment that looms as a result of Israel's unfaithfulness. The wider context of the quotation resonates with the hints of end of exile and salvation from sins that have already appeared in Matthew's narrative. Matthew, however, transfigures Hosea's poignant recollection of how God called his "son" out of Egypt by reading it as an event that finds its fulfillment in the life of Jesus.[23] The calling of Jesus out of Egypt "fulfills" God's redemption of Israel from Egypt as well as his promises of faithfulness to Israel in Hosea. Matthew thereby introduces an Israel typology in which Jesus embodies the role and fate of the entire people. He is the son who will save his people from their sins. Hosea describes wayward Israel as God's own child whom he led out of Egypt, and in the remainder of the chapter this familial relationship between Israel and God is the ground for God's promise that he will "return them to their homes" (11:11). Matthew takes up this metaphor and weaves it into his catena of allusions to the end of exile, but now, instead of looking back at the nation as God's son, Hosea, on Matthew's reading, looks to the future when a son (cf., 3:17; 17:5) will embody the fate of Israel in himself.

We are now in a better position to see the significance of the following quotations of Jeremiah 31 and Isaiah 40. Three verses after citing Hosea 11, Matthew quotes another passage dealing with end of exile: Jeremiah 31. Herod's slaughter of children in Bethlehem fulfilled what was spoken through the prophet Jeremiah:

> A voice was heard in Ramah,
> Wailing and loud lamentation,
> Rachel weeping for her children;

---

22 See Ploner (*Die Schriften Israels als Auslegungshorizont der Jesusgeschichte*, 286–292) on the allusions to Exodus in Matt 2:13–20.
23 Hays, "Reconfigured Torah," 173–74.

She would not be consoled,
Because they are no more.

Rachel, who was the wife of Jacob/Israel, here represents the figurative mother of the whole people.[24] She wailed for her children in Ramah, a location which was used to gather exiles for deportation to Babylon.[25] Matthew extends her weeping to the children of Bethlehem, thereby situating this atrocity against the backdrop of the exile in Jeremiah's time as well as Pharaoh's schemes against the Hebrew boy babies in Exodus.[26] Those familiar with Jeremiah 31 could hardly fail to notice that it is remarkably similar to Hosea 11. Both passages offer a respite amidst oracles of doom, describing the people as God's "son" whom he will bring home from exile.[27] Indeed, immediately following the weeping of Rachel it says: "Let your voice stop weeping, and your eyes from tears, because there is a wage for your works (μισθὸς τοῖς σοῖς ἔργοις) and they shall come back from the land of enemies. There is a place for your children" (31:16–17; 38:16–17 LXX). Thus, even the lamentation over the slaughtered infants evokes the promise of redemption.

God's words of comfort to Rachel are based on the fact that she has earned a "wage" that will bring the exile to an end. Not surprisingly, these words have elicited a multiplicity of interpretations from both ancient and modern commentators. J. A. Thompson, for instance, suggests that the wage is paid in return "for all Rachel's activity on behalf of her children."[28] According to *Lamentations Rabbah*, R. Schemuel ben Nah-

---

24 Christine Ritter, *Rachels Klage im antiken Judentum und frühen Christentum* (AGJU 52; Leiden: Brill, 2003), 121.

25 See Jer 40:1, 4.

26 Hays, "Reconfigured Torah," 175.

27 Hays: "Surely it is not merely coincidental that in consecutive formula quotations (Mt 2:15, 2:17–18) Matthew has linked these two very similar passages from Hosea 11:1–11 and Jeremiah 31:15–20. Both prophetic texts speak of the exile and suffering of an unfaithful people, and both declare that God will reach out in mercy and bring the people back from exile… This suggests that Matthew is not merely looking for random Old Testament proof texts that Jesus might somehow fulfil; rather, he is thinking about the *shape* of Israel's story and linking Jesus' life with key passages that promise God's unbreakable redemptive love for his people." Ibid., 176.

28 *The Book of Jeremiah* (NICOT; Grand Rapids, MI: Eerdmans, 1980), 574. Tzvi Novick ("Wages from God: The Dynamics of a Biblical Metaphor," *CBQ* 73 [2011]: 708–22) suggests that Rachel's distress "constitutes the 'labor' for which she is to receive wages" (713).

man said it was Rachel's tolerant treatment of her sister that earned the capital necessary to repay Israel's debt of sin.[29] Another possible reading would be to understand Rachel as the metaphorical mother of the people as a whole, the wife of Israel who weeps over the suffering of her children throughout the centuries, and whose wage is therefore corporate.[30] Targum Jeremiah understands the verse accordingly: Rachel's mourning is the mourning of the people as a whole – denoted with "the house of Israel" and "Jerusalem." The wages are those earned by the fathers:

> Thus says the Lord: "The voice has been heard in the height of the world, the house of Israel who weep and lament after Jeremiah the prophet... and those who weep for the bitterness of Jerusalem, as she weeps for her children, refusing to be comforted for her children, because they have gone into exile."
>   Thus says the Lord: "restrain your voice from weeping, and your eyes from flowing with tears; for there is a reward for the deeds of your righteous fathers (אגר לעובדי אבהתד צדיקיא) says the Lord, and they shall return from the land of their enemies.[31]

The logic here is that of the "merits of the fathers."[32] Sin incurs a debt which must be repaid. Fortunately for Israel the wages of the fathers can be applied to this debt and so bring about an end to the exile.

It is impossible to say with certitude how the Evangelist understood the wages that precipitated the return from exile. Matthew 2:18 evokes this word of comfort, but does not comment on it. Nevertheless, it appears likely that something analogous to the Targum's interpretation is in view here. Jesus fulfills both Jeremiah 31:15 and Hosea 11:1 as a representative figure in whom the suffering and salvation of all Israel is recapitulated. He, like the people of Israel, was exiled amidst wailing and death, and he is the "beloved son" called out of exile. Nothing about wages is mentioned explicitly by Matthew at this point, but the reader knows that Jesus is to save his people from their sins and end the exile. Thus, the "wages of Rachel's works" could evoke the works of the people as a whole as embodied by Jesus, who, like the "righteous fathers" of the Targum, earns treasure in heaven for the whole people.[33]

---

29 *Lamentations Rabbah* (Buber) 24, end.
30 Hays, "Reconfigured Torah," 175.
31 Hayward, *The Targum of Jeremiah*.
32 Cf. Tg Jer 12:5.
33 Cf. Mark F. Whitters, "Jesus in the Footsteps of Jeremiah," *CBQ* 68 (2006): 229–47, esp. 235–37.

A more cautious alternative would be to note simply that Matthew's catena of pregnant biblical quotations suggests here that the end of exile is at hand, which is a wage for works.

A few verses later the account of John the Baptist begins, introducing John as the one spoken of in Isaiah 40:2:

> In those days John the Baptist appeared in the wilderness of Judea saying: "Repent! For the kingdom of heaven has come near." This is the one of whom it was spoken through the prophet Isaiah saying:

> A voice crying in the wilderness
> Prepare the way of the Lord,
> Make straight his paths. (3:1–3)[34]

Needless to say, this is yet another biblical quotation dealing with end of exile. The reason that exile is coming to an end is stated in the preceding verse:

MT[35]	LXX
Speak tenderly to Jerusalem, and cry to her that she has served her term, that her penalty is paid, that she has received from the LORD's hand double for all her sins. (NRSV)[36]	O priests, speak to the heart of Jerusalem; comfort her, because her humiliation has been fulfilled, her sin has been annulled (λέλυται αὐτῆς ἡ ἁμαρτία), because she has received from the Lord's hand double that of her sins.

As noted above, Isaiah 50:1 portrays Israel's exile in Babylon as debt-bondage. Something similar seems to be the case here. Exile is at an

---

34 Note that Matthew omits the words from Malachi (Mark 1:2) thereby increasing attention on Isaiah. Matthew returns to these words from Malachi, however, while discussing John the Baptist in 11:10.

35 Extant Greek and Hebrew traditions differ in this verse and 1QIsa^a supports the Masoretic reading. Though it is generally agreed that Matthew's version of the Scriptures generally agreed with septuagintal readings, this is not always the case (e.g., Hos 11:1 in Matt 2:15). It would seem prudent, therefore, to take the Masoretic reading into consideration in this case.

36 See Blenkinsopp (*Isaiah 40–55*, 180) or, more exhaustively, Anderson (*Sin*, 44–54) for a defense of the interpretation presupposed by the NRSV's rendering. Cf. Chilton, (*The Isaiah Targum*, 77): "Speak to the heart of Jerusalem and prophesy to her that she is about to be filled with people of her exiles, *that her debts* (חובהא) *have been remitted* (אשתביקו) *her*, that she has taken a cup of consolations before the LORD as if she suffered two for one for all her sins" (alt.).

end because Jerusalem's sin has been "annulled" by the punishment she endured in exile. In verse 10 the herald goes on to say, "See, the Lord comes with strength (κύριος μετὰ ἰσχύος ἔρχεται) and his arm with authority. See, his wages (ὁ μισθός) are with him, and his work before him."

Old Testament scholars sometimes understand the "wages" of the Lord in Isaiah 40:10 to be the returning exiles themselves, the people ransomed from captivity who follow him on the journey home.[37] This possibility resonates with Matthew's emphasis on the coming salvation from sins. Yet, readers who have just been reminded of the wages of the "double" punishment that paid the debt of sins would perhaps associate these "wages" with the recompense that the Lord will pay the people when he comes.[38] The Targum interprets the verse in this latter sense ("…behold, the wage of those who perform his Memra is with him, all those whose deeds are disclosed before him)," as do some texts of the Septuagint ("His wages are with him and the work of each [ἑκάστου] is with him").[39] It may be that the ambiguity of the Lord as either the recipient or the repayer of wages is itself significant; as noted in chapter 2, Matthew portrays Jesus not only as the one who will return to repay everyone according to their deeds but also as an earner of heavenly wages. The message of the coming kingdom is an urgent call to repentance in the face of coming judgment, but Matthew adds to this the news that Jesus would save from sins.

This very ambiguity plays a role in the following exchange between John the Baptist and Jesus. John the Baptist arrives calling people to repent in light of the nearness of the kingdom. His warnings about the coming Lord place all the emphasis on the Lord as the one who comes to repay people for their deeds:

> But when he saw many Pharisees and Sadducees coming for baptism, he said to them, "Brood of vipers! Who warned you to flee from the coming wrath? Bear fruit worthy of repentance and do not suppose to say to yourselves, 'We have Abraham as our father'; for I tell you, God is able from these stones to raise up children for Abraham. Already the ax is lying at the root of the trees; every tree therefore that does not bear good fruit is cut down and thrown into the fire. I baptize you with water for repentance, but one who is more powerful than I is coming (ὁ … ἐρχόμενος ἰσχυ-

---

37   Blenkinsopp, *Isaiah 40–55*, 186.
38   Novick, "Wages from God," 721.
39   Chilton, *The Isaiah Targum*, 78 alt. See also the apparatus of the Göttingen LXX.

ρότερός) after me; I am not worthy to carry his sandals. He will baptize you with the Holy Spirit and fire. His winnowing fork is in his hand, and he will clear his threshing floor and will gather his wheat into the barn; but the chaff he will burn with inextinguishable fire." (3:7–12)

John is crying out in the wilderness to warn people that an agent of divine retribution for works is coming. The warnings of John, whom Matthew has identified as the herald in Isaiah 40, notably resemble the words of the herald in Isaiah. The herald speaks of the Lord coming with strength (μετὰ ἰσχύος ἔρχεται) and John warns of the stronger one who is coming (ὁ ... ἐρχόμενος ἰσχυρότερος). As the following discussion of 3:13–17 will show, however, Jesus problematizes John's straightforward understanding of the coming mighty one.

A brief summary of the picture that emerges from this investigation of 1:1–3:12 is in order. By the time the adult Jesus appears on the scene in 3:13, Matthew has described him as the Davidic messiah who will bring about the end of "exile." In addition, in 1:21 it is said that he will "save his people from their sins" (1:21), a theme to which Matthew will return at key points in the narrative. This emphasis on forgiveness of sins does not prescind from the themes of Davidic messiahship and end of exile but illuminates them: the unborn messiah will end the exile of his people precisely by rescuing them from their sins, a vocation that is written into his very name. The evocative biblical quotations in 1:1–3:12 bring further clarity to this picture, situating the coming redemption against the history of Israel's hope that their debts would finally be paid.

3.2 Filling Up All Righteousness (3:13–17)

As noted above, John the Baptist announces the coming mighty one who will give people their just deserts for their deeds, thereby initiating a theme that is central to Matthew's eschatology; Jesus will return and "repay to each according to his deeds" (16:27). Yet, the birth narrative also indicates that Jesus will save his people from their sins. It is not clear at this point in the narrative how these two vocations relate to one another, or even that they are not mutually exclusive. This tension becomes explicit when Jesus comes to John to receive his baptism of repentance: "Then Jesus came from Galilee to the Jordan to John to be baptized by him. But John was trying to prevent him, saying 'I need to be baptized by you, and you are coming to me?'" (3:13–14). John rightly views Jesus as God's agent of retribution and understandably objects to his undergoing a sign of repentance. Jesus' response is famously enigmatic. It is typically translated, "Let it be so now; for it is proper for us in this way to fulfill all righteousness."In the remainder of this chapter I shall argue that Jesus' response is the first indication how he will save his people from their sins.

Every word of Jesus' reply bristles with difficulties, but the lynchpin is arguably πληρόω.[40] There are two widespread interpretations of πληρόω here. One, advanced by John Meier among others, reads πληρῶσαι as a fulfillment of prophecy.[41] Matthew uses the word πληρόω sixteen times, twelve of which refer to the fulfillment of Scripture (1:22; 2:15, 17, 23; 4:14; 8:17; 12:17; 13:35; 21:4; 26:54; 26:56; 27:9). Ἀναπληρόω in 13:14 may be added to this list. Meier proposes that this idiosyncratic use of πληρόω indicates that πληρῶσαι πᾶσαν δικαιοσύνην refers to the fulfillment of Scripture.[42] The obvious objection to this proposal is the fact that, while the theophany following the baptism is indeed rich with scriptural allusions, the direct object of πληρῶσαι is not Scripture or prophecy but righteousness. Meier attempts to harmonize the idea of the fulfillment of prophecy with δικαιοσύνη by arguing that, in 3:15 at least, δικαιοσύνη means not "man's moral conduct" but God's saving activity.[43] Yet, in every other case Matthew uses δικαιοσύνη in the former sense.[44] Moreover, even if one were to accept this doubtful interpretation of δικαιοσύνη here, it is not clear that this would help Meier's case, for fulfilling *righteousness* (in the sense of God's saving activity) is not the same as fulfilling *Scripture*. Thus, while πληρῶσαι πᾶσαν

---

40 For thorough but dated descriptions of contemporary interpretations see O. Eissfeldt, "Πληρῶσαι πᾶσαν δικαιοσύνην in Matthäus 3:15," *ZNW* 61 (1970): 209–15, and Jacques Dupont, *Les Béatitudes III* (Bruges: Abbaye de Saint-André, 1973), 225–45.

41 Meier, *Law and History in Matthew's Gospel* (AnBib 71; Rome: Biblical Institute Press, 1976), 76–80; Davies and Allison, *Matthew*, 1.326–27; more cautiously, John Nolland, *The Gospel of Matthew: A Commentary on the Greek Text* (NIGTC; Grand Rapids, MI: Eerdmans, 2005), 153–54.

42 Meier, *Law and History*, 79.

43 Meier, *Law and History*, 79–80. "It is our contention, then, that taking *plērōsai pasan dikaiosynēn* in a prophetic or *heilsgeschichtliche* sense (instead of reducing it to a question of obedience and moral example) provides the whole pericope with a closely woven, unified motif." (80).

44 Benno Przybylski, *Righteousness in Matthew and His World of Thought* (New York: Cambridge University Press, 1980), 78–98. See chapter two above for a refutation of the view that 5:6 is an exception.

δικαιοσύνην may evoke Scripture fulfillment, this is unlikely to be its most immediate referent.[45]

Another common interpretation, defended by Ulrich Luz and others, takes πληρόω to mean "to do what is required"; the phrase πληρῶσαι πᾶσαν δικαιοσύνην would therefore mean "to do all righteousness."[46] In support of this interpretation is the fact that Matthew may use πληρόω in this way when Jesus says he "fulfills the law" in 5:17, though even this example is doubtful, and, as Luz himself admits, this use of πληρόω would be unusual, not only in Matthew but in other literature as well.[47] More importantly, there are dozens of instances where Matthew speaks unambiguously of "doing that which is required" and in all of these ποιέω or τηρέω is used.[48] Thus, while it is possible that πληρῶσαι πᾶσαν δικαιοσύνην means "to do all righteousness," this would go against the grain of typical Matthean usage.

Luz's interpretation also faces logical problems: what does it mean to say that Jesus and John do all righteousness in Jesus' baptism? Luz suggests that "Nicht in der Johannestaufe *besteht* 'alle Gerechtigkeit', sondern sie gehört nur zu ihr."[49] In other words, *all* righteousness is not accomplished in this baptism, but Jesus needed to be baptized because it is one of God's many requirements. This presumes, however, that Jesus was obligated to submit himself to John's baptism of repentance. Yet, baptism for repentance was not a requirement of Torah. Rather, in

---

45 Luz writes, "Primär an die Erfüllung von prophetischen Weissangungen zu denken...ist m.E. vom Objekt δικαιοσύνη ausgeschlossen" (*Matthäus*, 1.213).

46 Luz: "Auszugehen ist im Kontext von der Bedeutung 'erfüllen' im Sinne von 'verwirklichen'. Die Wortwahl mußte aber einem damaligen Hörer oder Leser auffallen" (*Matthäus*, 1.213); R. T. France, *The Gospel of Matthew* (NICNT; Grand Rapids: Eerdmans, 2007), 119–20; Robert H. Gundry *Matthew: A Commentary on His Handbook for a Mixed Church under Persecution* (2d ed; Grand Rapids, MI: Eerdmans, 1994), 50. Warren Carter (*Matthew: Storyteller, Interpreter, Evangelist* [Peabody, Mass.: Hendrickson Publishers, 1996], 129) combines these two interpretations: "Using contextual clues the audience knows from the four previous uses of the key word "fulfill" (1:22; 2:15, 17, 23) that this verb means to enact or carry out God's saving will according to the scriptures."

47 See the discussion of 5:17 in chapter 1 above.

48 See, e.g., 6:1 ("Be careful not to do righteousness (τὴν δικαιοσύνην ὑμῶν μὴ ποιεῖν) before people...") or 23:3 "Do and observe (ποιήσατε καὶ τηρεῖτε) whatever [the scribes and Pharisees] tell you." See also, for ποιέω: 1:24; 3:3, 8, 10, 5:19, 46–47; 6:2–3, 7:12, 17–19, 21–22, 24, 26; 8:9; 12:50; 19:16; 21:6, 31, 43; 23:23; 24:46; 25:40, 45; 26:19. And for τηρέω: 19:17; 28:20.

49 *Matthäus*, 1.213.

Matthew John's baptism was a necessity only in light of the coming of the mighty one who would separate the wheat from the chaff (3:12). Jesus, of course, is the coming mighty one. It would be odd, then, to say he needed to repent to prepare for coming judgment. Indeed, Jesus' baptism appears to be an act of supererogation rather than the completion of a requirement.

I would like to propose another interpretation of πληρόω, one that has rarely been considered: that of filling something up.[50] The phrase would then be translated "to fill up all righteousness." Matthew himself uses the word this way in 13:48 to refer to a fish-net becoming full, and in 23:32 when Jesus tells the scribes and Pharisees to "fill up (πλη-ρώσατε) the measure of [their] fathers." According to this proposal, "filling up all righteousness" would be the exact inverse of the filling up of the scribes and Pharisees; they fill up the measure of sin, but Jesus and John the Baptist fill up the measure of righteousness. I shall provide three main arguments for this rendering.

First main argument: for Matthew, righteousness is something that can be "filled up" because righteous deeds earn wages that are stored up in heavenly treasuries.[51] In 6:1, for instance, Jesus says, "Take care not to do your righteousness before people in order to be seen by them. Otherwise, *you have no wage with your Father who is in the heavens* (μισθὸν οὐκ ἔχετε παρὰ τῷ πατρὶ ὑμῶν τῷ ἐν τοῖς οὐρανοῖς)." As noted in chapter 2, the words μισθὸν οὐκ ἔχετε παρὰ τῷ πατρὶ ὑμῶν τῷ ἐν τοῖς οὐρανοῖς are commonly translated "you *will* have no reward *from* your Father in heaven," thereby obscuring the fact that Matthew describes divine wages as (1) existing already in the present time rather than only in the future, and (2) *with* God in heaven, stored up to be repaid

---

50   It has been suggested that an eschatological filling up of time is in view in 3:15. Henrik Ljungman (*Das Gesetz Erfüllen* [Lund: C. W. K. Gleerup, 1954], 97–126) writes: "Der kommende Zorn, der Tag, an dem der Messias die Welt richten wird, steht bevor. Das ist das Ende der Zeit, da dieses Zeitalter aufhören soll. Es ist der Tag, an dem das Gericht vollendet werden und das Mass der Bosheit voll sein soll. Vor diesem Hintergrund zeichnen sich Jesu Worte vom Voll-Machen aller dikaiosyne ab" (118). The arguments presented here do not conflict with Ljungman's main thesis so much as add to it; the eschatological valence of πληρόω is an important aspect of Matthew's depiction of the filling up of righteousness.

51   Note that πληρόω can also mean "render, pay in full" (LSJ III.5). Moulton and Milligan note that "the meaning 'pay' is very common" in the papyri.

at the return of the Son of Man. The description of heavenly treasures that follows reinforces the point:

> Do not treasure up for yourselves treasures on earth (Μὴ θησαυρίζετε ὑμῖν θησαυροὺς ἐπὶ τῆς γῆς), where moth and rust destroy and where thieves break in and steal. Rather, treasure up for yourselves treasures in heaven (θησαυρίζετε δὲ ὑμῖν θησαυροὺς ἐν οὐρανῷ), where neither moth nor rust destroys and where thieves do not break in nor steal. For *where* your treasure is, there also will be your heart (ὅπου γάρ ἐστιν ὁ θησαυρός σου, ἐκεῖ ἔσται καὶ ἡ καρδία σου). (6:19–21)

The focus here is on the *location* of one's treasure, whether earth or heaven. It is better to stockpile treasures "in heaven" because heavenly treasuries are safe from corruption and theft. Similarly, in chapter 19 Jesus tells the rich young man: "If you wish to be perfect, go, sell your possessions, and give the money to the poor, and you will have treasure in heaven; then come, follow me." The young man refuses to acquire this heavenly treasure because he cannot bear to lose all that he has stockpiled on earth.

Matthew is not unusual in depicting divine recompense as existing in a particular space with God. As seen in chapter 1, early Jewish and Christian texts depict heavenly treasure variously as filling up treasuries, purses, baskets, or scales – all the locations where one would put earthly treasures. Consider Luke's parable of the rich fool. The rich man plans to build ever bigger barns to store his crops, but God says to him: "You fool! This very night your life is being demanded of you. And the things you have prepared, whose will they be?" Then Jesus adds "So it is with those who store up treasures for themselves but are not rich toward God." (12:20–21). This thought receives further elaboration a few verses later when Jesus says "Sell your possessions, and give alms. Make money-bags for yourselves that do not wear out, an unfailing treasure in heaven, where no thief comes near and no moth destroys" (12:33). Incorruptible money-bags are to be prized above earthly money bags because they can be counted on even after death.

In short: for Matthew, the wages of righteousness "fill up" heavenly treasuries. When Matthew makes "righteousness" the direct object of πληρόω, therefore, it is worth considering whether he is saying that Jesus "fills up" all righteousness.

Second main argument: as already noted, Matthew uses πληρόω in the way suggested here but in reference to sin rather than righteousness. In 23:32 Jesus ironically tells his opponents to "fill up (πληρώσατε) the measure of [their] fathers" and so receive the punishment for all the righteous blood that has been shed since Abel.[52] In chapter 2 it was argued that the measure in 23:32 is, like the measure in 7:2, a measure that records the amount that is owed. When Jesus tells the scribes and Pharisees to "fill up the measure of your fathers," he ironically tells them to bring the debt of their fathers to its limit, the point at which the creditor can tolerate it no more and steps in to collect what is due. Both 3:15 and 23:32 employ the spatial image of "filling up," but in 23:32 it is the "measure" (μέτρον) for recording the debt of sin.

One may object that the parallel with 23:32 is not quite exact; Matthew does not say that Jesus fills up *the measure* of righteousness. To be sure, if Matthew had written "it is fitting for us in this way to fill up the measure of all righteousness" then this verse would not be the notorious *crux interpretum* that it is. Nevertheless, the parallel should not be dismissed simply because 3:15 fails to mention a "measure"; references to the "completion" or "filling up" of sins usually lack explicit mention of a measuring device. For instance, 2 Macc 6:14 speaks simply of the filling up of sins (ἐκπλήρωσις ἁμαρτιῶν) that leads God to step in and punish a people.[53] *Epistle of Diognetus* 9:2 speaks of the filling up of unrighteousness (πεπλήρωτο ... ἡ ἡμετέρα ἀδικία) that brings the "wages of unrighteousness." There are numerous other examples.[54] The explicit mention of a measure in Matt 23:32, therefore, makes this saying unusual in its clarity. Jesus' words to John the Baptist in 3:15, on the other hand, are more similar to these other depictions of "filling up" with one important exception: Jesus and John the Baptist fill up righteousness rather than sin.

This raises the question of what the filling up of the debt of sin has to do with Jesus' baptism; after all, the phrase "to fill up all righteousness" clearly is not referring to sins reaching their full measure. Yet, it is the conception of sin as incurring a debt and the corresponding idea of righteousness as earning a wage that stands behind both; just as righteous deeds accumulate in heavenly treasuries, sins incur a debt that piles up until it is called due. As noted in chapter 1, in some cases a scale weighing sins on one side and righteousness on the other is envisioned; right-

---

52   Cf. also the expression "to complete/fulfill sins" (Gen 15:16; Dan 8:23; 9:24; 4Q388 col. 2 frag. 9:4–6; 1 Thess 2:15–16; L.A.B. 26:13; 36:1; 41:1), which refers to the moment when at debt reaches the point where the creditor (i. e., God) must step in to collect, or, depending on context, to the time when the debtor has fulfilled his obligation by repaying the debt.

53   See the discussion of this text in chapter 1.

54   See note 52 above and Anderson, *Sin*, 75–94.

eousness would be filled up when it outweighs sin, but sin would be filled up when it outweighs righteousness. For instance, Philo says Sodom
was destroyed because "no good could be found to put on the scale to
balance the unspeakable multitude of evils" (De sac. 1.122).[55] Similarly,
in Daniel 4 Daniel concludes his ominous interpretation of Nebuchadnezzar's dream with advice for how he could avoid the coming punishment: "Redeem your sins by giving alms and your iniquities with
mercy to the poor." Nebuchadnezzar found himself in tremendous
debt because of his sin, but he could have paid it down with alms.
Something similar can be seen in the Didache. In 4:5–7 the author says

> If you have [something] through the work of your hands, you shall give [it
> as] redemption of your sins (λύτρωσιν ἁμαρτιῶν σου). You shall not hesitate
> to give, and when you give you shall not grumble, for you will know who
> the good Repayer of wages is.

The author assumes that sin incurs a debt from which one needs to be
ransomed. By giving alms one is able to invest one's money in heaven,
thereby paying down one's debt. Filling up sins and filling up righteousness are therefore two sides of one conceptual coin – or, better, two
sides of one scale.

A narrative link has often been observed between 23:32 and the
preaching of John the Baptist.[56] In 3:7–12 John (A) calls the Pharisees
and Sadducees a "brood of vipers" (γεννήματα ἐχιδνῶν), (B) asks them
rhetorically "Who told you to flee from the coming wrath?", and (C)
warns them that they will not escape the coming wrath simply by rely-
ing on the fact that Abraham is their father. They must "bear fruit worthy of repentance" because God is able to raise up children of Abraham
from stones (3:8–9). In other words, it is not biology that determines
paternity but deeds.[57] The question of paternity and the coming judgment is also at stake in 23:31–33, where Jesus (A) calls the scribes
and Pharisees a brood of vipers (γεννήματα ἐχιδνῶν), (B) asks rhetorically,
"How will you escape the judgment of Gehenna?", and (C) warns them
that their actions show that they are the children (not of Abraham but)
of those who murdered the prophets, as their coming complicity in

---

55 See also t. Qidd 1:13–14, discussed in chapter 1.
56 Ljungman, Das Gesetz Erfüllen, 111; Pennington, Heaven and Earth in the Gospel
    of Matthew, 239.
57 This is in keeping with Matthew's overarching emphasis on the importance of
    right actions over presumptions of belonging.

Jesus' own death shows.[58] In short, 23:31–33 harks back to John the Baptist standing in the wilderness of Judea, thereby strengthening the connection between these two "filling-up" sayings.

Moreover, as noted in chapter 2, within the framework of Matthew's eschatology, both the debt of sin and the wages of righteousness are about to reach their full measure. For Matthew, the coming Parousia is the time when debts are collected and wise investments are rewarded. As the parable of the talents puts it, the master will return and settle accounts with his servants (25:19 cf. 18:23), taking what is owed to him, repaying faithful service, and punishing those who failed to earn money with the master's investment. Similarly, in 16:24–28 Jesus explains the necessity of cross-bearing in terms of the imminent eschatological recompense. Like the Markan parallel, this pericope explains that following Jesus entails giving one's life to gain it back, following Jesus who will be killed and then raised from the dead (see 16:21). Matthew, however, explicitly describes this "losing in order to regain" as repayment; those who lose their lives following Jesus will regain it because the Son of Man is about to "repay to each according to his deeds." For Matthew, the coming fullness of both sin and righteousness will be the time of sifting between those who kill the prophets and those who bear crosses, between the wheat and the weeds (13:24–30) or the sheep and the goats (25:31–46), between those who give the owner of the vineyard his fruit and those who kill his messengers (21:33–44).[59]

In short, Matthew's depiction of sin reaching its eschatological fullness, typified in Jesus' words "fill up the measure of your fathers," is the

---

58 Craig S. Keener argues that in both of these passages Matthew associates vipers with the question of parentage because vipers were widely thought to kill their mothers during birth. "'Brood of Vipers' (Matthew 3.7; 12.34; 23.33)," *JSNT* 28 (2005): 3–11.

59 The Zechariah traditions alluded to in 23:35 increase the ominous import of Jesus' words. Catherine Sider Hamilton ("His Blood Be upon Us": Innocent Blood and the Death of Jesus in Matthew," *CBQ* 70 [2008]: 82–100) notes that the Zechariah stories found in rabbinic literature and earlier (i.e., 2 Chron 24:20–22; *Lives of the Prophets* 23) make the murder of a prophet named Zechariah the sin that finally leads God to allow the temple to be destroyed. See also David M. Moffitt ("Righteous Bloodshed, Matthew's Passion Narrative, and the Temple's Destruction: Lamentations as a Matthean Intertext," *JBL* 125 [2006]: 299–320, esp. 305–9) on a possible allusion in Matt 23:35 to Lam 4:13, which says that Jerusalem was sacked because of the unrighteous priests who shed righteous blood.

mirror image of what I am proposing in 3:15; both wages and debts are "stored up" until the time of their fullness when the Son of Man comes to collect debts and pay wages.

Third main argument: Matthew describes Jesus' saving activity as a payment on behalf of others in the so-called "ransom saying" in 20:28. Fuller treatment of this verse must wait until the next chapter. For now it must be noted only that, regardless of the pre-Matthean history of the saying, the description of Jesus' gift of his life as a *ransom-price* (λύτρον) fits hand in glove with Matthew's grammar of sin and righteousness. For Matthew sin is thought of as debt, and Jesus was born to save his people from their sins. I propose that it is not a coincidence that this saving activity is described as a payment; Jesus gives his life as a ransom-price to pay the debt of "the many."[60]

What does this tell us about the baptism? It appears that these famously enigmatic sayings closely parallel and illuminate each other. At the beginning of the Gospel Jesus is depicted as one who will fill up the righteousness of the people; he is the beloved son who saves them from the debt of their sin by living a life of humble self-emptying. As the narrative progresses this mission comes into ever sharper focus. The pivotal moment comes in chapter 16 when he begins teaching the disciples that he and all who wish to follow him must take up their crosses so that they will be repaid in the coming repayment of deeds. This counter-intuitive catechesis reaches its climax when, just before entering Jerusalem, Jesus tells the disciples that he will give his life as a ransom, a payment for many. Or – if one includes the closely related statement at the Last Supper – one might say Jesus gives his life as a ransom-price for the payment of sins. These words explicate, from under the shadow of the cross, the full extent of what it means for Jesus to fill up all righteousness; he meekly submits, not only to baptism, but also to death on a cross, and so stores up treasure in heaven that overflows to those under the debt of sin.[61]

---

60 One might object that this proposal asks too much of the word λύτρον. Commentators frequently claim that in the Septuagint λύτρον and its cognates had lost any sense of an actual ransom-price, coming to refer simply to deliverance in a generic sense. One might also object that the ransom saying is simply detritus from the Markan narrative. Both of these claims will be dealt with in the next chapter.

61 It may be that a parallel filling up on behalf of others is in view in Colossians 1:24: Νῦν χαίρω ἐν τοῖς παθήμασιν ὑπὲρ ὑμῶν καὶ ἀνταναπληρῶ τὰ ὑστερήματα

The parallel between the "filling up" of Jesus' baptism and the ransom-price given at the cross raises the issue of whether 3:13–17 prefigures the cross in some way. Contemporary exegetes have tended to conclude that it does not. Luz, for instance, dismisses this suggestion as "eine verbreitete Eisegese in den Text."[62] Oscar Cullman argued that Jesus' baptism indicated that he would die to bring forgiveness of sins, but it is difficult to see how to sustain this reading without importing a Pauline link between baptism and death.[63] Indeed, 3:13–17, read in isolation, would seem not to contain any allusion to the cross. Nevertheless, it would be hasty to conclude on this basis that it does not prefigure his death. Matthew's prologue frequently hints at the events to come in the remainder of the story. There are a number of indications that similar foreshadowing is at work at the baptism. In verse 13 the adult Jesus appears for the first time. His first deed is to join those have come to be baptized in preparation for the coming of the Stronger One who will separate the wheat from the chaff. John recognizes the inappropriateness of this request; there is no sense in the coming agent of divine recompense himself submitting to baptism. Jesus' response – his first words in the Gospel – explains why he should be baptized in spite of his identity: this strange reversal is appropriate for the moment (ἄρτι) because by it they will fill up all righteousness. Then the Spirit descends on Jesus and a voice from the heavens thunders its approval: "This is my son, the beloved. In him I am well-pleased" (3:17). At the beginning of Jesus' ministry, then, he is revealed to be not only God's apocalyptic agent of recompense but also one who humbly stands alongside his people. In this way the baptism presages the whole of Jesus' identity and mission. While there is nothing in the baptism itself that leads inexorably to crucifixion, Jesus' submission to baptism indicates the nature of his mission, a mission which ends in Jesus giving his life.

These observations lead to an explanation of how the baptism itself fills up *all* righteousness. As noted above, Matthew features an Israel typology wherein the identity and fate of the whole people is embodied in Jesus. Small events, particularly in Jesus' early life and ministry, recall the

---

τῶν θλίψεων τοῦ Χριστοῦ ἐν τῇ σαρκί μου ὑπὲρ τοῦ σώματος αὐτοῦ, ὅ ἐστιν ἡ ἐκκλησία.

62 *Matthäus*, 1.214.

63 *Die Tauflehre des Neuen Testaments: Erwachsenen- und Kindertaufe* (ATANT 12; Zürich: Zwingli Verlag, 1948), 13–14.

past history of the people whom Jesus embodies while also presaging the coming redemption. One obvious example is the flight of the Holy Family into Egypt which is said to fulfill Hosea 11:1, "Out of Egypt I have called my son." What at first appears to be a superficial similarity – the boy Jesus, like the people of Israel, was called out of Egypt – becomes the basis of a fecund typological correspondence: the return of Jesus from Egypt recalls the redemption of the people whom he embodies while simultaneously pointing forward to the redemption that is at hand.

I would suggest that these examples show the sense in which the baptism fills up all righteousness. This one act of baptism does not per se fill up all righteousness any more than the boy Jesus led his people out of exile when he left Egypt. Rather, the baptism, like the flight into Egypt, symbolically enacts the nature of Jesus' identity and mission; Jesus is the beloved son who by his humble obedience will fill up the righteousness of a people crushed by the debt of sin. He goes beyond that which is required of him – presumably we are to understand from verse 14 that Jesus did not need John's baptism of repentance –in order to allow his righteousness to overflow to a people in need of ransom.

From this angle we can see the programmatic nature of Jesus' response to John. The birth narrative indicates that Jesus will bring the end of exile and also salvation from sins. Jesus' baptism – his first words and deed in the Gospel – indicates that Jesus will save his people from the debt of sin through the gift of his own superabundant righteousness.[64]

---

64   Leroy Huizenga (*The New Isaac: Tradition and Intertextuality in the Gospel of Matthew* [NovTSup 131; Leiden: Brill, 2009], 153–88) makes a compelling case that the heavenly voice in 3:17 ("This is my beloved son in whom I am well-pleased") evokes the Aqedah (see esp. Gen 22:2, 11–12, 15–16 LXX) and that by the first century Isaac was already viewed as a willing victim whose "death" was associated with Passover and the establishment of the temple cult. It is possible, then, that the evocation of the Aqedah would have reinforced the sense that Jesus' willing submission to baptism was efficacious for others. It is also interesting to note that later rabbinic texts read the Aqedah as accomplishing something very similar to a filling up of all righteousness; by willingly submitting to the sacrifice he earned merits for the whole people. Cf. Jon D. Levenson, *The Death and Resurrection of the Beloved Son: The Transformation of Child Sacrifice in Judaism and Christianity* (New Haven: Yale University Press, 1993), 173–99. See also the discussion of the Last Supper in chapter 5 below.

3.3 Conclusion

Matthew begins with a genealogy and birth narrative that repeatedly emphasizes that the end of exile is at hand with the birth of Jesus, the Davidic messiah, who will end the exile by saving his people from their sins. Woven into this story is a series of biblical quotations that deal with the coming restoration of the Davidic monarchy or the end of exile (Isa 7:14; Micah 5:1–3; 2 Sam 5:2; Hos 11:1; Jer 31:15; Isa 40:3; Isa 8:23–9:1). These evocative quotations name the history of God's faithfulness to Israel and the house of David as Jesus' "back-story" as well as the template for understanding the redemption that is at hand. Moreover, the citation of Jeremiah 31 and Isaiah 40 associates the end of exile with the "wages" due for works and the repayment of the debt of sin. John the Baptist, whom Matthew identifies as the herald of the end of exile and of the repayment of works, arrives on the scene announcing Jesus as the coming mighty one (3:11; Isa 40:10) who will throw every tree that does not bear fruit into the fire. As noted in chapter 2, Jesus' role as the coming repayer of wages is indeed a central Matthean proprium. Yet, the encounter with John the Baptist in 3:13–17 nuances this picture to include Jesus' vicarious action for others. John tries to prevent Jesus' baptism, but Jesus explains that in doing this they will "fill up all righteousness" – a statement that parallels both the ransom saying in 20:28 and, antithetically, Jesus' words to the scribes and Pharisees in 23:32.[65] Jesus is the beloved son who goes beyond what is required of him to fill up all righteousness, thereby liberating those trapped by the debt of sin.

---

65 Note that Jesus appears to include John in the filling up (οὕτως γὰρ πρέπον ἐστὶν ἡμῖν πληρῶσαι πᾶσαν δικαιοσύνην). Similarly, the ransom saying occurs in the context of exhortation; Jesus is telling the apostles not to lord it over each other but to be servants, just as he serves by giving his life as a ransom. Jesus' vicarious action for others does not exclude their participation – indeed, it demands it. I shall return to this point in the following chapter.

4 Wages of Cross-Bearing:
Eternal Life, Glorious Thrones, and the
Ransom-Price for Captive Debtors

4.1 Introduction

We arrive now at the heart of the argument. This chapter will examine the way salvation from sins and the payment of wages is developed in three key passages occurring after the pivotal moment when Jesus begins predicting his death and resurrection (16:13–28; 19:16–29; 20:17–28) with a particular focus on the ransom saying in 20:28. To anticipate the main conclusions: Matthew repeatedly sets forth a salvation-by-imitation schema in which both Jesus and all who would follow him must give their lives and be "repaid" with resurrection and participation in the coming triumph described in Daniel 7. On the other hand, however, there are indications that provision will be made for those without heavenly treasure. In 20:17–28 these two motifs converge, as Jesus reprimands the apostles for their posturing by explaining that he will give his life to earn the ransom-price for the many in debt-bondage.

Those who favor dividing Matthew into three parts according to the twice-repeated phrase ἀπὸ τότε ἤρξατο ὁ Ἰησοῦς will not fail to notice that in moving from the prologue to 16:13 I am jumping over the ostensible second part that begins when Jesus begins proclaiming "Repent! For the kingdom of heaven has come near!" (4:17) and ends when Jesus begins to show his disciples that it was necessary for him to die and be raised (16:21).[1] While I am not convinced that this three-fold division can account for all the major structural shifts in Gospel, it is undeniable that 4:17–22 marks a transition from an introduction to the person of Jesus to Jesus' teaching and deeds in Israel. Similarly, 16:21 marks the point when Jesus' death and resurrection begins to take center stage. It is not surprising, therefore, that 16:21 also marks the point at which the salvation from sins that Jesus will bring

---

1   E.g., Edgar Krentz, "The Extent of Matthew's Prologue: Toward the Structure of the First Gospel" *JBL* 83 (1964): 409–14; Jack Dean Kingsbury, *Matthew: Structure, Christology, Kingdom* (Philadelphia, Fortress, 1975; repr., 1991), 7–25.

comes to the fore. In other words, we have seen that the prologue presents Jesus as the one who will bring salvation from sins through the wages of his superabundant righteousness. This aspect of Jesus' identity does not reemerge with full force until Jesus turns his face to Jerusalem, where he will give his life as the ransom-price for many.

4.2 Cross-bearers will be Repaid with Eternal Life (16:21–28)

After Peter confesses Jesus as "the Christ, the Son of the living God" (16:16), Jesus begins to explain to the disciples what this means: "From then Jesus began showing his disciples that it was necessary for him to go to Jerusalem and to suffer many things from the elders and chief priests and scribes and be killed and on the third day be raised" (16:21).[2] Unsurprisingly, this prediction is repugnant to Peter: "And taking him aside Peter began to rebuke him saying 'Far be it from you Lord! This will certainly not happen to you!' But turning, Jesus said to Peter, 'Get behind me, Satan! You are a trap to me because you are not thinking the things of God (τὰ τοῦ θεοῦ) but the things of people (τὰ τῶν ἀνθρώπων)'" (16:21–23).[3] Peter's seemingly reasonable objection is condemned by Jesus as human rather than divine thinking.[4]

In the teaching that follows in 16:24–28 Jesus commences a bit of remediation for the disciples in "the things of God." Regardless of the

---

2   At first glance 16:21–28 would seem to have a tenuous relationship to the preceding material. The introduction of ἀπὸ τότε ἤρξατο makes the break between Peter's confession (16:13–20) and the first passion and resurrection prediction (16:21–28) stronger than in the Markan parallel (8:27–31). Moreover, verse 21 marks the beginning of Jesus' decisive turn to Jerusalem and the cross. Nevertheless, verses 21–28 continue both the topic (Jesus' identity) and the central players (Jesus and Peter) of the preceding section. Luz notes that vv.21–28 is a chiastic reversal of vv.13–20, *Das Evangelium nach Matthäus* (4 vols.; EKK 1/1–4; Düsseldorf: Benziger, 1990–2002), 2.486.

3   Cf. "The things of God" (τὰ τοῦ θεοῦ) that one must "repay" (ἀπόδοτε) in 22:21.

4   By calling Peter "Satan," Jesus indicates that Peter's opposition to his crucifixion is not only human but diabolical as well. Cf. the taunts of those witnessing the crucifixion (27:40–43) which repeat the tempting words of the devil in 4:3–6. See Ulrich Luz, *The Theology of the Gospel of Matthew* (Cambridge; New York: Cambridge University Press, 1995), 35–37.

pre-Matthean history of verses 24–28, they function in the narrative as Jesus' explanation of how to understand his fate. He begins by explaining that the path of death and resurrection is not his alone but theirs as well: "Then Jesus said to his disciples, 'If anyone wants to come behind me, let him deny himself and take up his cross and follow me'" (16:24). He then goes on to unfold the logic of these strange words.

> Then Jesus said to his disciples, "If anyone wants to come behind me, let him deny himself and take up his cross and follow me. For whoever wants to save his life (ψυχήν) will lose it, and whoever loses his life for my sake will find it. For what will it profit (ὠφεληθήσεται) a person if he gains (κερδήσῃ) the whole world but forfeits (ζημιωθῇ) his life (ψυχήν)? Or what will a person give (δώσει) in exchange (ἀντάλλαγμα) for his life (ψυχῆς)? For the Son of Man is about to come in the glory of his Father with his angels, and then he will repay to each according to his deeds (ἀποδώσει ἑκάστῳ κατὰ τὴν πρᾶξιν αὐτοῦ). (16:24–27)

The argument here is somewhat dense and requires unpacking. It is important to note the wordplay on the two different meanings of ψυχή, present earthly life and eternal life.[5] Jesus' disciples must follow him in losing their earthly lives to be repaid with eternal life. Using logic that is very similar to 6:19–21, verse 26 explains why one should take the bold step of following Jesus in his cross-bearing: "For what will it profit (ὠφεληθήσεται) a person if he gains the whole world but loses (ζημιωθῇ) his [eternal] life?"[6] It is folly to cling to "the world," including one's present life, because the more precious possession is one's ψυχή in the world to come. The next line develops this further: "Or what will a person give in exchange (ἀντάλλαγμα) for his [eternal] life? (16:26)." The implied answer to this rhetorical question is, of course, "nothing." No matter how much earthly wealth one amasses it can never purchase eternal life. As Psalm 49:7–9, a text which may have influenced this passage, puts it, "Truly, no ransom avails for one's life, there is no price one can give to God for it. For the ransom of life is costly, and can never suffice that one should live on forever and

---

5   R. T. France, *The Gospel of Matthew* (NICNT; Grand Rapids: Eerdmans, 2007), 636–40. This is an example of the ancient (and modern) rhetorical device known as antanaclasis. For another example of antanaclasis in the synoptic tradition see T. J. Lang, "'You will desire to see and you will not see [it]': Reading Luke 17.22 as Antanaclasis," *JSNT* 33 (2011): 281–302.

6   Ζημιόω is commonly used to refer to the loss of money. See LSJ II.

never see the grave" (NRSV).[7] In the day of judgment no one can present God with earthly treasures and purchase eternal life.[8] Thus, while it may seem ridiculous to those "thinking the things of people" to give one's present life, it is in fact the more prudent course of action. No one can store up enough earthly treasure to give in exchange for one's ψυχή. It makes more sense to follow Jesus in cross-bearing, to give one's life in order to find it in the resurrection.[9]

The traditions alluded to in verse 27 offer further illumination. The image of the Son of Man judging all people is drawn from Daniel 7, and Matthew's image of the Son of Man "repaying" everyone is similar to the Danielic imagery of the Similitudes of Enoch where it is said that God will place the Elect one on his "throne of glory" where he sits and "judge[s] all the works of the holy ones in heaven above, weighing in the balance their deeds" (61:5).[10] The phrase ἀποδώσει ἑκάστῳ κατὰ τὴν πρᾶξιν αὐτοῦ occurs so often with slight variations in early Jewish and Christian literature that Davies and Allison suggest that it is a stereotyped phrase rather than a biblical quotation.[11] Regardless of whether this is true, one of the texts where this phrase occurs, Psalm 62, is strikingly similar to Matthew 16:24–28:

> For God alone my soul waits in silence, for my hope is from him.
> He alone is my rock and my salvation, my fortress; I shall not be shaken.
> On God rests my deliverance and my honor; my mighty rock, my refuge is in God.
> Trust in him at all times, O people; pour out your heart before him; God is a refuge for us. Selah
> People are but a breath, mortals are a delusion; in the balances they go up;

---

7 Davies and Allison, *A Critical and Exegetical Commentary on the Gospel according to Saint Matthew* (3 vols; ICC; Edinburgh: T&T Clark, 1988–1997), 2.674.

8 Cf. Luke 12:13–21; 17:33.

9 Daniel Marguerat, *Le Jugement dans L'Évangile de Matthieu* (2nd ed.; MdB 6; Genève: Labor et Fides, 1995), 90–91, 99.

10 The significance of the Danielic imagery is developed further below in connection with 19:16–29 and 20:17–28.

11 Davies and Allison, *Matthew*, 2.676. They cite LXX Ps 61:13; Prov 24:12; Sirach 35:24; *T. Job* 17:3; *L.A.B.* 3:10; Rom 2:6; 2 Tim 4:14; Rev 2:23; *Apoc. Pet.* 1; *Ps. Sol.* 17:8–10; 2 Cor 11:15; 1 Pet 1:17; 1 Clem 34:3; 2 Clem 11:6; Herm. *Sim.* 6.3.6; *Acts Thom.* 29. One might argue that the "stereotyped phrase" occurs regularly in these later texts precisely because it *is* a biblical quotation. Kyoung-Shik Kim (*God will Judge Each One According to Works: Judgment According to Works and Psalm 62 in Early Judaism and the New Testament* [BZNW 178; Berlin/New York: Walter de Gruyter, 2011], 158) argues that Matthew used the Hebrew text of Ps 62.

they are together lighter than a breath.
Put no confidence in extortion, and set no vain hopes on robbery; if riches
increase, do not set your heart on them.
Once God has spoken; twice have I heard this: that power belongs to God.

Covenant faithfulness (חסד/τὸ ἔλεος) belongs to you, O Lord, for you repay
to all according to their work (כי־אתה תשלם לאיש כמעשהו/ὅτι σὺ ἀποδώσεις
ἑκάστῳ κατὰ τὰ ἔργα αὐτοῦ). (62:5–12 NRSV alt.)[12]

The Psalm contrasts the unwavering faithfulness and reliability of God
with the ephemerality of people and their wealth. People are so insub-
stantial that "in the balances they go up," that is, weighed on a scale they
inevitably do not have enough weight – or one might say they do not
have enough credit – to push down the scale. Their money is not worthy of trust. One thinks of Matthew's rhetorical question, "What will a
person give in exchange for his life?", which assumes that no one has
anything costly enough to exchange or weigh down the scale. God,
however, is faithful and will demonstrate his חסד or ἔλεος by repaying
to each according to his deeds. To be sure, the focus of the Psalm is
not the same as Matthew 16; the former is stressing God's faithfulness
whereas the latter is calling the disciples to follow Jesus in losing their
lives. Nevertheless, both texts are saying that one's possessions are not
costly enough to purchase anything of ultimate significance. Matthew
makes explicit what is arguably implied by the Psalm: one should
focus one's energy on storing up the treasure that God will repay, rather
than fleeting earthly riches. Regardless of whether there is a conscious
allusion to Psalm 62 here, both Psalm 62 and 49 are particularly clear
articulations of "the things of God" that Peter had failed to grasp.

Two other details in this passage need to be noted. First, eternal life
is the "repayment" that cross-bearers will receive when the Son of Man
returns and repays everyone for their deeds. It was noted in chapter 2
that Matthew describes heavenly treasure as that which determines
whether one enters the kingdom (e.g., 25:14–30), but also as something enjoyed while already in the kingdom (e.g., 19:28). In this passage, the emphasis is decidedly on the former, as the only wages that
are explicitly mentioned are the "life" that one receives in exchange
for losing one's life. Those who take up their crosses and follow Jesus
will be repaid with eternal life when the Son of Man returns. Although
the description of eternal life as the *repayment* for cross-bearing is clearer
in Matthew than in the other Gospels (see esp. Mark 8:34–9:1; Luke

---

12   In v.12 ולך־אדני חסד is taken with what follows in agreement with the MT.

9:23–27), this idea was fairly common in early Jewish literature. Second Maccabees 12:45 refers to resurrection as the "splendid favor that is stored up for those who sleep in godliness." Wisdom of Solomon 2:22 describes the afterlife of the godly as the "wages of holiness (μισθός ὁσιότη-τος)." *Psalms of Solomon* 9:5 says that "The one who does righteousness treasures up life for himself with the Lord." First Timothy 6:19 says that those who give alms store up a foundation that allows them to take hold of true life.[13] Matthew's version of Jesus' exhortation brings it more clearly into conformity with this line of thinking; eternal life is the payment received by those who deny themselves and follow Jesus.

The second detail that needs to be noted is this: when Jesus says that anyone who would follow him must give her life and so receive it in the coming repayment, he is explaining not only the logic of Christian faithfulness and resurrection but also his own mission. There is a tight, organic unity between Jesus' first passion and resurrection prediction in 16:21–23, and the explanation that follows in verses 24–28.[14] The latter section is an explanation of the path that Jesus and all who follow him must take against Peter's human thinking; total self-abandonment is necessary because stockpiles of earthly possessions will be useless in the eschatological repayment of deeds. An important implication of the unity of verses 21–28 is the fact that it is not only the eschatological repayment of Jesus' followers under discussion but the repayment of Jesus himself as well – indeed, it is Jesus' claim that he will die and be raised that initiates the discussion. It is the message of Jesus' coming death and resurrection to which Peter objects and which Jesus defends. Thus, it is not only followers of Jesus who will be repaid for their cross-bearing with eternal life but also Jesus, as the passive infinitive ἐγερθῆναι indicates.[15] As noted in chapter 2, Matthew repeatedly

---

13   See chapter 1 for more examples.
14   Luz, *Matthäus*, 2.486–87.
15   This point is obscured by the scholarly habit of referring to Jesus' passion and resurrection predictions as "passion predictions." Three out of four of Matthew's passion predictions also contain a prediction of the resurrection. 26:2, which appears to be redactional, only predicts the passion. This is probably for narrative reasons. The following verses depict the chief priests and elders of the people conspiring to kill Jesus. The addition of 26:2 frames their actions as taking place within the divine plan and Jesus' foreknowledge. See Holly J. Carey on the distorting effect of the title "passion prediction" with reference to the Markan narrative, *Jesus' Cry from the Cross: Towards a First-Century Understanding of the Intertextual Relationship between Psalm 22 and the Narrative of Mark's Gospel* (LNTS 398; London & New York: T & T Clark, 2009), 46–47.

portrays Jesus doing the very things that Jesus says earn heavenly treasure. Differently put, the life to which the Matthean Jesus calls his disciples is the life that he himself lives. An important and neglected implication of verses 21–28 taken as a whole is that Jesus' resurrection is the repayment he will receive from his Father for obediently submitting to rejection and death (26:39, 42).

4.3 The Thrones of the Son of Man and the Apostles (19:16–29)

The close link between Jesus' fate and the fate of the disciples continues to unfold in the account of the rich young man. After telling the disciples about his coming death and resurrection for the first time in 16:21, he repeats the prediction in Galilee in 17:22. Then they go to Judea where they encounter the rich young man immediately before Jesus predicts his death and resurrection for the third time and ascends to Jerusalem. The passage begins with the man's quest for "eternal life": "Teacher, what good must I do to have eternal life?" (19:16). Jesus responds by first telling him to obey the commandments and then by calling him to "go sell your possessions and give to the poor, and you will have treasure in the heavens (ἕξεις θησαυρὸν ἐν οὐρανοῖς), then come, follow me." This call to renunciation recalls Jesus' earlier words to the disciples: "If anyone wants to come behind me, let him deny himself and take up his cross and follow me" (16:24). Self-denial, for the rich man, means giving away all his possessions. Like 16:21–28, then, this passage describes the self-denial that is necessary to follow Jesus and earn the heavenly treasure necessary to enter the kingdom. Moreover, like the Markan parallel, the passage appears after the first two passion and resurrection predictions and immediately before the third; the placement of the story suggests it is a specific example of how a would-be follower of Jesus may take up his cross.[16]

---

16 Commenting on the Markan parallel, Gary Anderson notes that the juxtaposition of this encounter with the passion predictions is not without significance: "The giving up of all one's wealth was construed to be one way of losing one's life on behalf of the gospel. Just as the inner core of the disciples found the crucifixion to be shocking, so the young man finds the giving up of all his wealth to be a sacrifice beyond calculation." *Sin: A History* (New Haven: Yale University Press, 2009), 167–68.

The discussion that ensues after the young man goes away offers further illumination of the links between cross-bearing, heavenly treasure, and eternal life. When Jesus declares the impossibility of a rich person's entering the kingdom, Peter asks, "Behold, *we* have left everything (ἡμεῖς ἀφήκαμεν) and followed you. What then will there be for us?" (19:27). Jesus' reply underscores again what the first passion and resurrection prediction emphasized: those who follow Jesus will be recompensed like Jesus. A new element emerges in this passage, however; Jesus says that in the new age the apostles will share not only in his resurrection but also in his rule as Son of Man:

> Truly I say to you that you who have followed me, in the new age when the Son of Man sits on his throne of glory, you yourselves also will sit on twelve thrones judging the twelve tribes of Israel.[17] And whoever left houses or brothers or sisters or father or mother or children or fields on account of my name will receive a hundred times as much and will possess eternal life" (19:28–29).

For the moment Jesus does not address the disciples' ongoing failure to grasp that following him means bearing crosses.[18] Instead, he responds quite straightforwardly to Peter, promising the apostles thrones alongside the Son of Man.

What does this mention of the enthronement of the Son of Man evoke at this point in the narrative? Most agree that Daniel 7 has had some influence on this passage, though opinions differ as to whether this is a clear allusion or a faint echo.[19] Daniel 7 depicts four beasts that represent Gentile kings making war against "the holy ones" (7:25; OG 7:8). Then Daniel goes on to report:

---

17 David C. Sim's study, "The Meaning of παλιγγενεσία in Matthew 19.28," *JSNT* 50 (1993): 3–12, remains convincing; Matthew 5:18 and 24:35 show that Matthew did hold to the common belief in the re-creation of the cosmos after its destruction at the eschaton. It is probable that παλιγγενεσία refers to this event here. In light of Matthew's emphasis on end of exile, however – including the union of the twelve tribes in this very verse – this sense of the word need not exclude the hint of the rebirth of the nation after exile, which is how Josephus (*Ant.* 11:66) uses the word, albeit in a non-eschatological context.

18 Though the following parable (20:1–16) corrects the idea that only those who have practiced radical renunciation may enter the kingdom. See chapter 2.

19 E.g., Hagner (*Matthew 14–28* [WBC 33b; Dallas: Word Books, 1995] 565) says that this saying "alludes to Dan 7:9." Gundry (*Matthew*, 393) is less confident: "Jesus seems to have drawn his promise from Dan 7:9–27." Other commentators simply make no mention of Daniel 7 here.

I kept watching
  until thrones (θρόνοι) were set,
  and an ancient of days sat...
A thousand thousands were waiting on him,
And ten thousand times ten thousand stood attending him.
And books were opened,
  and a court sat in judgment...
    I was watching in the night visions
and lo, as it were a son of Man
    was coming upon the clouds of heaven (ἐπὶ τῶν νεφελῶν τοῦ οὐρανοῦ ὡς
υἱὸς ἀνθρώπου ἤρχετο).
And he came as far as the ancient of days,
and the attendants were present with him.
And royal authority was given to him (ἐδόθη αὐτῷ ἐξουσία),
and all the nations of the earth according to posterity,
and all honor was serving him (καὶ πᾶσα δόξα αὐτῷ λατρεύουσα).
And his authority is an everlasting authority (καὶ ἡ ἐξουσία αὐτοῦ ἐξουσία
αἰώνιος),
which shall never be removed
    and his kingdom which will never perish (καὶ ἡ βασιλεία αὐτοῦ ἥτις οὐ μὴ
φθαρῇ)

And as for me, Daniel, since I was exhausted by these things, by the night
vision, I approached one of those standing and was seeking the truth from
him about all these things. So answering, he spoke to me and disclosed to
me the meaning of the words: "These great beasts are four kingdoms,
which shall perish from the earth. And holy ones of the Most High will
receive the kingdom and possess the kingdom forever – forever and
ever." (7:9 – 10, 13 – 17 NETS translation of OG).

Many have argued that in Daniel the one like a son of man is a symbol
for all Israel rather than a messianic figure, noting that the kingdom
given to him is subsequently given to "the holy ones of the Most
High."[20] At least as early as the first century, however, Jews and Christians read this passage as an enthronement of the Messiah.[21] Daniel 7 is
an important messianic text in Matthew, conspicuously recurring at a

---

20 See Joel Marcus's appendix on "the Son of Man" in *Mark 1 – 8: A New Trans-
    lation with Introduction and Commentary* (AB 27a; New Haven: Yale University
    Press, 2000), 528 – 32, esp. 528. Others have suggested that the holy ones are
    angels. See John J. Collins, *Daniel: A Commentary on the Book of Daniel* (Her-
    meneia; Minneapolis: Fortress Press, 1993), 304 – 18.

21 Donald Juel, *Messianic Exegesis: Christological Interpretation of the Old Testament in
    Early Christianity* (Philadelphia: Fortress, 1988), 162 – 64; Marcus, *Mark 1 – 8*,
    528 – 32.

number of key points in the narrative. The following three unmistakable instances occur after 19:28:

> And then the sign of the Son of Man will appear in heaven, and then all the tribes of the earth will mourn and they will see '*the Son of Man coming on the clouds of heaven*' with power and much glory (τὸν υἱὸν τοῦ ἀνθρώπου ἐρχόμενον ἐπὶ τῶν νεφελῶν τοῦ οὐρανοῦ μετὰ δυνάμεως καὶ δόξης πολλῆς). (24:30)

> And when the Son of Man comes in his glory and all the angels with him, then he will sit on the throne of his glory (Ὅταν δὲ ἔλθη ὁ υἱὸς τοῦ ἀνθρώπου ἐν τῇ δόξῃ αὐτοῦ καὶ πάντες οἱ ἄγγελοι μετ' αὐτοῦ, τότε καθίσει ἐπὶ θρόνου δόξης αὐτοῦ). (25:31)

> And the chief-priest said to him, "I adjure you by the living God that you tell us if you are the Christ, the Son of God." Jesus said to him, "You said it. But I tell you, from now on you will see *the Son of Man* sitting at the right hand of Power and *coming on the clouds of heaven* (τὸν υἱὸν τοῦ ἀνθρώπου καθήμενον ἐκ δεξιῶν τῆς δυνάμεως καὶ ἐρχόμενον ἐπὶ τῶν νεφελῶν τοῦ οὐρανοῦ)." (26:63–64)

The recurrence of allusions and quotations of Daniel 7 in passages referring to Jesus' coming triumph increases the likelihood that other, less obvious allusions are significant, such as the risen Jesus' claim that "All authority in heaven and on earth has been given to me (ἐδόθη μοι πᾶσα ἐξουσία ἐν οὐρανῷ καὶ ἐπὶ τῆς γῆς)" (28:18), or the reference to the Son of Man (ὁ υἱὸς τοῦ ἀνθρώπου) "coming" (ἔρχεσθαι) in "glory" (ἐν τῇ δόξῃ) to render judgment on all people (16:27).[22] As James D. G. Dunn notes,

> Within the Gospel tradition, the influence of Dan 7:9–14 is most noticeable in regard to Matthew …[T]hree of Matthew's allusions to Daniel 7 are distinctive to Matthew [10:23; 25:31; 28:18], Matthew strengthens the Daniel 7 allusion in another four verses [16:27–28; 19:28; 24:30], and two verses show awareness of the way the Similitudes of Enoch developed Daniel's son of man vision [19:28; 25:31].[23]

---

22 The argument from recurring or clustering was articulated first by Richard B. Hays, *Echoes of Scripture in the Letters of Paul* (New Haven: Yale University Press, 1989), 30. The concise formulation in *The Conversion of the Imagination: Paul as Interpreter of Israel's Scripture* (Grand Rapids, MI.: Eerdmans, 2005), is helpful: "When we find repeated Pauline quotations of a particular OT passage, additional possible allusions to the same passage become more compelling" (37).

23 "The Danielic Son of Man in the New Testament," in *The Book of Daniel: Composition and Reception* (2 vols.; ed. John J. Collins and Peter W. Flint; Leiden/Boston: Brill, 2001), 2.538. Juel (*Messianic Exegesis*, 158–61) considers Matthew 16:27–28, 19:28, 24:27–44, 25:31, 26:64 all "indisputable" allusions to Daniel 7. He considers 10:23, 24:44, and 28:18 "likely" allusions.

Dunn's redactional argument complements the argument from recurrence; Matthew depicts Jesus' triumph in language drawn from Daniel 7's narrative of a triumphant "Son of Man" to whom authority and kingship are given.

The probable Danielic background of Jesus' words in 19:28–29 illuminates Jesus' claim that the twelve will receive thrones when the Son of Man sits on his throne of glory. The plural "thrones" in Daniel 7:9 has engendered a great deal of speculation about who exactly would sit on them.[24] For Matthew, the thrones are for Jesus, who will sit at the right hand of his Father (26:64; cf. Ps 110:1), and for the twelve apostles who will join him. The apostles' thrones are given to them as recompense for following Jesus. In addition to this, anyone (πᾶς ὅστις) who leaves possessions behind will receive a hundred times as much and eternal life. This underscores once again the unity between the path that Jesus takes and what he requires from his followers. In 16:21–28, Jesus explains that, just as he must die and be raised to life, all who would follow him must lose their lives and so regain them when the Son of Man returns to repay everyone for their deeds. The discussion following the departure of the rich young man brings further clarity to this picture; those who leave everything behind and follow Jesus will be repaid with a share in his rule as Son of Man.

The tone of 19:27–29 is almost triumphalistic. Despite the unwarranted conjecture of numerous scholars, there is no hint that Peter's question is in any way unseemly.[25] Jesus' response is disarmingly straightforward; Peter and the other apostles will take thrones alongside of the Son of Man, and everyone who leaves their possessions behind will receive a hundred times as much. The contrast with 16:21–28 is striking; that passage also spoke of the recompense that followers of

---

See also Jonathan T. Pennington, "Refractions of Daniel in the Gospel of Matthew," in *Early Christian Literature and Intertextuality* (ed. Craig A. Evans and H. Daniel Zacharias; vol. 14 of *Studies in Scripture in Early Judaism and Christianity*; LNTS 391; London: T & T Clark, 2009), 65–86.

24 On the interpretation of the "thrones" in the NT and rabbinic literature see Craig A. Evans, "Daniel in the New Testament: Visions of God's Kingdom," in *The Book of Daniel: Composition and Reception*, 516–19.

25 E.g., France (*Matthew*, 741) who writes "Peter's words sound both smug (*we*, unlike that young man, have done what you asked) and mercenary (God owes us). The reader is being prepared for v. 30 (and the parable that follows), where Peter's simplistic calculation will be challenged." See the treatment of the parable in chapter 2 for a rebuttal.

Jesus would receive, but the accent was on the necessity to follow Jesus in giving one's life in order to receive it back, a message that disturbs the apostles (cf. also 17:22–23) and incites conflict between Jesus and Peter. In 19:16–29, however, there is no explicit mention of the cross— though Jesus defined "following" as cross-bearing in 10:38 and 16:24 – and Peter seems blithely unaware that following the Son of Man and sharing his enthronement means giving one's life.

This passage leaves one obvious loose thread that will become important in 20:17–28. While the emphasis of 19:16–29 is on the danger of wealth and the generous repayment awaiting those who renounce their possessions to follow Jesus, verse 26 dangles a hint that some provision will be made for those who, like the rich young man, do not store up treasure in heaven because "all things are possible with God." This point is further developed in the following parable, which indicates that God will indeed pay his workers as he promised, but that he is also inclined to pay those who have done less work far more than they deserve. At this point in the narrative this generosity is hinted at, but not explained in detail, though, as we saw in chapter 3, Jesus has been described as the one who will save his people from their debts.

4.4 Contrast with Gentile kings (20:17–28)

The discourse following the rich young man's departure concludes with the parable of the workers in the vineyard. It is followed by the third, final, and most detailed passion and resurrection prediction (20:17– 19), which marks Jesus' decisive and final move toward Jerusalem.[26] Im-

---

26 Apart from 20:17–19 all of 19:16–20:28 is united by the theme of God's repayment for following Jesus. For this reason, W. F. Albright and C. S. Mann consider this final passion and resurrection prediction a foreign insertion that breaks the flow of thought (*Matthew: A New Translation with Introduction and Commentary* [AB 26; Garden City, NY: Doubleday, 1971], 239). Yet, from the first prediction in 16:21 onward, Matthew shows that it is those who follow Jesus in cross-bearing who have treasure in heaven and eternal life. Thus, Albright and Mann ironically repeat the failure of the disciples to see that heavenly thrones are attained by way of the cross. Cf. Luz: "Wie auch immer die schwierigen traditionsgeschichtlichen und historischen Fragen, die dieses Wort stellt, zu beurteilen sind, im matthäischen Kontext ist klar, daß das Menschensohnwort V 28 kein äußerlich angehängter Fremdkörper, sondern die Spitze eines organischen Gedankengangs ist, der mit dem Leiden des Menschensohns beginnt (V 18) und schließt (V 28)." *Matthäus*, 3.165. Warren Car-

mediately afterward (τότε) Jesus is accosted by the mother of the sons of Zebedee, who has apparently heard about the thrones the Twelve are to receive in the coming kingdom and wants the best ones to be given to her sons.[27]

> Then the mother of the sons of Zebedee came to him with her sons, kneeling before him and asking something from him. And he said to her, "What do you want?" She said to him, "Declare that these two sons of mine will sit one on your right and one on your left in your kingdom."But answering Jesus said, "You do not know what you are asking (οὐκ οἴδατε τί αἰτεῖσθε). Are you able to drink the cup which I myself am about to drink?" They said to him, "We are able." He said to them, "You will drink my cup, but to sit at my right and at my left is not mine to give, but is for those for whom it has been prepared by my Father." (20:20–23)

While Mark 10:17–45 features a similar discussion of cross-bearing and repayment, Matthew's inclusion of Jesus' promise in 19:27 that the Twelve will sit on thrones foreshadows the coming dispute about who will have the best places alongside Jesus in 20:20–28, thereby tightening the narrative unity and increasing the Danielic overtones. The link between 19:27 and 20:20–28 also shows that Matthew was not following Mark passively, but is carefully amplifying Mark 10:17–45.

Since 16:21 Jesus has explained to the disciples that he and everyone who would follow him must give their lives in order to be repaid. Yet, it would seem that the only part of this that James and John have grasped is that they were to have one of the thrones mentioned in Daniel 7. Jesus' response cuts straight to the heart of the matter: "You [plural] do not know what you are asking."[28] If James and John had understood what Jesus taught them, they would have realized that enthronement with the Son of Man is the repayment for following him in his cross-bearing, a point that is further underscored by the language of sitting

---

ter notes that the three subsections of vv.17–19, 20–23, and 24–28 are united by the themes of Christology, discipleship, and rule (*Households and Discipleship: A Study of Matthew 19–20* [JSNTSup 103; Sheffield: Sheffield Academic, 1994], 162–63).

27 Gundry (*Matthew*, 401) notes that "The story of the request for places of honor on Jesus' right and left begins with a replacement of καί and τότε... This favorite conjunction of Matthew correlates the prediction of Jesus' passion (20:17–19) with the teaching of service to others: the former illustrates the latter."

28 Unlike the Markan parallel (10:35), Matthew portrays the mother of the sons of Zebedee asking for the best thrones on behalf of her sons (20:20). Jesus' responds in the plural, thereby including the sons in his rebuke.

at Jesus' right and left (εἷς ἐκ δεξιῶν σου καὶ εἷς ἐξ εὐωνύμων σου), which is the same as the description of the revolutionaries crucified at Jesus' right and left: σταυροῦνται σὺν αὐτῷ δύο λῃσταί, εἷς ἐκ δεξιῶν καὶ εἷς ἐξ εὐωνύμων.[29] Jesus then clarifies the nature of James' and John's misapprehension: "Are you able to drink the cup which I myself am about to drink?" In the prophets and post-biblical Jewish and Christian literature "cup" could refer to God's judgment or more generally to a person's fate or death.[30] Raymond Brown pointed out that James and John are probably not being invited to drink the cup of God's wrath for sin but are rather challenged to drink the cup of suffering that Jesus will drink.[31] Jesus thus intimates that they are, in effect, asking to be crucified with him (cf. 26:39). The thrones are to be repayment for cross-bearing.

The request incites discord among the disciples, who become angry with James and John (20:24). Jesus continues his catechesis, this time contrasting the Son of Man with the Gentile kings:

> You know that the rulers of the Gentiles rule them, and great ones (οἱ μεγάλοι) exercise dominion over them. It will not be so among you; but whoever wishes to be great among you must be your servant, and whoever wishes to be first among you must be your slave; just as the Son of Man came not to be served but to serve, and to give his life a ransom-price for many (ὥσπερ ὁ υἱὸς τοῦ ἀνθρώπου οὐκ ἦλθεν διακονηθῆναι ἀλλὰ διακονῆσαι καὶ δοῦναι τὴν ψυχὴν αὐτοῦ λύτρον ἀντὶ πολλῶν). (20:25−28)[32]

In correcting the disciples Jesus makes a distinction drawn from Daniel 7; one can hardly join the Son of Man in his glory by emulating the Gentile kings he opposes.[33] If the Twelve would occupy twelve thrones

---

29 Keener, *Matthew*, 486; Davies and Allison, *Matthew*, 3.88. Matthew provides another link between these passages: unlike Mark he says that the mother of the sons of Zebedee witnessed the crucifixion (27:56).

30 *T. Ab.* 1:3; 16:11−12; *Tg. Yer. I, Tg. Yer. II,* and *Tg. Neof. I* on Gen 40:23; *Tg. Neof.* on Deut 32:1; *Mart. Pol.* 14:2. Luz, *Matthäus*, 3.161−62.

31 *Death of the Messiah* (2 vols.; ABRL; New York: Doubleday, 1994), 1.169−70.

32 Note that Matthew tightens the link between Jesus' coming gift of his life and the life that is necessary for the disciples by changing Mark's καί to ὥσπερ. Also, as is often noted (e.g., Hagner, *Matthew 14−28*, 582; Gundry, *Matthew*, 404), the καί that introduces the final phrase is epexegetical; the Son of Man came to serve by giving his life.

33 Brant Pitre's (*Jesus, the Tribulation, and the End of the Exile* [Grand Rapids: Baker, 2005], 390) comments on the Danielic imagery in the Markan parallel apply: "The images of the disciples 'sitting' (presumably on 'thrones') (Dan 7:10, 26; Mark 10:37) with a 'son of man' (Dan 7:14; Mark 10:45) who has been given 'glory' (Dan 7:14; Mark 10:37) − all of these presume the Danielic

along with the Son of Man then they must give their lives as he does rather than ruling as do the Gentiles.[34] Here the link between wage-earning behavior and Jesus' own actions is finally made explicit; the path to ruling with the Son of Man is in following him in giving one's life for others. Even the wage that Jesus earns is not for himself, at least not primarily, but is the ransom-price for others.

A brief summary is in order: in 16:13–28 Jesus announces that he is going to be killed and raised from the dead and that his followers must do likewise because cross-bearers will be "repaid" with eternal life, a treasure that no earthly possession could purchase (cf. 5:2–12; 6:1– 24; 13:44–46). In 19:16–29 further nuance is provided: those who re-nounce their possessions to follow Jesus will be repaid not only with eternal life but also with a share in the coming reign of the Son of Man, including thrones for the apostles. Then, in 20:17–28 the sons of Zebedee attempt to seize the best thrones for themselves. Jesus coun-ters this request by intimating that they are asking to be crucified with him and telling all the apostles yet again that to rule with the Son of Man they must give their lives. In nuce: *these three passages indicate that Jesus and his followers must give their lives in order to be repaid with resurrection and the reign spoken of in Daniel 7.* Or, as Jesus puts it at the conclusion of the Beatitudes, "Blessed are those who are persecuted on account of righteousness, for theirs is the kingdom of the heavens. Blessed are you when people revile you and persecute you and say all kinds of evil against you falsely on my account. Rejoice and be glad, for your wage is great in the heavens" (5:10–12).

---

vision of the 'people of the saints of the Most High' being given the eternal 'kingdom' (Dan 7:27, cf. 18, 22)…[E]ven Jesus' image of 'the great' (οἱ μεγάλοι) Gentiles kings 'lording it over' [κατακυριεύω] their subjects (Mark 10:42) may also be drawing on the Danielic images of the 'great beasts' – who are, of course, *Gentile kings* (Dan 7:3) – and those Gentiles rulers who will 'lord it over many' during the end times (Dan 11:39 LXX Theod.)."

34 Since Kenneth W. Clark's study ("The Meaning of [κατα]κυριεύειν" in *Studies in New Testament Language and Text: Essays in Hour of George D. Kilpatrick on the Occasion of his sixty-fifth Birthday* [NovTSup 44; ed. J. K. Elliot; Leiden: Brill, 1976], 100–105) most have agreed that κατακυριεύω lacked the negative force of the English idiom "to lord it over." The contrast in this passage, then, is not between abuse of power and right lordship, but on ruling as do the Gentiles and Jesus, who gives his life. In other words, the critique of Gentile rulers is more profound than a condemnation of corruption; any that do not follow Jesus in giving in their lives cannot lead.

A new element emerges in 20:28, however; the repayment that Jesus earns by giving his life is described as a λύτρον for many. In other words, the "wage" or "repayment" or "treasure" that Jesus' cross-bearing earns is not only for himself but for others as well. In this verse, then, the two key Matthean themes of earning treasure in heaven by imitating Jesus and of Jesus' vicarious action for others converge. Before unpacking the significance of this for the larger argument it is necessary to take a closer look at the meaning of the ransom saying itself.

4.5 The Ransom-Price for Many

There is a vast amount of scholarly literature on Matt 20:28//Mark 10:45, much of which is not directly relevant here because it focuses on the pre-Markan origins of the saying and the question of whether or not the saying was originally drawn from Isaiah 53.[35] Davies and Allison list a number of intriguing parallels between the saying and the Hebrew text of Isaiah,[36] but, as has often been noted since C. K. Barrett and Morna Hooker made their classic cases against dependence on Isaiah

---

35 E.g., Scot McKnight, "The Authenticity of the Ransom Sayings," in *Jesus and His Death: Historiography, the Historical Jesus, and Atonement Theory* (Waco, TX: Baylor University Press, 2005); William H. Bellinger, Jr. and William R. Farmer, ed., *Jesus and the Suffering Servant: Isaiah 53 and Christian Origins* (Harrisburg, PN.: Trinity, 1998); Max Wilcox, "On the Ransom-Saying in Mark 10:45c, Matt 20:28c," in *Geschichte-Tradition-Reflexion: Festschrift für Martin Hengel zum 70. Geburtstag* (ed. Hubert Cancik et al.; 3 vols.; Tübingen: Mohr Siebeck), 1996), 173–86. Peter Stuhlmacher, "Vicariously Giving His Life for Many, Mark 10:45 (Matt 20:28)," in *Reconciliation, Law, and Righteousness* (Philadelphia: Fortress Press, 1986), 16–29; Joachim Jeremias, "Das Lösegeld für Viele (Mk 10.45)," in *Abba: Studien zur neutestamentilichen Theologie und Zeitgeschichte* (Göttingen: Vandenhoeck & Ruprecht, 1966), 216–29; Morna Hooker, *Jesus and the Servant: The Influence of the Servant Concept of Deutero-Isaiah in the New Testament* (London: S.P.C.K., 1959); C. K. Barrett, "The Background of Mark 10:45," in *New Testament Essays* (ed. A. J. B. Higgins; Manchester: Manchester University Press, 1959), 1–18. For a discussion of Luke's transformation of the saying see Nathan Eubank, "Bakhtin and Lukan Politics: A Carnivalesque Reading of the Last Supper in the Third Gospel," *JGRChJ* 4 (2007): 32–54, esp. 38–40.

36 *Matthew*, 3.95–97. The words ἀντὶ πολλῶν are reminiscent of לרבים in Isaiah 53:11–12; the words δοῦναι τὴν ψυχὴν αὐτοῦ λύτρον ἀντὶ πολλῶν are similar to אם-תשים אשם נפשו in Isaiah 53:10; διακονῆσαι evokes the עבד in 52:13 and 53:11.

53, there are few verbal links between the saying and Isaiah 53 LXX. It seems likely that Isaiah's description of vicarious suffering had some influence on the saying, though neither Matthew nor Mark appears to have been interested in drawing attention to this link. More importantly, however, the debate over Isaianic influence is something of a red herring, distracting scholars from a number of important clues to the meaning of the saying in its Matthean context.[37] Regardless of whether the saying alludes more or less faintly to Isaiah, Jesus' gift of his life as a ransom-price is in deep continuity with Matthew's description of the plight of those Jesus came to save and with the recompense of righteous cross-bearing.

Discussion of the ransom saying has been distracted not only by a preoccupation with Isaiah (and a corresponding neglect of its relationship to the Matthean narrative as a whole) but also by a tendency to equate λύτρον with several of its cognates, especially λυτρόω. Since David Hill's 1967 study, *Greek Words and Hebrew Meanings*, many scholars have claimed that the word λύτρον does not necessarily involve an actual exchange or payment.[38] Rather, it is claimed that in the Septuagint λύτρον and its cognates were used to refer to "deliverance" or "salvation" without any hint of a ransom-price being paid. For instance, while commenting on Matt 20:28, Eugene Boring writes:

> Matthew adopts Mark's picture of Jesus' life as a "ransom," but does not elaborate it into a doctrine of the atonement (as Mark does not). The fact that Jesus' death effects forgiveness of sins and entering into a new covenant life with God (26:28) is important to Matthew, but he is not concerned to speculate on *how* this is "explained." *"Ransom" (λύτρον lytron) in the LXX had already lost its specific idea of release by paying off the captor*

---

37 Brant Pitre (*Jesus, the Tribulation, and the End of the Exile*, 405) has suggested that the debate over the Isaianic background has served as a red herring, distracting exegetes from the way the saying evokes numerous other Old Testament texts describing God's "ransoming" of his people. In the following I concur with this judgment but extend it to include the Gospel itself.

38 *Greek Words and Hebrew Meanings: Studies in the Semantics of Soteriological Terms* (Cambridge, Cambridge University Press, 1967). Hill concluded, "the λύτρον-words" should be interpreted "in terms of 'deliverance' or 'emancipation', except when the context expresses or implies a payment made to gain freedom" (81). See also Stanislas Lyonnet and Léopold Sabourin, *Sin, Redemption, and Sacrifice: A Biblical and Patristic Study* (Rome: Biblical Institute Press, 1970), 79–103.

and had come to mean simply "rescue," "deliver" as an act of God's power (e. g., Exod 6:6; Deut 7:8).[39]

More recently, Charles Talbert has argued that "There is nothing in the term [λύτρον] that demands an elaborate soteriological theory. It simply means that Jesus is acting on others' behalf in his ministry."[40] Like Boring, Talbert appeals to the LXX to substantiate his claim:

> In Jer. 15:20–21 LXX, Yahweh says to Jeremiah, "I am with you to save you and to deliver you…and I will ransom [λυτρώσομαι] you." In the parallelism, save, deliver, and ransom are synonyms. In Jer. 27:34 LXX (50:34 Eng.), when Yahweh says he is the one who ransoms [ὁ λυτρούμενος] Israel, it is in the context of his defeat of Israel's enemies (deliverance). In Jer. 38:11 LXX (31:11 Eng.), when the Lord has ransomed [ἐλυτρώσατο] Jacob, it means that Yahweh has delivered him out of the hands of stronger foes (return from exile). Ransom is, then, synonymous with salvation and deliverance.[41]

There is an initial plausibility to Boring and Talbert's argument. In addition to denoting the payment of the price of release (e. g., Lev 25:48), the verb λυτρόω in the middle voice is indeed also used in the LXX as a synonym of ῥύσομαι, that is, with no apparent reference to the payment of any price.

Surprisingly, however, neither Boring nor Talbert cites a single verse that actually includes the word λύτρον, the word Matthew uses.[42] There is good reason for this odd omission: λύτρον is never used in the LXX, Josephus, Philo – or, according to BDAG and Liddell and Scott, anywhere else – to mean simply "rescue" or "deliver" as Boring and Talbert claim. It always refers to some price or exchange. In the LXX λύτρον denotes the price paid to redeem the life of the negligent owner of a deadly ox (Exod 21:30), the price paid to avert a plague (Exod 30:12), the price to redeem a slave (Lev 19:20; 25:51–52; Isa 45:13), the price paid to regain land (Lev 25:24–26), the price to recover the tithe from the land (Lev 27:31), the payment, paid either

---

39 "The Gospel of Matthew," *The New Interpreter's Bible* 8 (Nashville: Abingdon, 1995), 399. Emphasis added
40 *Matthew* (Paideia Commentaries on the New Testament; Grand Rapids, MI.: Baker Academic, 2010), 241. See also France, *Matthew*, 761.
41 Ibid.
42 E.g., Exod 6:6, cited by Boring, where God says "I will deliver you from slavery and will redeem (καὶ λυτρώσομαι) you with a raised arm and great judgment." Similarly, Deut 7:8 says "the Lord brought you out with a strong hand and raised arm and redeemed (ἐλυτρώσατο) you from a house of slavery."

with money or with the lives of the Levites, to redeem the lives of the first-born of Israel (Num 3:12, 46, 48–49, 51; 18:15), the price paid to redeem the life of a murderer (Num 35:31–32), the price paid to appease a cuckolded husband (Prov 6:35), and the money that a rich person may be forced to pay if threatened (Prov 13:8). Other relevant literature reveals more of the same.[43] In short, λύτρον always refers to some sort of payment or exchange.[44] The claims of Talbert, Boring, Hill and others, therefore, that no payment is in view in Matthew 20:28 are utterly without warrant, being based on a fallacious equation of λύτρον with λυτρόω, aided, perhaps, by the fact that the English word "ransom" is used to translate both the noun and the verb.[45]

It is not difficult to ascertain why λυτρόω came to be used in contexts where there is no payment in view, while λύτρον always retained the clear sense of some payment. If λυτρόω originally meant to pay a price for deliverance it would not be hard for its range to expand to include deliverance in the generic sense. The cognates λύτρωσις and ἀπολύτρωσις are abstract and could expand on the same lines. Λύτρον, however, denoted the price itself and was therefore less susceptible to being used to refer to redemption without an actual payment or exchange. For this reason, and in light of the ambiguity of the English word ransom, which, like λυτρόω, can denote redemption with or without payment, it would seem best to translate λύτρον as "price of release," as LSJ suggests, or as "ransom-price."

Having addressed the question of Isaianic influence and the misconceptions about the semantic range of λύτρον, we are now in a position to discuss the significance of the saying against the backdrop of the narrative. The ransom saying evokes two major motifs in the Gospel: (1) the deliverance from captivity and (2) the earning of heavenly treasure.

---

43 E.g., Josephus uses λύτρον to refer to the price paid to free captives (*Ant.* 12:28, 33, 46; 14:371; 15:156; *J.W.* 1.274; 1.384, 419), the price paid to recover a brother's dead body (*J.W.* 1.325), a costly item given to save other costly items: λύτρον ἀντὶ πάντων (*Ant.* 14:107).

44 Wilcox rightly takes the concreteness of λύτρον seriously, but then reads the saying to mean that Jesus gives himself as the ransom-price that helps his followers avoid being captured, a proposal with no merit as far as the First Gospel is concerned ("On the Ransom-Saying in Mark 10:45c, Matt 20:28c").

45 Hill's lengthy study adduces only one example, Prov 13:8, of the noun λύτρον being used without any hint of payment or exchange (*Greek Words*, 61). Yet, even this verse refers to the money a rich person may be forced to pay if threatened.

4.5.1 Deliverance from Captivity

As already noted, the word λύτρον was commonly used to refer to the price paid to free a captive, whether prisoners of war, slaves, or debtors.[46] For instance, Josephus says that Ptolemy gained the release of the Jewish slaves in Egypt by paying λύτρα to the soldiers who had captured them (*Ant.* 12:28, 33, 46).[47] As noted above, the LXX also frequently uses λύτρον to refer to the money paid to redeem slaves (Lev 19:20; 25:51−52; Isa 45:13), as well as the payment, paid either with money or with the lives of the Levites, to redeem the lives of the first-born of Israel (Num 3:12, 46, 48−49, 51; 18:15).

The link between the gift of a λύτρον and the end of captivity is strengthened by the many biblical texts that describe God ransoming Israel from exile using the verb λυτρόω.[48] For instance, in Exodus 6:6 God tells Moses to tell the Israelites, "I will ransom (λυτρώσομαι) you with uplifted arm." In Micah 6:4 God recalls the Exodus: "For I brought you from the land of Egypt and ransomed (ἐλυτρωσάμην) you from the house of slavery."[49] Unsurprisingly, prophecies of the end of later exiles use this same language. In the promise of restoration in Isaiah 43:1 God says, "Fear not, for I have ransomed (ἐλυτρωσάμην) you." Jeremiah 31:11 (38:11 LXX) says that "the Lord has ransomed (ἐλυτρώσατο) Jacob and has delivered him from stronger hands." Similarly, Micah 4:10 promises that "the Lord your God will ransom (λυτρώσεται) you from the hand of your enemies." Other examples could be cited.[50] Combined with Matthew's description of Jesus as the one spoken of by the prophets who would save his people from exile, it is likely that Jesus' claim to give the ransom-price for the many evokes the Septuagintal "ransoming" of the people, a biblical echo that is reinforced by the lan-

---

46 See LSJ; K. Kertelge, "*Lytron*," *EDNT* 2:364−66.

47 See also *Ant.* 14:371; 15:156; J.W. 1.274; 1.384, 419. Gustav A. Deissman noted that the ubiquity of the term in reference to the manumission of slaves would have made it a particularly vivid image in early Christian circles, *Light from the Ancient East: The New Testament Illustrated by Recently Discovered Texts of the Graeco-Roman World* (trans. Lionel R. M. Strachan; New York: George H. Doran, 1927), 327−30.

48 *Jesus, the Tribulation, and the End of the Exile*, 404−17.

49 See also Psalms 78:42−55; Isaiah 51:10−11.

50 Zech 3:1; 10:8; Isa 44:21−23; 51:11; 62:12; Jer 50:33−34; Lam 5:8; Hos 13:14; Zeph 3:15.

guage of "the many," a term commonly used to refer to exiles.[51] One might object that to shed light on Matthew 20:28 by appealing to the common Septuagintal use of λυτρόω is to commit the same blunder as Boring and others, namely, confusing the verb λυτρόω with the noun λύτρον. On the contrary, the suggestion here is that Jesus' gift of his life as the price of release (λύτρον) for the many echoes the numerous biblical references to God "ransoming" (λυτρόω) his people. The switch from noun to verb could weaken the strength of the echo, but not eliminate it. Boring and others note that λυτρόω is sometimes used without any sense of payment or exchange and then assume that λύτρον was used in the same way. As we have seen, this assumption is mistaken.

The ransom-price for many would seem to presuppose that "the many" are enduring some sort of captivity from which they need to be ransomed. Yet, scholars have generally agreed that this apparent presupposition is never fleshed out in the course of the narrative. That is, the suggestion that Jesus gives his life as the price of release suggests that "the many" endure some sort of captivity, but Matthew never develops or explains this suggestion. Davies and Allison state the problem clearly: "almost every question we might ask remains unanswered. What is the condition of 'the many'? Why do they need to be ransomed?"[52] In the absence of any explanation the ransom saying would seem to be "only an unexplained affirmation."[53]

Over the course of this study, however, we have seen that Matthew repeatedly describes the plight of those Jesus came to save in terms of captivity. Sin is debt, and the punishment for unresolved sin is debt-bondage. The prologue of the Gospel describes Jesus' people as in exile, and promises that Jesus will save them from their sins (1:21). Isaiah and other texts already described exile as a kind of debt-bondage, and Matthew's citation of Jeremiah 31 and Isaiah 40 associates the end of exile with the "wages" due for works and the repayment of the debt of sin. In 5:21–26 Jesus says that even the smallest sins against a brother

---

51 See Isa 52:14–15; 53:11–12; Dan 12:1–3; 1Q28 VIII, 12–14; IX, 18–20. Pitre, *Jesus, the Tribulation, and the End of the Exile*, 413–14.
52 *Matthew*, 3.100
53 Ibid. See also Luz, *Matthäus*, 3.166; John T. Carroll and Joel B. Green, "His Blood on Us and On Our Children: The Death of Jesus in the Gospel according to Matthew" in *The Death of Jesus in Early Christianity* (John T. Carroll and Joel B. Green, eds.; Peabody, Mass.: Hendrickson, 1995), 44; John Nolland, *The Gospel of Matthew: A Commentary on the Greek Text* (NIGTC; Grand Rapids, MI: Eerdmans, 2005), 826.

will be repaid in Gehenna down to the last penny. In the Lord's Prayer Jesus teaches his followers to pray "cancel our debts (τὰ ὀφειλήματα) for us, as we also cancel for those in debt to us (τοῖς ὀφειλέταις)" (6:12). This claim is given vivid expression in the parable of the unforgiving servant, which says that debtors (i. e., those with unforgiven sin) who do not cancel the debts of others will be thrown into prison and will not get out until they repay all that they owe (18:34). *In sum: captivity for the debt of sin is the plight of both Jesus' "people" who are in exile and of individual sinners.* To return to Davies and Allison's question, then: what is the condition of "the many"? It is debt-bondage and exile because of their sins. To whom is the price of release paid? For Matthew, it is paid to God, the "creditor" whom Jesus' disciples ask to cancel their debts, and who will settle accounts with his servants (18:23; 25:19). This does not exclude the fact that, for Matthew, Jesus rescues his people from the power of the devil (e. g., 4:1−11; 8:28−34; 12:22−28) and from wicked human authorities (e. g., 2:1−23; 20:25−28; 21:12−21:46). To the perennial question of whether Jesus gives a ransom-price to God or the devil, however, Matthew gives an unequivocal answer: the λύτρον is paid to God. In sum: attention to the role of Matthew 20:28 in the narrative as a whole reveals that Jesus gives his life as the price of release for the many in debt-bondage.

4.5.2 The price of release as heavenly treasure

Another major question raised by the ransom-saying is how Jesus generates the price of release for the many. In other words, in light of the fact that λύτρον denotes some sort of payment to release captives, one must ask what this payment consists of and how Jesus earns it. Does Matthew answer this question, or is this a traditional logion that is not integrated into the narrative?

It was noted in the conclusion to chapter 2 that time and again Matthew depicts Jesus doing the things that earn heavenly wages. In other words, Jesus does the very things that he teaches his disciples to do in order to store up heavenly treasure. Having examined Jesus' interactions with his disciples from 16:21 to 20:28, it is possible to shed further light on the link between what Jesus does and what he tells his followers to do. Jesus earns the price of release by doing the very thing he told his followers they must do to earn heavenly treasure: by taking up his cross and giving his life. After the first passion and resurrection predic-

tion in 16:21, Jesus tells the disciples that they must take up their cross
to find their lives (16:24–25). As noted above, Matthew provides a rationale for this claim: the Son of Man is about to repay everyone according to their deeds. In other words, the exhortation following the
first passion and resurrection prediction is based on the promise that
those who follow Jesus in his cross-bearing will be repaid at the Parousia. As Jesus makes his way to Jerusalem this claim surfaces again: those
who deny themselves and follow Jesus will receive a hundred times as
much in return, and the apostles will receive thrones alongside the
Son of Man (19:27–28). Immediately after this there erupts the dispute
over who will receive the thrones closest to Jesus. In correcting the disciples Jesus points them again to his own mission: the Son of Man who
triumphs over the Gentile kings did not come to be served but to serve
and to give his life as the price of release for the many. These words recall the message that Jesus has been repeating again and again: those who
give up their lives will be repaid in the eschaton. Though the pre-his-
tory of the ransom saying remains mysterious, the logic of these words
in Matthew's narrative is clear. *Jesus will earn the ransom-price for those trapped by the debt of sin by giving his life, just as he calls all who would follow him
to earn heavenly treasure by giving their lives.*[54]

To anyone familiar with Daniel's description of the Son of Man
being "given dominion and glory and kingship, that all peoples, nations,
and languages should serve him" (7:14), Jesus' claim that the Son of
Man came not to be served but to serve by giving his life would have
been jarring, almost as if Jesus was deliberately contrasting his own
identity with the figure in Daniel 7.[55] Yet, as already noted, Matthew
repeatedly describes Jesus' coming triumph as the triumph of the figure
in Daniel 7, so it would seem that in applying this text to Jesus, Matthew
does not deny that "all authority in heaven and on earth" is given to him
(28:18). How does the Son of Man as servant relate to the Son of Man
as the wielder of all authority? This is, I would suggest, the implicit
question running throughout 16:21–28, 19:16–29, and 20:17–28.
How is it possible that Jesus, the Christ, who is also the Son of Man

---

54 Thus, even if λύτρον could be used to mean "deliverance" or "redemption"
    with no exchange in view as Boring and others wrongly assert, the Matthean
    context would bring the importance of paying an actual price back to the fore-
    ground.

55 For a discussion of this issue in the Lukan parallel see my "Bakhtin and Lukan
    Politics," 48–53.

of Daniel 7, will reign if he is going to be crucified when he goes to Jerusalem? Jesus answers this question several times while always keeping the similar destiny of his followers in view. In 16:21–28 he says that those who give their lives will be repaid with eternal life. Earthly possessions do not add up to eschatological victory. The treasure that matters is the treasure gained by cross-bearing. Then, in 19:16–20 Jesus says that those who renounce their possessions to follow him will receive a hundred times as much and eternal life, and the twelve apostles will receive twelve thrones alongside the Son of Man. It is implicit, then, that the Son of Man receives his throne from God in return for his renunciation. Finally, in 20:17–28 Jesus explains again that the Son of Man, unlike the Gentile kings he opposes, conquers by giving his life. Or, if one combines this saying with the pericopae leading up to it, Jesus gives his life and is repaid with a glorious throne, eternal life, and with heavenly treasure that redounds not only to his own benefit but to those in arrears because of sin. Thus, the economy of divine recompense running throughout Matthew illuminates how the serving Son of Man becomes the triumphant Son of Man.[56]

Matthew's repeated emphasis on debt-bondage and the divine repayment of cross-bearing also sheds light on the meaning of the preposition ἀντί in the phrase λύτρον ἀντὶ πολλῶν. There are a number of possible ways to understand the price of release being given ἀντί here, the most popular probably being that of "substitution," that is, Jesus dies "in place of" the many.[57] Matthew uses ἀντί this way in 2:22 ("Archelaus reigned over Judea in place of [ἀντί] his father Herod") and in 5:38 ("You have heard that it was said, 'An eye for [ἀντί] and eye, an a tooth for [ἀντί] a tooth'"). Yet, ἀντί could also be used with a slightly different nuance that may be more appropriate for the context in Matthew 20: that of "payment for." For example, in 17:27 Jesus tells Peter to take the shekel he finds in the mouth of a fish and "give it to them for me and for you" (δὸς αὐτοῖς ἀντὶ ἐμοῦ καὶ σοῦ). The shekel is given to pay the debt that Jesus and Peter are thought to owe. As we have seen, within Matthew "the many" are in debt-bondage, and the ransom-price is paid to set them free. Thus, ἀντί in this passage chiefly in-

---

56   Augustine's comment on Jesus' glorification in John 17:1 and Phil 2 (*Tract. Ev. Jo.* 104.3) is apropos: "Humility earns glory; glory is the recompense of humility" (*humilitas, claritatis est meritum; claritas, humilitatis est praemium*).

57   E.g., Hagner, *Matthew 14–28*, 583; Keener, *Matthew*, 488. See BDAG ἀντί II.

dicates "payment for."[58] At the same time, however, it would be over-zealous to exclude the sense of substitution entirely. The idea of payment or exchange is but a hair's breadth away from substitution, and the various possible meanings of words are not hermetically sealed off from each other in everyday speech. Nevertheless, Matthew's emphasis is decidedly on payment; "the many" are in bondage because of the debt of sin, and cross-bearing earns the λύτρον, the price of their release. For Matthew it is not the mere fact of Jesus' death that earns the ransom-price. There is little if any hint here that the crucifixion atones by absorbing God's wrath, or that the effects of sin required that God crush someone and so Jesus received this punishment instead of the many. Rather, it is Jesus' active, obedient giving of his life that earns a surplus of heavenly treasure.[59]

I have suggested that the description of Jesus' gift of his life as the "ransom-price" be taken to mean that Jesus' obedient cross-bearing earns wages with God that repay the debt of sin of the many, thereby saving them. There are two potential objections to this conclusion that need to be addressed before going on. The first is that this reading is simply too clever. It is unlikely, one might protest, that Matthew would have set forth any "elaborate soteriological theory," to use Talbert's phrase.[60] There are three things to say in response to this. First, the argument is not that Matthew provides an elaborate theory. The narrative does not evince systematic reflection on the plight of humanity before God. Matthew's "soteriology" – if such a word is appropriate – leaves a number of significant questions unanswered.[61] But Matthew's description of Jesus' saving activity is coherent.[62] That is, it is based on a few core assumptions that manifest themselves quite predictably throughout the narrative. People find themselves in bondage due to the debt of sin. Jesus was born to save them. He teaches them to earn

---

58 BDAG ἀντί III; LSJ ἀντί III.3.
59 Matthew's narrative soteriology thus bears a certain resemblance to Anselm's satisfaction theory as articulated by David Bentley Hart ("A Gift Exceeding Every Debt: An Eastern Orthodox Appreciation of Anselm's *Cur Deus Homo*," *Pro Ecclesia* 7 [1998]: 333–49) in contrast to penal substitution.
60 *Matthew*, 241.
61 I shall return to some of these questions in the conclusion.
62 As noted in the Introduction, I use the word "coherent" in contradistinction to "systematic" following E. P. Sanders, "Did Paul's Theology Develop?" in *The Word Leaps the Gap: Essays in Scripture and Theology in Honor of Richard B. Hays* (ed. J. Ross Wagner et al.; Grand Rapids: Eerdmans, 2008), 325–50.

treasure in heaven and avoid debt-bondage, and in 20:28 he says that
the gift of his life – an action that Matthew repeatedly describes as
wage-earning – is the price of release for the many. This is *how* Jesus
saves his people from their sins. Again, questions remain: how do debtors receive this ransom-price? How does this vicarious payment relate
to Matthew's many claims that earning heavenly treasure is necessary
to enter the kingdom? Why do the scribes and Pharisees fill up the
measure of their sin? Why does Matthew exclude them from receiving
the ransom-price? Matthew provides no clear answers to these and
other questions.[63] Again, this is no elaborate soteriological theory. It is
only this: the people are God's debtors and they find themselves in
debt-bondage. Jesus takes up his cross to earn their ransom-price
while also teaching them to do likewise.

The second response to the charge that this reading is too clever is
this: though this study follows primarily a narrative approach rather than
a redaction-centered one, the occasional redaction-critical glance can be
quite instructive. Most of the key passages informing the argument are
found only in Matthew. The focus on end of exile, the repayment of
wages, and the promise that Jesus will "save his people from their
sins" (1:21) in the birth narrative is of course uniquely Matthean, and
Jesus' claim that he and John the Baptist will "fill up all righteousness"
is redactional. Much of the material on earning treasure in heaven in the
Sermon on the Mount is only found in Matthew. Matthew alone describes the fate of unresolved sinners as debt-bondage two times
(5:26; 18:23–35).[64] Only the Matthean Jesus teaches his followers to
pray for debt cancellation (6:12). Matthew's discussion of the wages
of missionaries and those who receive them (10:40–42) is much
more extensive than in Mark and Luke. Only Matthew includes the
parable of the hidden treasure (13:44), the parable of the pearl
(13:45–46), the parable of the unforgiving servant (18:23–35), the
parable of the workers in the vineyard (20:1–16), and the sheep and
the goats pericope (25:31–46). The discussions revolving around the
passion and resurrection predictions and the journey to Jerusalem follow

---

63   To hazard a preliminary response to the question of the Jewish leaders Matthew
     opposes: it was argued in chapter 2 that 25:29 is probably the best summation of
     wages in Matthew: "For to everyone who has will more be given, and he will
     have abundance; but from him who has not, even what he has will be taken
     away." Thus, those who oppose Jesus, who do not even try to "earn more tal-
     ents," would be beyond the pale.

64   Cf. Luke 12:59.

the basic Markan template, but it is Matthew alone who explains that cross-bearing is necessary because the Son of Man is about to "repay to each according to his deeds" (16:27), that is, to repay cruciform lives with resurrection. Matthew alone expands the teaching on treasure in heaven in 19:27–28 to make it clear that the apostles, like Jesus, will be repaid with Danielic thrones.[65] This Matthean addition ties that passage together with the dispute over the best thrones in 20:17–28. It is impossible to deny, therefore, that Matthew has a special interest in sin as debt, cruciform deeds as earning wages, and in the redemption from sin that Jesus accomplished.[66] The ransom-saying is of course not unique, being found in Mark and possessing a number of parallels in other early Christian literature.[67] But only the most flat-footed redaction critic could claim that Matthew drowsily copied the Markan text in 20:28 when the saying fits so perfectly with scores of uniquely Matthean details leading up to it. Is it not more plausible that this uniquely Matthean material comprises the Evangelist's interpretation of the traditional Christian belief that Christ gave himself up as a ransom-price?

A third and final response to the charge that this reading is too clever is this: New Testament scholars resist attributing elaborate soteriological theories to early Christian texts because they are rightly wary of reading later theological concerns back into early Christianity. Yet, the soteriological schema described here is not drawn from the categories of later Christian theology but from Matthew's late first-century Jewish-Christian milieu. Like many other Jewish texts, Matthew assumes that sin incurs a debt and that righteous deeds earn treasure in heaven. Moreover, like many other Jewish texts, Matthew assumes that one's heavenly account is not simply a matter between the individual and God but that it is possible to benefit from the heavenly treasure earned by others. Matthew shares these common Jewish beliefs about sin, debt, and redemption but refracts them through the decisive event of Jesus' death and resurrection. Far from importing later Christian theology, then, this proposal situates the Gospel squarely in its historical context.

Now for the second potential objection: one might argue – and some have – that 20:28 cannot possess any great soteriological signifi-

---

65 See the very different treatment of a similar saying in Luke 22:28–30.
66 In addition to the preceding, see the catalogue of uniquely Matthean economic language in the Introduction.
67 See the discussion below.

cance because it occurs in the context of exhortation.[68] It is a word of exhortation, some would claim, rather than speculation on how Jesus saves his people. There are two things to be said in response. First, Matthew's moral vision is relentlessly christological. This can be seen in the myriad of connections between what Jesus himself does and what he tells his followers to do. In the series of exhortations leading up to Jesus' entry into Jerusalem Jesus repeatedly demands that his disciples follow him in losing their lives and then being repaid. Like the Christ hymn in Philippians 2:1–11, then, Matthew admonishes followers of Jesus to do what he did. Neither Matthew nor the letter to the Philippians reflects on Christ's kenosis and following glorification as would a systematic theologian – beginning from first principles and treating the Christ event and the Christian life in separate chapters – but this should not be confused with a lack of interest in Christ's work itself.[69] Far from undercutting its soteriological significance, the hortative context of 20:28 presents Jesus saving work as both vicarious and as the template for the self-giving required of Jesus' followers. In Matthew, Jesus "saves" by showing his followers how to earn wages with God, but also by doing it for them.

Second, this objection assumes that the work of vicarious atonement is not something that Jesus' followers are able to participate in. As Talbert puts it, the ransom-saying "simply means that Jesus is acting on others' behalf in his ministry…If 20:28 gives Jesus's example for disciples to follow, it cannot include more than disciples can follow."[70] This idea may be correct in some theological systems, especially those that emphasize the complete inability of humankind to participate in their own salvation, but one should not assume this is the case in early Christian texts. To take one particularly vivid example, in Colossians 1:24 the author says "now I rejoice in my sufferings for your sake, and in my flesh I fill up (ἀνταναπληρῶ) what is lacking in Christ's afflictions for the sake of his body, that is, the church." Here Paul suffers vicariously on behalf of the church, seeing his trials as somehow contributing to the

---

68 E.g., Talbert, *Matthew*, 241.
69 *Pace*, Keener (*Matthew*, 488), who says "As in Philippians 2:1–11, however, the evangelists treat their audiences to this summary of Jesus' mission not to rehearse soteriology but to provide an active model for Christian living." The assumption that exhortation betrays a lack of interest in Jesus' work is unwarranted. See also J. Christopher Edwards, "Pre-Nicene Receptions of Mark 10:45// Matt. 20:28 with Phil. 2:6–8," *JTS* 61 (2010): 194–99.
70 *Matthew*, 241.

benefits wrought by Christ's trials. Similarly, given the fact that Matthean ethics are cruciform in nature, that is, the disciples are told to do what Jesus in fact does, it is at least implicit that the apostles are to follow Jesus in storing up treasure in heaven not just for themselves but for others. Instead of rejecting the soteriological significance of 20:28 because it occurs in the context of exhortation, it makes more sense to see Jesus' words as a call to the apostles to join him in earning heavenly treasure not only for themselves but for others. They are to follow him in giving their lives and then receiving "a hundred times as much" in return, heavenly treasures that overflow to the benefit of the many, just as Paul filled up what was lacking for the sake of the church, and just as the merits of the patriarchs accrued to the benefit of Israel.[71]

This final admonition to the disciples before entering Jerusalem unites Matthew's depiction of Jesus as savior with the depiction of Jesus as exemplar and teacher. Before 20:28 Matthew stresses, on the one hand, what we might call salvation by imitation of Jesus, by taking up one's cross like him in order to receive many times as much. On the other hand, however, there are indications, especially in the prologue of the Gospel, that, through Jesus, provision will be made for those without heavenly treasure: most notably, the prophecy that Jesus would save his people from their sins (1:21), his claim to fill up all righteousness (3:15), and the hint that God is able to save those who have done little worthy of heavenly treasure (19:26; 19:30–20:16).[72] In 20:28 these two motifs, which wind their separate ways through the Gospel, finally converge and illuminate each other. Jesus' righteous deed is here described not just as an example – though it is that too – but as a vicarious payment on behalf of others.

To sum up: scholarly discussion of Matthew 20:28 has been distracted by an erroneous equation of λύτρον with the verb λυτρόω and by neglect of the considerable light that the preceding narrative sheds on the saying. The word λύτρον always denotes some sort of price, frequently the price paid to free a captive. Jesus' claim to give his life as a λύτρον for many thus raises two obvious questions: why do "the many" need to be ransomed, and how does Jesus' gift of his life accomplish this? The prologue shows that "the many" are in exile because of the

---

71 Something similar appears in the baptism as well; Jesus says that it is fitting "for us" – namely Jesus and John the Baptist – to fill up all righteousness.
72 See also Jesus' forgiveness of sin in 9:1–6.

debt of sin, and the narrative subsequently describes the punishment for
"debts" (i. e., sins) as debt-bondage. He earns the ransom-price for them
by doing the very thing he taught his followers to do to earn heavenly
treasure: he gives his life. It is Jesus' obedient giving of his life that earns
the ransom-price rather than the mere fact of his death per se.

4.6 Excursus: similar early Jewish and Christian references to atoning death

The two most important pre- or para-Christian parallels to Matthew
20:28 are found in 2 and 4 Maccabees. The book of 2 Maccabees is
commonly dated to the second century B.C.E. In chapter 7 the youngest
of the martyred brothers reproaches Antiochus with the following
words before his death:

> What are you waiting for? I will not obey the king's command, but I obey
> the command of the law that was given to our fathers through Moses. But
> you, who have contrived all sorts of evil against the Hebrews, will certainly
> not escape the hands of God. For we are suffering because of our own sins
> (ἡμεῖς γὰρ διὰ τὰς ἑαυτῶν ἁμαρτίας πάσχομεν). And if our living Lord is
> angry for a little while, to rebuke and discipline us, he will again be recon-
> ciled with his own servants. But you, unholy wretch, you most defiled of
> all men, do not be elated in vain and puffed up by uncertain hopes, when
> you raise your hand against the children of heaven. You have not yet es-
> caped the judgment of the almighty, all-seeing God. For our brothers
> after enduring a brief suffering have drunk of everflowing life under
> God's covenant; but you, by the judgment of God, will receive just pun-
> ishment for your arrogance. I, like my brothers, give up body and life for
> the laws of our fathers (ἐγὼ δέ καθάπερ οἱ ἀδελφοί καὶ σῶμα καὶ ψυχὴν προ-
> δίδωμι περὶ τῶν πατρίων νόμων), appealing to God to show mercy soon to
> our nation and by afflictions and plagues to make you confess that he alone
> is God, and through me and my brothers to bring to an end the wrath of
> the Almighty (στῆσαι τὴν τοῦ παντοκράτορος ὀργήν) which has justly fallen
> on our whole nation. (7:30–38 NRSV).

In this passage the last brother to be killed takes up the theodical explanation offered in the previous chapter: God waits to allow the sins of the
other nations to pile up and reach their "full measure" (6:14–15) before
taking vengeance on them, but God frequently disciplines the Jewish
people with calamities so that their punishment will not be severe. Eleazar and the seven brothers suffer for "our own sins" – that is, the sins of
the whole people – and give their "body and life" (σῶμα καὶ ψυχήν) for
the laws of their fathers, thereby bringing an end to the wrath of God.

Then, in the following passage, the tide turns in favor of the Jews "for the wrath of the Lord had turned to mercy" (8:5). Thus, by giving their lives for the Law the martyrs endured the chastisement and prevented the sins of the people from accumulating any further, while also meriting their own resurrection from the dead (see 7:9, 23, 29, 36).

The mechanics of atonement are less clear in 2 Maccabees than in Matthew. The language of debt and repayment is present, but it is very faint. The martyrs give up (προδίδωμι) body and life (σῶμα καὶ ψυχήν) for the laws of the fathers (περὶ τῶν πατρίων νόμων) and end the wrath that comes because of accumulating sin, whereas in Matthew Jesus gives (δοῦναι) his life (τὴν ψυχὴν αὐτοῦ) as the price of release for many (λύτρον ἀντὶ πολλῶν). Sin is described as something that builds up, possibly recalling debt language, but it is less clear how the giving of body and life averts God's wrath.[73] It may be that the martyrs endure the punishment that God intended for the entire people and so end the chastisement – that is, something like penal substitution – whereas Matthew describes Jesus' giving of his life as a currency-generating act (rather than a punishment-absorbing one).[74]

In 4 Maccabees, which is commonly dated to the mid to late first century, Eleazar utters the following prayer before he dies:

> You know, O God, that though I might have saved myself, I am dying in burning torments for the sake of the law (διὰ τὸν νόμον). Be merciful to your people, and let our punishment suffice for them (ἀρκεσθεὶς τῇ ἡμετέρᾳ ὑπὲρ αὐτῶν δίκῃ). Make my blood their purification (καθάρσιον), and take my life in exchange for theirs (καὶ ἀντίψυχον αὐτῶν λαβὲ τὴν ἐμὴν ψυχήν). (6:27–29 NRSV)

A related statement appears in 17:20–22 when the narrator comments on the deaths of Eleazar and the other martyrs:

> These, then, who have been consecrated for the sake of God, are honored, not only with this honor, but also by the fact that because of them our enemies did not rule over our nation, the tyrant was punished, and the home-

---

73 On the Deuteronomistic scheme of disobedience, suffering, and reconciliation in 2 Maccabees see Daniel R. Schwartz, *2 Maccabees* (CEJL; Berlin/New York: Walter de Gruyter, 2008), 298–99; Jonathan A. Goldstein, *2 Maccabees: A New Translation with Introduction and Commentary* (AB 41 A; Garden City, NY: Doubleday, 1983), 296.

74 *Pace* Sam K. Williams, who argues that the martyrs' deaths are not atoning in 2 Maccabees, *Jesus' Death as Saving Event: The Background and Origin of a Concept* (HDR 2; Missoula, Mont.: Scholars Press for Harvard Theological Review, 1975), 76–91.

land purified (καθαρισθῆναι) – they having become, as it were, an exchange for the sin of our nation (ὥσπερ ἀντίψυχον γεγονότας τῆς τοῦ ἔθνους ἁμαρτίας), and through the blood of those devout ones and their death as an atoning sacrifice (διὰ τοῦ αἵματος τῶν εὐσεβῶν ἐκείνων καὶ τοῦ ἱλαστηρίου τοῦ θανάτου αὐτῶν), divine Providence preserved Israel that previously had been mistreated. (NRSV)[75]

Like 2 Maccabees, these passages indicate that the martyrs die for the Law, bring peace to the people, and merit their own post-mortem reward.[76] In the final chapter the narrator goes on to say:

Therefore those who gave over their bodies in suffering for the sake of religion (διὰ τὴν εὐσέβειαν) were not only admired by mortals, but also were deemed worthy to share in a divine inheritance (θείας μερίδος κατηξιώθησαν). Because of them the nation gained peace, and by reviving observance of the law in the homeland they ravaged the enemy. (18:3–4 NRSV).

There are also important differences between 2 and 4 Maccabees. Fourth Maccabees introduces cultic language, speaking of purification (καθάρσιος) and atoning death (τοῦ ἱλαστηρίου τοῦ θανάτου). Fourth Maccabees also uses clearer language of substitution, twice describing the martyrs as the ἀντίψυχος of the people, and stating that the punishment (δίκη) endured by the martyrs was on behalf of the whole people (ὑπὲρ αὐτῶν).[77] Indeed, one might call the atonement effected by the

---

75 The NRSV's translation of ἀντίψυχον as "ransom" is here changed to "exchange." The word ἀντίψυχος is a neologism which appears to denote a life given in place of another (J. Lust, *Greek-English Lexicon of the Septuagint* [Stuttgart: Deutsche Bibelgesellschaft, 2003]). Many scholars have the odd habit of comparing the "ransom" in 4 Maccabees to the "ransom" in Matt 20:28/Mark 10:45 without reflecting on the possible differences between the Greek words. At the risk of belaboring the point, a life given to earn a ransom-price (λύτρον) could also be called a life given in place of others, an ἀντίψυχος, but a life given in place of others is not necessarily given to earn a ransom-price.

76 See also 13:9; 1:8 (ὑπὲρ ἀρετῆς); 1:10 (ὑπὲρ τῆς καλοκἀγαθίας); 9:6, 18:3 (διὰ τὴν εὐσέβειαν); 16:25 (διὰ τὸν θεόν).

77 M. De Jonge, "Jesus' Death for Others and the Death of the Maccabean Martyrs," in *Text and Testimony: Essays on New Testament and Apocryphal Literature in Honour of A. F. J. Klijn* (ed. T. Baarda et al.; Kampen: Kok, 1988), 142–52, 150–51. Jan Willem van Henten points out that, unlike 2 Maccabees, 4 Maccabees does not describe the punishment endured by the people as disciplinary. *The Maccabean Martyrs as Saviours of the Jewish People: A Study of 2 and 4 Maccabees* (Supplements to the Journal for the Study of Judaism 57; Leiden: E. J. Brill, 1997), 184–86.

martyrs "penal substitution," because it is explicit that they endure the punishment intended for the entire people.[78]

There are intriguing similarities between 4 Maccabees and Matthew; both texts depict the giving of life (ψυχή) in obedience to God to save the people from their sins.[79] But the similarities should not be exaggerated. In 4 Maccabees the martyrs endure the punishment that was coming because of the sins of the whole people, absorbing God's wrath so it did not fall on everyone else. In Matthew, Jesus gives his life to earn the price of release of the many in debt-bondage.[80] This is the difference between what later theologians would call penal substitution and satisfaction.

The closest parallel to Matthew 20:28 in early Christian literature is of course Mark 10:45, which differs only by one word. Mark, however, lacks Matthew's emphasis on end of exile, debt-bondage, and the heavenly wages one earns by giving one's life.[81] It is possible that early auditors of Mark would have understood the Markan ransom saying to mean Jesus earns heavenly currency for those in the debt of sin by giving his life, but Mark, unlike Matthew, does not provide enough information to warrant any firm conclusion on the matter.

Indeed, most of the parallels to Matthew 20:28 in the New Testament resemble the Markan version in that it is possible they would have evoked something similar to what we see in Matthew, but not enough information is given to make this conclusion. For instance, Paul admonishes the Corinthians to shun immorality, reminding them that, "You are not your own; for you were bought with a price (ἠγοράσθητε γὰρ

---

78 *Pace*, once again, Williams (*Jesus' Death as Saving Event*, 165–202), who downplays the atoning significance of the martyrs' deaths in 4 Maccabees, arguing that their deaths are merely exemplary. Despite this conclusion, Williams argues that 4 Maccabees had an enormous influence on emerging Christian understandings of Jesus' death. In 4 Maccabees, early Christians would have encountered the idea that "a human death could be beneficial for others because it was regarded by God as effective for the ransom of their lives, the expiation of their sins. Whatever the correct explanation for the dynamics underlying the formulation of this concept…, having once been formulated it was there, a given conceptual entity with its own autonomous existence…free to exert its powerful influence among Jews and Christians as an exciting new 'doctrine.' (253)."

79 David A. deSilva, *4 Maccabees* (Guides to Apocrypha and Pseudepigrapha; Sheffield, Eng.: Sheffield Academic Press, 1998), 140.

80 Again, this difference is obscured by the common translation of ἀντίψυχος in 17:21 as "ransom."

81 See, however, Mark 10:17–30.

τιμῆς). Glorify God, then in your body" (1 Cor 6:19b-20)." Similarly, in chapter 7 Paul advises slaves to become free if they find the opportunity:

> Were you a slave when called? Do not be concerned about it. But if you can gain your freedom, avail yourself of the opportunity. For whoever was called in the Lord as a slave is a freed person belonging to the Lord, just as whoever was free when called is a slave of Christ. You were bought with a price (τιμῆς ἠγοράσθητε); do not become slaves of human masters. (7:21-23)

In both of these passages Paul gives instructions drawn from the fact that the Corinthians were bought with a "price" (τιμή).[82] As Richard B. Hays notes, "The metaphorical picture is of the purchase of slaves by a new master" (cf. Rom 6:18). Jesus' death "paid the terrible price to ransom us from bondage to the powers of sin and death; consequently, we now belong to him and not to ourselves."[83] Note that Paul assumes the Corinthians will know what he means when he refers to this price. This is suggestive; it could imply that the narrative of Christ giving his life to earn a price to purchase the church from (debt?)-slavery was a basic element of Paul's preaching.[84]

There are a number of similar statements in the so-called deutero-Pauline epistles. As noted in chapter 1, Colossians 2:14 says that God canceled the χειρόγραφον (bond of indebtedness) by nailing it to the cross. It is possible that this presupposes that the cross became the means of doing away with the bond of indebtedness and its stipulations (i. e., the right of execution) because Jesus' death generated the "currency" needed to rescue humanity from insolvency. Titus 2:14 says that Christ "gave himself for us (ἔδωκεν ἑαυτὸν ὑπὲρ ἡμῶν) in order to redeem (λυτρώσηται) us from all lawlessness." Again, though λυτρόω need not refer to the payment of an actual price, it frequently does, and a price is in fact mentioned: Christ gave "himself."

Similarly, 1 Timothy 2:6 states that Christ "gave himself as a ransom-price on behalf of all (ὁ δοὺς ἑαυτὸν ἀντίλυτρον ὑπὲρ πάντων). This verse is the closest parallel to the ransom saying in the Matthew and Mark:

---

82 On τιμή in the papyri see Deissman, *Light from the Ancient East*, 324.
83 *First Corinthians* (*Int*; Louisville, KY: John Knox, 1997), 106.
84 W. D. Davies argued that Paul understood Jesus' death as an act of obedience the merits of which redound to others. See his discussion of Rom 5 and Phil 2 in *Paul and Rabbinic Judaism: Some Rabbinic Elements in Pauline Theology* (Philadelphia: Fortress, 1948; repr., 1980), 268-73.

1 Timothy:	ὁ δοὺς ἑαυτὸν		ἀντίλυτρον ὑπὲρ πάντων
Matthew/Mark:	δοῦναι τὴν ψυχὴν αὐτοῦ λύτρον	ἀντὶ πολλῶν

The most substantial difference here is the use of the rare compound ἀντίλυτρον in place of λύτρον, which may be due to nothing more than the predilection for compound words in the Pastoral Epistles.[85] Like Mark, 1 Timothy gives no explanation of what is meant here. Why is a ransom-payment needed? How does Christ's self-giving earn this price? The author does not say. It is worth noting, however, that the author did have a robust sense of the salvific effects of almsgiving, claiming that the rich should "do good, to be rich in good works, generous, and ready to share, thus storing up for themselves the treasure of a good foundation for the future, so that they may take hold of the life that really is life" (ἀποθησαυρίζοντας ἑαυτοῖς θεμέλιον καλὸν εἰς τὸ μέλλον, ἵνα ἐπιλάβωνται τῆς ὄντως ζωῆς) (6:18−19 NRSV).[86] If the author believed that by giving alms one could treasure up a foundation that allows one to attain true life, perhaps his imagination was shaped more generally by the cluster of economic metaphors that were so common in early Judaism. It is possible, then, that 1 Timothy assumes a scheme similar to the one Matthew makes explicit – that is, the bondage of debt and the wage-earning of giving one's life – but it is impossible to say with confidence.

In 1 Peter 1:17−19, the author says

> And if you invoke as Father him who judges each one impartially according to his deeds, conduct yourselves with fear throughout the time of your exile, knowing that not with perishable things such as silver or gold were you ransomed (ἐλυτρώθητε) from the futile ways inherited from your fathers, but with the costly blood (τιμίῳ αἵματι) of Christ, like that of a lamb without blemish or spot.

Like most translations the NRSV renders the adjective τίμιος as "precious," a word with largely sentimental connotations in contemporary English, but the primary meaning of τίμιος, like the Vulgate's pretioso, is "costly" or "of great worth." In concert with the "ransoming" and the contrast with silver and gold – a contrast that is reminiscent of Mat-

---

85 Benjamin Fiore, *The Pastoral Epistles: First Timothy, Second Timothy, Titus* (SP 12; Collegeville, MN.: Liturgical Press,1991), 60. Jeremias influentially argued that the version in 1 Timothy is a hellenization of the more Semitic version found in Matthew, "Das Lösegeld für Viele (Mk 10.45)" (225−26).

86 See 6:6−19. Nathan Eubank, "Almsgiving is 'The Commandment': A Note on 1 Timothy 6.6−19," *NTS* 58 (2012): 144−50.

thew's claim that earthly treasures are not efficacious – it is clear that some sort of exchange is in view. Similarly, in Revelation 5:9 the four living creatures and the twenty-four elders sing, "You are worthy to take the scroll and to open its seals, for you were slaughtered and by your blood (ἐν τῷ αἵματί σου) you purchased (ἠγόρασας) for God saints from every tribe and language and people and nation." As in 1 Peter, the currency that is used to "purchase" people for God is Jesus' blood.

4.7 Conclusion

This chapter, which has focused on three key passages that occur when Jesus begins predicting his death and resurrection (16:13–28; 19:16–29; 20:17–28), is central for this study's overarching argument regarding the significance of Matthew's grammar of sin and righteousness. These three passages indicate that Jesus and his followers must give their lives in order to be repaid with resurrection and the reign spoken of in Daniel 7. In 16:13–28 Jesus announces his coming death and resurrection and then explains that any who would follow him must also take up their crosses and lose their lives because the Son of Man is about to repay those who have given their present lives with eternal life. Then, in 19:16–29 Jesus says that those who renounce their possessions, give the money to the poor, and follow Jesus will be repaid with eternal life and a share in the rule of the Son of Man.

The emphasis in these passages is on finding eternal life by imitating Jesus' obedient self-giving. Yet, as noted in the previous chapter, Matthew describes the people as in exile or debt-bondage due to sin and Jesus as the one would save them. To be sure, his teaching and example throughout the Gospel is part of this saving, but there are numerous hints of hope for those who fail to give up everything for Jesus' sake (1:21; 3:15; 10:40–42; 19:23–26; 20:1–16). In 20:17–28 these two motifs finally converge and illuminate each other. Jesus' righteous deed is here described not just as an example – though it is that too – but as a vicarious payment of the ransom-price to liberate the many trapped by the debt of sin. Sinners are in debt to God and find themselves in debt-bondage. Jesus gives his life for them, earning their ransom-price, and commands his followers to do likewise. It is Jesus' obedient cross-bearing that earns the price of release rather than the mere fact of his suffering and death.

5 "Behold, Your Savior Comes, His Wage is with Him": The Passion and Resurrection

5.1 Introduction

It is a curious fact that all of Matthew's explicit economic language is found on the lips of Jesus. In the passion and resurrection narrative, Jesus speaks less than he does throughout most of the rest of the Gospel, and he says nothing at all about heavenly wages and debts. Indeed, Matthew follows the Markan narrative very closely here, and none of the Matthean additions mention treasure in heaven and the like. At first glance, then, it would seem that chapters 26–28 have little, if anything, to add to this study.

If the passion and resurrection narrative is read as a solitary fragment then there is indeed little to say. But to read the conclusion of the Gospel in isolation from the preceding narrative would be to read it in a way that runs contrary to numerous hints in the story itself that it was written as a coherent whole.[1] Throughout Matthew, Jesus' self-giving on the cross is foreshadowed, interpreted, and defended.[2] The account of Her-

---

1   See the discussion of method in the Introduction.
2   For Matthew's "defense" of the cross, see esp. the discussion of 16:24–28 in chapter 4 above. One is reminded of the exaggerated but incisive claim of Martin Kähler that the Gospels are passion narratives with extended introductions (*Der sogenannte historische Jesus und der geschichtliche biblische Christus* [Leipzig: Deichertsche Verlagsbuchhandlung, 1896], 33). This famous overstatement emerged from Kähler's critique of the tendency of the historical Jesus scholars of his day to deemphasize the significance of Jesus' death, and many subsequent New Testament scholars have cited it approvingly, noting that the Gospels are indeed oriented to the cross from the beginning. There is little doubt that this judgment applies to Matthew, which contains numerous hints of this coming fate beginning with the birth narrative, and which is explicitly preoccupied with Jesus' coming death and resurrection from chapter sixteen onwards. Even Matthew's great blocks of teaching material, much of which is often thought to derive from the sayings-source Q, foreshadow Jesus' coming death and vindication. E.g., 5:10–11; 10:37–39. See John S. Kloppenborg on the significance of Jesus' death in "Q" (*Excavating Q: The History and Setting of the Sayings Gospel* [Minneapolis: Fortress, 2000], 369–74).The purpose of this chapter is to read the passion narrative in light of its "introduction."

od's attempt on Jesus' life (2:16−18), for instance, is not simply a story about a cruel king's attempt to eliminate an infant rival. To reduce the import of the episode to its explicitly articulated details in this way would be to misunderstand it; the full significance of this story can be grasped only in light of the narrative as a whole, wherein it becomes clear that this deadly conflict pitting Herod and "all of Jerusalem" (2:3) against Jesus foreshadows Jesus' crucifixion. Similarly, to attend only to the explicitly cited details of the passion and resurrection − that is, to read with self-imposed amnesia regarding the preceding narrative − would be a certain path to misunderstanding. To take one example, when the risen Jesus appears to the eleven he describes himself in language redolent of the triumph of the Son of Man in Daniel 7 (Matt 28:16−20). Of course, when Jesus and the apostles were on their way to Jerusalem he had told them that the recompense for following him in giving their lives would be thrones alongside of the Son of Man (19:27−29; 20:17−28). To read 28:16−20 with intential disregard for these earlier passages would be to forfeit important insights into Matthew's portrayal of Jesus' resurrection. Indeed, this uniquely Matthean resurrection appearance is not a free-standing monad any more than is Herod's attempt to kill Jesus. Thus, the goal of this chapter, as in the rest of this study, is to read Matthew as a coherent whole, not because of some prior theory of narrativity, but because of the abundant clues within Matthew itself that it was written to be read in this way.

In light of this brief *relecture* of the method employed throughout this study, it is now possible to state the thesis to be argued in this chapter. In the preceding chapter we saw that the Matthean Jesus claims he will give his life and be repaid with (1) resurrection, (2) rule as Son of Man, and (3) the ransom-price for his people in debt-bondage. By reading the passion narrative in light of Matthew's careful preparation for it, I shall argue, among other things, that it depicts the threefold repayment of Jesus' cross-bearing. This conclusion does not spring from the passion and resurrection narrative alone but depends on the conclusions of the earlier parts of this study, especially chapter 4. Nevertheless, the thoroughgoing redaction critic may take heart in the fact that most of the crucial links between the passion and resurrection and the preceding narrative are uniquely Matthean, a point to which I shall return. Before turning to the passion narrative, however, it is necessary to take note of a neglected feature of Matthew's version of the triumphal entry.

5.2 Behold, your king comes with his wage in his hand (21:5)

The discourse leading up to the ransom-saying (20:17−28) is the last private discussion between Jesus and the apostles before they enter Jerusalem. After healing the two blind men Jesus enters Jerusalem meekly, seated on an ass rather than a war-horse. Matthew alone among the Synoptic Gospels describes this event as the fulfillment of Scripture: "This happened to fulfill what was spoken by the prophet, saying 'Behold your king is coming to you, humble, and mounted on an ass, and on a colt, the foal of an ass'" (21:5). Commentators have tended to fixate on the question of whether Matthew thought Jesus rode two animals at the same time,[3] neglecting the fact that the quotation combines two remarkably similar passages − Isa 62 and Zech 9 − that describe the coming of Zion's king to ransom the people from captivity and repay their deeds. The phrase εἴπατε τῇ θυγατρὶ Σιων is a verbatim quotation of Isa 62:11. The remainder of Matt 21:5 is from Zech 9:9. There is good reason to believe that the wider contexts of these passages are being evoked: first, Jesus has just said he would go to Jerusalem to pay the ransom-price for the many. It is fitting, then, that his entry into Jerusalem is said to fulfill two prophetic texts describing God or the messiah coming to ransom the people. Second, Matthew's use of these prophetic texts closely parallels the use of Scripture in the prologue; as noted in chapter 3, Matthew there cites seven passages that deal with either the end of exile or Davidic messiahship, and two of these passages, Jer 31 and Isa 40, attribute the end of exile to the repayment of deeds. In 2:6 Matthew also conflates Mic 5 and 2 Sam 5 to show that the messiah had to be born in Bethlehem. The addition of 2 Sam was unnecessary as far as birth in Bethlehem is concerned, but the wider context from which this added line is taken, David's enthronement, served to deepen the messianic overtones. The citation of Isa 62 and Zech 9 in the triumphal entry is, therefore, formally and materially parallel to Matthew's use of Scripture in the prologue; formally, because in both places events in Jesus' life fulfill a series of biblical texts that closely resemble each other and possess deep thematic unity with the larger Matthean narrative; materially, because in both the prologue and 21:5, the biblical texts cited deal with the end of

---

3   See the judicious treatment of John Nolland, *The Gospel of Matthew: A Commentary on the Greek Text* (NIGTC; Grand Rapids, MI: Eerdmans, 2005), 836−37.

the people's captivity through the repayment of deeds and Davidic messiahship. A closer look at the context of these passages is therefore required.

Isaiah 62 describes the coming of YHWH to Zion in language recalling Isa 40, a passage which is itself evoked by Matthew in 3:3. The
coming savior is again portrayed as the redeemer of the captive people:

> Say to daughter Zion, "See, your savior comes; his reward (שכרו/ τὸν ἑαυ-
> τοῦ μισθόν) is with him, and his recompense (ופעלתו/τὸ ἔργον) before him."
> They shall be called, "The Holy People, The Redeemed (גאולי/λελυτρω-
> μένον) of the LORD"; and you shall be called, "Sought Out, A City Not For-
> saken." (62:11–12 NRSV)

Joseph Blenkinsopp argues that the wage God brings is the wage due to
the people who are to be redeemed.[4] This is a possible construal; the
parallel passage in Isaiah 40 begins by telling the people that they had
paid the penalty for all their sins. Another possibility, however, emerges
in light of the prophet's claim that the people will bear the title "The
Redeemed by the Lord" (גאולי/λελυτρωμένον). As noted in the previous
chapter, the verb λυτρόω, following the Hebrew גאל, can refer to redemption of slaves or captives through the payment of some price of release, or it can refer to redemption in contexts where no payment is
made. In this passage, the people are given the title "Redeemed by
the Lord" immediately after being told that the savior comes with his
wages. The juxtaposition of "wages" brought by the savior with the language of redemption suggests that the usual, payment-based meaning of
λυτρόω/גאל is in view here. This opens up the possibility that the wages
brought by the Lord are not only, or even primarily, the wages earned
by the exiles. Indeed, the image here is that of the redemption of captives by the payment of some price; the Lord comes to Jerusalem with
wages that he will pay in order to "redeem" the people from captivity.
In Matthew's narrative, of course, Jesus has just informed the disciples
that he is going to Jerusalem to give his life as the ransom-price for
the many. Now, when he enters the city he is described as the fulfillment of Isa 62, where the Lord comes with a payment in hand.

The fulfillment quotation combines Isa 62 with Zech 9:

> Rejoice greatly, O daughter Zion! Shout aloud, O daughter Jerusalem!
> Lo, your king comes to you; triumphant and victorious is he,[5] humble

---

4   *Isaiah 56–66: A New Translation with Introduction and Commentary* (AB 19B;
     New York: Doubleday, 2003), 244.
5   LXX: "just and saving is he" (δίκαιος καὶ σῴζων). Cf. Matthew 1:21; 27:19.

and riding on a donkey, on a colt, the foal of a donkey. He will cut off the chariot from Ephraim and the war-horse from Jerusalem; and the battle bow shall be cut off, and he shall command peace to the nations; his dominion shall be from sea to sea, and from the River to the ends of the earth. As for you also, because of the blood of my covenant with you (בְּדַם־בְּרִיתֵךְ/ἐν αἵματι διαθήκης), I will set your prisoners free from the waterless pit (מִבּוֹר אֵין מַיִם בּוֹ/ἐκ λάκκου οὐκ ἔχοντος ὕδωρ). Return to your stronghold, O prisoners of hope; today I declare that I will repay you double (מִשְׁנֶה אָשִׁיב לָךְ/διπλᾶ ἀνταποδώσω σοι). (9:9–12 NRSV)[6]

Like Isa 62, this passage declares the coming of a savior – here a Davidic king rather than God himself – who comes to repay the people and set them free from captivity.[7] Zechariah 9 also shares with Matthew a striking number of themes in addition to the repayment and redemption of the people. The most obvious is the explicitly cited claim that the entering king is humble (πραΰς), which recalls Matthew 11:29. Jesus comes not as one who bears the sword (cf. 26:52) but in peace (cf. 5:9, 43–48). Then there is the promise that this peace will extend over the whole of a reunified Israel (i. e., Ephraim and Jerusalem) and over the nations as well, ruling "from sea to sea."[8] Matthew has already said that the apostles will reign over the twelve tribes of Israel (19:28), and the coming inclusion of the Gentiles has been hinted at since the birth narrative. Zechariah's "waterless pit" (מִבּוֹר אֵין מַיִם בּוֹ/ἐκ λάκκου οὐκ ἔχοντος ὕδωρ) recalls the waterless pit (וְהַבּוֹר רֵק אֵין בּוֹ מָיִם/ὁ δὲ λάκκος κενός ὕδωρ οὐκ εἶχεν) into which Joseph was thrown by his brothers (Gen 37:24). The words translated "pit" here (בּוֹר/λάκκος) are also used as synonyms of Sheol (Isa 14:15; 38:18; Ps 28:1), the realm of the dead, and early Christian interpreters routinely understood this passage to be

---

6 Slight alteration: the NRSV's rendering of אָשִׁיב as "restore" has been changed to "repay" as befits both the context (cf. Exod 21:34) and the Septuagintal interpretation (ἀνταποδώσω). Paul Foster ("The Use of Zechariah in Matthew's Gospel," in *The Book of Zechariah and its Influence* [ed. Christopher Tuckett; Burlington, VT: Ashgate, 2003], 65–85) rightly argues that Matthew's citation resembles the MT more closely than the LXX but that there is not enough information here to determine the form of the text that Matthew knew.

7 On the Davidic overtones see Carol L. Meyers and Eric M. Meyers, "The term *melek* ('king') itself is a loaded one on the present context, which is unmistakably eschatological and which foreshadows the emergence of messianic language in intertestamental literature and the New Testament." *Zechariah 9–14: A New Translation with Introduction and Commentary* (AB 25C; New York: Doubleday, 1992), 123.

8 Carol L. Meyers and Eric M. Meyers, *Zechariah 9–14*, 133.

referring to redemption from death.[9] Given Matthew's description of
Gehenna as a prison for debtors and Jesus as the one who frees them
(5:21–26; 18:23–35), it is probable he would have read this passage accordingly.[10]

Finally, Zechariah says that this redemption from captivity will be a
"repayment" and also says that it will happen "by the blood of the covenant" (ἐν αἵματι διαθήκης). The only other time the phrase "blood of the
covenant" occurs in the Hebrew Bible is the covenant ceremony at
Sinai in Exod 24:8, where Moses takes the blood from the offerings
of the twelve tribes and throws half of it on the altar and half on the people saying, "Behold the blood of the covenant (הברית-דם/τὸ αἷμα τῆς
διαθήκης) which the LORD has made with you in accordance with all
these words" (NRSV). The implication in Zechariah is that God's repayment of the people takes place because of the covenant that was
cut at Sinai. The repeat reader of Matthew, as well as any reader who
has been initiated into the eucharistic practice that Matthew presupposes, knows that before Jesus dies in Jerusalem he will call his blood "the
blood of the covenant" (τὸ αἷμά μου τῆς διαθήκης) that is poured out for
many for the forgiveness of sins (26:28).

It is difficult to say how much of all this the evangelist himself hoped
to evoke, and even more difficult to ascertain what the first auditors of
the Gospel would have understood. At minimum, one must allow that
the combination of two passages describing the coming king who will
redeem the captives as a payment for wages is hardly accidental, particularly in light of the deep thematic unity with the whole of the Gospel
and the appearance of this same exegetical technique in the prologue.
Thus, Jesus enters Jerusalem as the humble savior spoken of by the
prophets who comes to redeem the people with the wages he has
earned.

---

9 E.g., Cyril of Jerusalem (*Catechetical Lecture* 12.10) says that the waterless pit is
    where the holy ones who rise in Matthew 27:52–53 had been. Didymus
    (*Comm. Zach.* 3.160–163) notes that the rich man in Luke 16:19–31 desires
    a drink of water because he is in the "waterless pit." See also Epiphanius, *Tes-
    timonia ex divinis et sacris scripturis*, 85.3; Theodoret, *Interpretatio in xii prophetas
    minors*, 81.1924.
10 See below on Matthew 27:52–53.

5.3 The passion and resurrection narrative (26:1–28:20)

5.3.1 The Last Supper

In 26:1–16 the stage is set for the crucifixion; the chief priests and elders make a plan (26:1–4), Jesus is anointed for burial (26:6–13), and Judas strikes a deal with the chief priests (26:14–16). Then, on the first day of Unleavened Bread, Jesus tells the disciples to go ahead of him and prepare the Passover.[11] During the meal Jesus predicts his betrayal and then the following episode occurs:

> Jesus took bread, and after blessing it he broke it, gave it to the disciples, and said, "Take, eat; this is my body." Then he took a cup, and after giving thanks he gave it to them, saying, "Drink from it, all of you; for this is my blood of the covenant, which is poured out for many for the forgiveness of sins (τοῦτο γάρ ἐστιν τὸ αἷμά μου τῆς διαθήκης τὸ περὶ πολλῶν ἐκχυννόμενον εἰς ἄφεσιν ἁμαρτιῶν). (26:26–28)

Though there may be an echo of the "new covenant" of Jer 31 (LXX 38) here, it is widely recognized that Matthew's words over the cup, like Mark's, are closer to Exod 24:8: "And taking the blood Moses scattered it on the people and said 'Behold the blood of the covenant (τὸ αἷμα τῆς διαθήκης) that the Lord made with you concerning all these words.'"[12] Matthew's well-known Moses typology also increases the likelihood of a connection.[13] Also, as noted above, this passage is cited only once in the Old Testament, in Zech 9, which is quoted as Jesus enters Jerusalem.

The words εἰς ἄφεσιν ἁμαρτιῶν are unique to the Matthean Last Supper, which is not surprising given Matthew's interest in the cancellation of sins that Jesus effects.[14] In the Hebrew Bible, the sacrifices at Sinai sig-

---

11 Jesus' instructions in 26:17–19 would seem to recall the similarly mysterious instructions that Jesus gave the disciples prior to their entry into Jerusalem. Timothy C. Gray (*The Temple in the Gospel of Mark: A Study in Its Narrative Role* [Grand Rapids: Baker, 2010], 100–102) argues that the parallels between the two passages in Mark encourage the reader to view Jesus' denunciation of the temple and the Last Supper in parallel.

12 See, however, the evocative quotation of Jer 31 in Matt 2:17–18 discussed in chapter 3 above.

13 See Dale C. Allison, *The New Moses: A Matthean Typology* (Minneapolis: Fortress Press, 1993).

14 This same phrase appears in Mark 1:4 to describe John's baptism. It is conspicuously absent from the Matthean parallel in Matthew 3.

nify the blood guilt incurred by parties who break the covenant.[15] In early Judaism and Christianity, however, the blood of the covenant in Exodus came to be seen as expiatory. Targum Onkelos and Pseudo-Jonathan describe the covenant sacrifice accordingly: "Moses took the blood and sprinkled (it) on the altar as an atonement (לכפרא) for the people. He said, 'This is the blood of the covenant which the Lord has made with you concerning all these things.'"[16] Hebrews 9:19–22 shows that this interpretation of the Sinaitic covenant existed in the first century and in Christian circles.[17]

In 20:28 Jesus explained that he would give his life to pay the price of release for the many in bondage. At the Last Supper he offers another interpretation of his coming death, here describing his coming death as a covenant sacrifice "for the cancellation of sins." Though Matthew lacks the words "Do this in my remembrance" (Luke 22:19; 1 Cor 11:24–25), the ongoing celebration of the Eucharist is presupposed.[18] One must ask, then, how the ransoming and the covenant sacrifice relate to each other. Is the cultic and covenantal interpretation given at the Last Supper a parallel or alternative explanation to Jesus' storing up of treasure in heaven on behalf of those in debt-bondage? In the previous chapter it was argued that the ransom-saying is in deep continuity with

---

15 William H. C. Propp, *Exodus 19–40: A New Translation with Introduction and Commentary* (AB 2 A; New York: Doubleday, 2006), 308–309.

16 Israel Drazin, *Targum Onkelos to Exodus: An English Translation of the Text with Analysis and Commentary* (Hoboken, NJ: Ktav Publishing, 1990), 238.

17 "For when every commandment had been told to all the people by Moses in accordance with the law, he took the blood of calves and goats, with water and scarlet wool and hyssop, and sprinkled both the scroll itself and all the people, saying, 'This is the blood of the covenant (τοῦτο τὸ αἷμα τῆς διαθήκης) that God has ordained for you.' And in the same way he sprinkled with the blood both the tent and all the vessels used in worship. Indeed, under the law almost everything is purified with blood, and without the shedding of blood there is no forgiveness of sins (χωρὶς αἱματεκχυσίας οὐ γίνεται ἄφεσις)" (NRSV).

18 Davies and Allison note, "[A]ll commentators presume that Matthew's first readers saw in the last supper the foundation of the Lord's Supper: 26.26–9 is an aetiological cult narrative. While agreeing, we observe that the text does not say this about itself. Jesus does not invite repetition of his actions…The last supper is then an example of how the text gives its full meaning only to readers who bring to it extra-textual knowledge, in this case knowledge of the Christian celebration of the eucharist." *A Critical and Exegetical Commentary on the Gospel according to Saint Matthew* (3 vols; ICC; Edinburgh: T&T Clark, 1988–1997), 3.465.

the Matthean narrative as a whole. Does the sacrificial "pouring out" of Jesus' blood relate in any definable way to the rest of the narrative?

It was noted in the discussion of the Sermon on the Mount in chapter 2 that the exchanges of the divine economy – the payment of treasure in the heavens in return for righteous deeds – take place within a familial relationship. The God who repays is repeatedly called "Father" (5:16, 45, 48; 6:1, 4, 6, 8–9, 14–15, 18, 26, 32; 7:11, 21), and those who do his will are called "sons" (5:9; 5:45). Those who do what the Sermon teaches are imitating the very qualities of their heavenly Father (5:48), qualities which are exemplified by Jesus himself as the narrative progresses. I would suggest that the Last Supper further nuances Matthew's portrait of Jesus as the one who pays the ransom-price for those in exile. In the Old Testament, God's ransoming of the people is frequently presented as a covenantal-familial act. One of the best examples of this is in Zech 9, a text echoed here at the Last Supper and at the triumphal entry: "By the blood of my covenant with you (בדם-בריתך/ἐν αἵματι διαθήκης), I will set your prisoners free from the waterless pit. Return to your stronghold, O prisoners of hope; today I declare that I will repay you double (משנה אשיב לך/διπλᾶ ἀνταποδώσω σοι)" (9:11–12). In this text the covenant is the means by which God ransoms the people.[19] Like Matt 26, this text points back to the covenant at Sinai, naming this bond between Israel and God as the ground of the redemption that God would bring and of God's double repayment of their meritorious works. God's repayment and deliverance of Israel are therefore acts of covenant faithfulness. Psalm 130:7 encapsulates this point well: "O Israel, hope in the LORD! For with the LORD there is covenant faithfulness (החסד/τὸ ἔλεος), and with him is a great redemption (פדות/λύτρωσις)." The potency of the image of redemption as a covenant act is increased by the biblical expectation that family members will pay the price to redeem kinsmen from debt slavery (Lev 25:47–49), and by the first-century practice of imprisoning debtors to compel them or their families to pay their debts.[20]

The picture that emerges from Matthew's twin descriptions of Jesus' giving on behalf of the many could be summarized as follows: Jesus

---

19 Both the Hebrew preposition ב and the Greek ἐν + dative could be taken instrumentally, i.e., God redeems the people *by means of* the blood of the covenant, or locatively, i.e., God redeems the people *in the context of* the covenant relationship.

20 See the discussion of 5:21–26 and 18:23–35 in chapter 2 above.

gives his life and so earns the ransom-price to redeem the many in debt-bondage. But, like God's previous saving acts on Israel's behalf and like kinsmen redeemers who pay the price to release debtors, this is an act of covenantal and familial faithfulness rather than an anonymous exchange between disinterested parties. His death is a covenant sacrifice that creates a bond which is the context of Jesus' ransoming and of all subsequent cross-bearing of his followers.

5.3.1.1 Excursus: treasure in heaven and sacrifice

Before going on, it is worth considering another, more tentative link between Jesus' death as earning superabundant treasures in heaven and Jesus' death as sacrifice. Biblical and post-biblical sources that link the binding of Isaac to the daily temple sacrifices and the Passover offer a possible analogy for how Jesus' self-giving might relate to the cultic pouring out of his blood. 2 Chronicles 3:1 claims that the mountain where Solomon built the temple was Mount Moriah, the very mountain where the near-sacrifice of Isaac had occurred.[21] As Jon D. Levenson has noted, this detail betrays an effort

> to endow Abraham's great act of obedience and faith with ongoing significance: the slaughter that he showed himself prepared to carry out was the first of innumerable sacrifices to be performed on that site... [J]ust as Abraham's intention met with divine favor and secured a rich blessing on his descendants, so would their own acts of service in the Temple prove acceptable to God and merit his continued good will toward them.[22]

By the time of *Jubilees* the Akedah was already seen as the basis of the Passover sacrifice, and rabbinic literature routinely bases the daily lamb sacrifices on it as well.[23] Targum Neofiti on Lev 22:27 explains that sacrificial lambs are used in order to

> remember the merit (למדכרא זכותא) of a man, the unique one (יחידה), who was bound on one of the mountains like a lamb for a burnt offering upon the altar. But (God) delivered him in his good mercies, and when his sons pray they will say in their hours of tribulation: "Answer us in this hour and

---

21   For our purposes it matters not if "Mount Moriah" was added to Genesis 22 to connect to 2 Chronicles or vice versa.

22   *The Death and Resurrection of the Beloved Son: The Transformation of Child Sacrifice in Judaism and Christianity* (New Haven: Yale University Press, 1993), 174.

23   *Jubilees* 17–18. See also *Tg. Onq.* and *Tg. Ps.-J* on Genesis 22, especially verse 14.

listen to the voice of our prayer and remember in our favor the binding of
Isaac our father."[24]

All sacrificial lambs recall the merit of Isaac, provoking God to remember him and so answer the prayers of his children. Similarly, when Lev
1:11 says the daily lamb offering must be slain on the north (צפנה) side of
the altar, *Leviticus Rabbah* vocalizes צפנה as the feminine passive participle
"hidden" to refer to the feminine noun Akedah, thereby making the
binding of Isaac the unseen source of the efficacy of the sacrifice:

> When our father Abraham bound Isaac his son, the Holy One (blessed be
> He!) established the institution of the two lambs, one in the morning and
> one in the evening [Exod 29:38–42]. Why so much? Because when Israel
> would sacrifice the daily offering on the altar and recite this verse ['hidden
> before the Lord'], the Holy One (blessed be He!) would remember the
> binding of Isaac.[25]

Whenever the sacrifice was made God would remember the merits of
Isaac "hidden" in heaven. To be sure, though Isaac was thought to be
a willing participant in his sacrifice and the mountain of the Akedah
was already understood to be the future site of the temple by the first
century, the efficacy of the temple sacrifices is not explicitly attributed
to Isaac's merits until much later. Indeed, one cannot exclude the possibility that this explanation of the efficacy of the temple cult was influenced by Christian claims about the salvific self-giving of Jesus, especially in the aftermath of the temple's destruction. Nevertheless, the
traditions linking Isaac's sacrifice to the temple sacrifice – which are
at least as old as 2 Chronicles – offer an intriguing analogy for thinking
about how Jesus' death as an act of meritorious self-giving might relate
to Jesus' death as a sacrifice. Matthew presents Jesus storing up treasure
in heaven for the many in debt, but also as a sacrifice for the forgiveness
of sins. Perhaps the emerging Christian cult was seen as a ritual appropriation of the merits of Christ stored up in the heavens, just as the temple cult was seen as an appropriation of the merits of Isaac.[26] Though

---

24 Robert Hayward, *Targum Neofiti 1: Leviticus. Translated, with Apparatus* (ArBib
    3; Collegeville, MN: Liturgical Press, 1994), 87. See also Levenson, *Death and
    Resurrection of the Beloved Son*, 184.

25 Translation from Gary Anderson's *Sin: A History* (New Haven: Yale University
    Press, 2009), 201. See also the discussion of this passage in Levenson, *Death and
    Resurrection of the Beloved Son*, 184–85.

26 Leroy Huizenga (*The New Isaac: Tradition and Intertextuality in the Gospel of Mat-
    thew* [NovTSup 131; Leiden: Brill, 2009]) argues that Isaac traditions play a sig-
    nificant role in Matthew.

this analogy from Akedah traditions is suggestive, I hasten to point out that it is speculative and should not distract from Jesus' redeeming gift as a covenantal-familial act, which is built on much firmer exegetical ground.

5.3.2 Gethsemane (26:36–56)

After the Last Supper Jesus goes with his disciples to Gethsemane and then tells them to stay put while he goes and prays. He takes Peter, James, and John with him, but then leaves even them and prays alone (26:39), just as he taught others to do if they would receive a wage with their Father in the heavens (6:5). The allusions to prior points in the narrative continue in what follows:

> Then he said to them, "I am deeply grieved, even to death; remain here, and stay awake with me." And going a little farther, he threw himself on the ground and prayed, "My Father (πάτερ μου), if it is possible, let this cup (ποτήριον τοῦτο) pass from me; yet not what I want but what you want." Then he came to the disciples and found them sleeping; and he said to Peter, "So, could you not stay awake with me one hour? Stay awake and pray that you may not come into the time of trial (προσεύχεσθε ἵνα μὴ εἰσέλθητε εἰς πειρασμόν); the spirit indeed is willing, but the flesh is weak." Again he went away for the second time and prayed, "My Father (πάτερ μου), if this cannot pass unless I drink it, your will be done (γενηθήτω τὸ θέλημά σου)." Again he came and found them sleeping, for their eyes were heavy. So leaving them again, he went away and prayed for the third time, saying the same words. (26:38–44 NRSV)

The cup that Jesus dreads drinking is of course the cup that he spoke of in 20:17–28 (esp. vv.22–23) while explaining that ruling with the Son of Man is payment for giving one's life.[27] Jesus' prayers recall the prayer

---

27 Though it is sometimes denied there is any connection with the cup that Jesus calls the blood of the covenant which is poured out for the many for the forgiveness of sins (26:27–28), the repeated association of Jesus' death with a cup are mutually reinforcing, even if the cup at the Last Supper is used to depict the sacrificial pouring out of blood, whereas the cup in 20:22–23 and in Gethsemane is a metaphor for the grisly fate that awaits Jesus. As noted in chapter 4, the cup metaphor is not necessarily a cup of God's wrath. See *T. Ab.* 1:3; 16:11–12; *Tg. Yer. I, Tg. Yer. II,* and *Tg. Neof. I* on Gen 40:23; *Tg. Neof.* on Deut 32:1. Luz, *Matthäus,* 3.161–62.

he taught to his followers.[28] He begins πάτερ μου, just as the Lord's Prayer begins πάτερ ἡμῶν. He tells Peter, James, and John to "pray that you may not come into the time of trial (προσεύχεσθε ἵνα μὴ εἰσέλθητε εἰς πειρασμόν)," recalling the last line of the Lord's Prayer: καὶ μὴ εἰσενέγκῃς ἡμᾶς εἰς πειρασμόν. Finally, in verse 42 Jesus quotes the Lord's Prayer: "My Father (πάτερ μου), if this cannot pass unless I drink it, your will be done (γενηθήτω τὸ θέλημά σου)." In the Lord's Prayer the words γενηθήτω τὸ θέλημά σου articulate the Matthean tension between the heavens, the realm where God's will is done, and earth, where God's will does not yet hold sway. Despite his agony (26:27 – 38), Jesus prays for his Father's will to be done on earth as it is in heaven. The tension between the heavens and earth that runs throughout Matthew comes to the fore here, as Jesus finds himself thinking "the things of people (τὰ τῶν ἀνθρώπων)" that had made Peter a trap to him.[29] In praying that God's will be done he renounces this earthly thinking to embrace the cross. Thus, Jesus exemplifies both the pattern of prayer and the self-renunciation that, according to Matthew, are repaid with treasure in heaven.

5.3.3 Enduring persecution (26:57 – 27:50)

After Jesus is arrested he is taken before "Caiaphas the high priest, where the scribes and elders had gathered" (26:57), at which point "the high priest and the whole Sanhedrin" began "seeking a false testimony against Jesus (ψευδομαρτυρίαν κατὰ τοῦ Ἰησοῦ)," bringing forward many false witnesses (ψευδομαρτύρων) so they could put him to death. This hearkens back once again to the Sermon on the Mount and the "great wage in the heavens" that is due when people "speak all kinds of evil against you falsely (καθ' ὑμῶν ψευδόμενοι)" (5:11).[30]

---

28 See Stephen Hultgren, *Narrative Elements in the Double Tradition: A Study of Their Place within the Framework of the Gospel Narrative* (BZNW 113; Berlin/New York: Walter de Gruyter, 2002), 290–301.

29 Cf. Athanasius, "And as for his saying 'if possible, let this cup pass,' see how, though having said these things, he rebuked Peter, saying 'You are not thinking the things of God, but the things of people.' For he desired what he entreated (God) to avoid, for on account of this he had come" (*C. Ar.* 26).

30 D and a handful of old Latin manuscripts (b c gl h k) lack ψευδόμενοι in 5:11. This purely Western variant is probably best explained as a harmonization to the

Following the trial before the Sanhedrin, Matthew continues to intimate that by going to the cross Jesus will be repaid with enthronement. After Pilate has scourged Jesus and handed him over to be crucified his soldiers bring Jesus to the governor's palace where an entire cohort of soldiers (600 to 1000 men) is gathered to pay fake homage as Jesus is stripped naked and given a scarlet robe and a crown of thorns. Matthew expands the sham coronation by adding the words "they put... a reed (κάλαμον) in his right hand, and kneeling before him they mocked him, saying 'Hail, King of the Jews!'" (27:29).[31] This unforgettable burlesque of Jesus' apparent lack of authority would perhaps recall the scepter of power (ῥάβδον δυνάμεως) that, according to the Psalm cited by Jesus in 26:64, the Lord sends out from Zion: "Sit at my right hand, till I make your enemies a footstool for your feet.' The Lord will send out from Sion a scepter of your power; rule in the midst of your enemies!" (Ps 109:1−2 LXX).[32] For the soldiers, the royal aspirations of this condemned prisoner are worthy only of gallows humor. For the readers of Matthew, however, a deeper irony lurks, as Jesus is about to be enthroned precisely because of the wages that he now stores up in the heavens.[33]

The parodic coronation in 27:27−31 is followed by a parodic enthronement in 27:38−44. Jesus is crucified with the charge "This is Jesus the King of the Jews" above his head, and with brigands at his right and left (εἷς ἐκ δεξιῶν καὶ εἷς ἐξ εὐωνύμων), recalling the request of the mother of James and John that they would take the thrones at Jesus' right and left (20:21).[34] Then the chief priests, scribes, and elders appear again, this time joining the crowd in mocking Jesus' claim to be God's son:

> Those passing by derided (ἐβλασφήμουν) him, shaking their heads and saying, "You who would destroy the temple and build it in three days, save yourself (σῶσον σεαυτόν)! If you are the Son of God, come down from the cross." Likewise also the chief priests along with the scribes and elders

---

parallel in Luke 6:22, aided, perhaps, by a desire to expand the opportunities for earning wages in heaven.

31   The words χαῖρε, βασιλεῦ τῶν Ἰουδαίων appear in Mark 15:18 as well.

32   In Matthew's quotation of Isaiah 42:1−4 (12:20) a reed is used as a symbol of vulnerability: κάλαμον συντετριμμένον οὐ κατεάξει.

33   See Joel Marcus, "Crucifixion as Parodic Exaltation," *JBL* 125 (2006): 73−87.

34   See the discussion of 20:21 in the previous chapter. Note also that, unlike Mark, Matthew says that the mother of the sons of Zebedee witnessed Jesus' crucifixion (27:56).

were mocking him, saying, "He saved others; he cannot save himself (ἄλλους ἔσωσεν, ἑαυτὸν οὐ δύναται σῶσαι). He is the King of Israel; let him come down now from the cross, and we will believe in him. He trusts in God; let God deliver him now, if he wants him; for he said, 'I am God's Son.'" The brigands who were crucified with him also taunted (ὠνείδιζον) him in the same way. (27:39–44)

The echoes of earlier points in the story continue, as Jesus endures taunting (ὠνείδιζον), which earns a great wage in the heavens (5:11–12). Jesus is told to save himself (σῶσον σεαυτόν) and is mocked for saving others but not being able to save himself (ἄλλους ἔσωσεν, ἑαυτὸν οὐ δύναται σῶσαι). The Gospel begins with the angelic promise that Jesus "will save (σώσει) his people from their sins" (1:21), and over the course of the narrative it has been revealed that Jesus saves them precisely by giving his life. Unlike Mark, Matthew also portrays Jesus being mocked for claiming to be the Son of God (27:40, 43). In chapter 4, the devil claims that if Jesus is the Son of God he should perform miraculous deeds on his own behalf (4:3, 6), and then at Caesarea Philippi and before the Sanhedrin Jesus' identity as Son of God is revealed to be inextricable from his death on the cross. Many have noted the irony of Jesus, the true king, being mocked as a messianic pretender. Less often noticed is the way the narrative as a whole prepares for this moment. Jesus begins his ministry by claiming that those who are persecuted on account of righteousness are blessed because "theirs is the kingdom of the heavens" (5:11) and ends it by teaching his followers that those who forsake their possessions and their lives will share in his rule. The irony here is, therefore, much richer than commentators have usually seen: when Jesus endures mockery and beatings as a sham king, he is enduring the suffering that God will repay with an actual kingship.[35]

---

35 Marcus ("Crucifixion as Parodic Exaltation") notes that victims of crucifixion sometimes resisted being mocked by exhibiting "unaccountable dignity," for instance, by laughing or singing songs of victory as they are crucified (e.g., B.J. 3.321; Geog. 3.4.18). "In such situations," Marcus writes, "the height of the cross might undergo a transvaluation and be seen to point toward the spiritual eminence rather than the arrogance of the victim" (87). Marcus concludes his essay by suggesting, "For many early Christians, this reversal of a reversal, which turned penal mockery on its head, was probably the inner meaning of Jesus' crucifixion" (ibid.). Marcus presents the "mockery of mockery" in the gospels as if it were in perfect continuity with the other historical examples of resistance to the degradation of crucifixion. Unlike these historical analogues, however, the Jesus of the gospels, especially Matthew and Mark, does not respond to crucifixion with "unaccountable dignity." Rather than singing songs

5.3.4 The death of Jesus and the preliminary repayment of heavenly treasure (27:45–28:20)

We arrive now at Jesus' death and the extraordinary phenomena that follow it. In the following I shall argue that Matthew depicts the first-fruits – or, better, the down payment – of the eschatological repayment of deeds. Scholars are not in agreement regarding the eschatological significance of Jesus' death, so before going on it is necessary first to ascertain whether Matthew does in fact present Jesus' death as an eschatological event.

Many scholars affirm that Matthew portrays Jesus' death as an apocalyptic-eschatological event of great import; the darkness, the earthquake, and Jesus' resurrection among other things are clear signs that something eschatological is taking place.[36] At the same time, however, Matthew frequently looks toward Jesus' future Parousia as the moment when he will appear in sight of all peoples and judge them (7:15–23; 13:24–30, 36–43, 47–50; 16:27; 25:31–46). The question that emerges in view of these apparently contradictory Matthean emphases is how Jesus' death and resurrection relate to the eschaton itself. Differently put, what is the relationship between realized and unrealized eschatology in Matthew?

John P. Meier, who argues that Matthew presents Jesus' death and resurrection as *die Wende der Zeit*, is a good representative of the view

---

of victory or smiling as he is nailed to the cross, Matthew presents Jesus remaining silent until he cries out in despair (27:46). For Matthew the transformation from parodic exaltation (i.e., mocking the victim's kingly aspirations) to ironic exaltation (i.e., the mocked victim is actually exalted) is not based on Jesus' bravado in the face of death, but on the obedience that the readers know is about to be repaid. Jesus enacts "the things of God" (16:21–28).

36 Davies and Allison (*Matthew*, 3.639) claim that the signs in 27:51–53 "are eschatological in nature. It follows that the Day of the Lord dawns on Golgotha: the divine judgment descends, and the first-fruits of the resurrection are gathered. The end of Jesus is the end of the world in miniature." Nolland (*Matthew*, 1214) writes: "With the opening of the tombs as the third element, the eschatological potential of the earth being shaken and the rocks being split is now clearly activated. But Matthew makes it quite plain that he is concerned here with proleptic manifestations of eschatological realities, not with the full substance of those realities." See also David Hill, "Matthew 27:51–53 in the Theology of the Evangelist," *IBS* 7 (1985): 76–87; Raymond E. Brown, *The Death of the Messiah*, (2 vols.; ABRL; New York: Doubleday, 1994), 2.1126.

that the end has in some sense already arrived.[37] Meier's main evidence is 27:51–54, 28:2–3, and 28:16–20. The tearing of the temple veil (27:51) is notoriously ambiguous, being interpreted variously as the sign of free access to God for all, or as a warning of God's judgment against the temple and its coming destruction in 70 c.e.[38] In any case, the temple, one of the foundations of the world, will not continue to function.[39] The Matthean additions in vv.51b-54 provide further support: the earthquake is a common apocalyptic motif denoting God's judgment on the old aeon. The resurrection of the holy ones (27:52–53) is as bold an eschatological sign as one could hope for, indicating that the resurrection of the dead takes place proleptically at the death of Christ. The addition of an earthquake and an angel in 28:2–3 extends eschatological imagery into the resurrection. Following C. H. Dodd and R. H. Lightfoot, Meier labels the final appearance of the risen Lord in 28:16–20 a "proleptic parousia," wherein Jesus declares his own enthronement in the language of Daniel 7 (28:18b) and declares that he will always be present with the church (28:20b).[40] Meier concludes: "Mt sees the death-resurrection as an eschatological event in which the Kingdom breaks into this aeon in a new, fuller way."[41]

At the same time, Meier is careful to distinguish between his characterization of Matthean eschatology and the Gospel according to John, contending that while Matthew's eschatology is more realized than is usually admitted and that it might be fair to say that Matthew is moving toward John's position, he still awaits the "end of the age" (συντέλεια τοῦ αἰῶνος) (28:20):

> The breaking-in of the Kingdom has put an end to the old aeon in principle, but not in full-blown reality. The old age continues, the world is a *corpus mixtum* in which the devil as well as the Son of Man can plant

---

37 *Law and History in Matthew's Gospel* (AnBib 71; Rome: Biblical Institute Press, 1976), 30–40.

38 See also Daniel M. Gurtner, *The Torn Veil: Matthew's Exposition of the Death of Jesus* (SNTSMS 139; Cambridge: Cambridge University Press, 2007).

39 Meier cites *Pirke Avot* I, 2.

40 Dodd, "Matthew and Paul," in *New Testament Studies* (Manchester, Manchester University Press, 1968), 55; Lightfoot, *Locality and Doctrine in the Gospels* (London: Hodder & Stoughton, 1938), 67–72. Gerhard Barth reaches the same conclusion, "Law and Christology," in *Tradition and Interpretation in Matthew* (Philadelphia: The Westminster Press, 1963), 133–34.

41 *Law and History*, 38.

seed (Mt 13:36–43). The final, visible separation that destroys the old age once and for all still lies in the future, since the harvest is expressly said to be the *synteleia aiōnos* [13:30–40].[42]

Yet, the promise of the risen Lord's presence with his followers and the signs of God's eschatological judgment (rending of the veil, earthquake, resurrection from the dead, angels, and the enthronement of the Son of Man) means that even as Jesus' followers await the end of the age, the end has already begun.

David C. Sim has objected to this proposal, arguing that "Meier has clearly exaggerated the importance of the eschatological nature of the death and resurrection of Jesus."[43] Sim's main counterargument is that Matthew stresses the coming Parousia more than the other evangelists and that Matthew does not portray heaven and earth "passing away" as he would have done if Jesus' death and resurrection truly ushered in the end of all things. These arguments miss their target because Meier does not deny the importance of the coming Parousia and the coming passing away of heaven and earth. Sim points to Matthew's unrealized eschatology without addressing the crucial question of why there are so many indicators in the passion narrative that something eschatological is happening.

The context of the debate for Sim is the question of whether the Matthean community was Law-observant. Against Meier's proposal that 5:18 ("not one iota or pen-stroke will pass from the Law until all is accomplished") refers to Jesus' death and resurrection, Sim argues that this interpretation "cannot be squared with the clear meaning of 5:17. If the Matthean Jesus claims in 5:18 that the law does become invalid with this death or resurrection, then he obviously did come to abolish the law, and this is a patent contradiction of what he says in the preceding verse."[44] This argument seems correct so far as it goes. It does not necessarily follow, however, that just because "all things" are not yet accomplished in Jesus' death and resurrection that Meier is

---

42   *Law and History*, 38–39. Meier notes that phrase συντέλεια τοῦ αἰῶνος is peculiar to Matthew in the NT.
43   "The Meaning of παλιγγενεσία in Matthew 19.28," *JSNT* 50 (1993): 3–12, 10. See also his remarks in *The Gospel of Matthew and Christian Judaism: the History and Social Setting and Social Setting of the Matthean Community* (Edinburgh: T&T Clark, 1998), 124–25.
44   *The Gospel of Matthew and Christian Judaism*, 124–25.

mistaken in saying that Jesus' death brings about the in-breaking of the Kingdom, even if the church must await the end of the age.

Another significant proponent of a non-eschatological reading of the passion narrative is Ulrich Luz, who makes three arguments: (1) some of the phenomena following Jesus' death, such as the earthquake and the opening of the tombs, could be taken to indicate the apocalyptic *Weltenwende* had occurred, but others, such as the tearing of the veil, are not traditional eschatological signs; (2) the fact that the resurrected holy ones do not appear in heaven but in the earthly city of Jerusalem suggests that their rising does not indicate an eschatological turning point;[45] (3) other passages in Matthew clearly indicate that the apocalyptic *Weltenwende* will occur in the future at the Parousia of the Son of Man.[46] In response to the first argument, one might ask how many eschatological signs are necessary before one admits that something eschatological is happening. Let us suppose for the sake of argument that the tearing of the veil was not a traditional eschatological sign; with an earthquake, the opening of tombs, resurrections, and the enthronement of the Son of Man, would one need the additional support of an eschatological tearing of the veil? It is also worth noting that Gurtner has argued that the tearing of the veil, which was sometimes associated with the heavenly firmament from Genesis 1:6, connotes the opening of heaven, a well-attested eschatological image.[47] Moreover, inasmuch as the rending of the veil presages the temple's coming destruction, it is for Matthew an eschatological sign, since the temple's destruction is closely as-

---

45 "Daß die Auferstandenen nach V 53 nicht ins himmlische Jerusalem eingehen, sondern im irdischen Jerusalem den Menschen des alten Äons ersheinen, spricht gegen eine Interpretation des Texts als Weltenwende" *Das Evangelium nach Matthäus* (4 vols.; EKK 1/1–4; Düsseldorf: Benziger, 1990–2002), 4.370.

46 *Matthäus*, 4.370.

47 See Isa 64:1. Gurtner concludes: though there was no pre-Matthean precedent to indicate what a torn temple veil might symbolize, "there *is* evidence for what the veil itself symbolizes. Though a few early texts present it as representing the temple itself, we saw that as early as Mark or Josephus, and probably earlier, the veil of the temple was part of a larger Jewish cosmology, dating perhaps to Ezekiel but surely at least to Ben Sira. This cosmology saw the different parts of the temple as representative of different parts of the universe; the veil, in this scheme, represented the heavenly firmament from Gen. 1:6... Its rending then connoted the opening of heaven, a well-attested apocalyptic image introducing a revelatory assertion" (*The Torn Veil*, 200–201).

sociated with the Parousia in the eschatological discourse.[48] Luz's second and third arguments, like Sim's, assume that Matthean eschatology must be either entirely realized or unrealized. It is true that the resurrected holy ones are not portrayed entering heaven, but in depicting a mini-resurrection from the dead, one might say that Matthew has shown heaven entering earth. The consummation is not complete, and most of the dead remain in their tombs, but by claiming that "the bodies of many holy ones who had been asleep were raised …and appeared to many in the holy city" (27:52) Matthew depicts another visible sign that the eschaton has broken in, even if the end of the age remains in the future. There is no gainsaying Matthew's emphasis on the future Parousia, but the clear eschatological signs in the passion narrative remain. The modern exegete may find these two emphases contradictory, but there they are.[49]

Meier and others − such as Davies and Allison, Senior, Nolland, Brown, and Gurtner − who see some sort of eschatological in-breaking in the events surrounding Jesus' death and resurrection would seem to be correct. One final argument should put to rest any lingering doubts on this point. During the eschatological discourse in chapter 24, Jesus describes the coming of the Son of Man that will occur after the great tribulation:

> Immediately after the tribulation of those days the sun will be darkened, and the moon will not give its light; the stars will fall from heaven, and the powers of the heavens will be shaken. And then the sign of the Son

---

48   Luz (*Matthäus*, 4.363), Donald Senior (*Matthew* [ANTC; Nashville: Abingdon Press, 1998], 334), and Davies and Allison (*Matthew*, 3.630−31) argue that the veil's rending foreshadows or symbolizes the coming destruction of the temple, an event that Jesus had prophesied and which is recalled by the passers-by taunting Jesus (27:40). Gurtner argues that the rending marks the eschatological turning of the ages and the removal of cultic barriers between the holy and the less holy. If the cultic function of the temple were to cease, however, the temple itself would, from a theological point of view, be as good as destroyed, i.e., the difference between this proposal and that of Luz et al. is only a difference of emphasis.

49   Ronald L. Troxel has argued that the events of 27:51−53 do not infuse Jesus' death with eschatological significance but are rather intended to provoke the centurion's confession of Jesus as the Son of God in verse 54 ("Matt 27.51−4 Reconsidered: Its Role in the Passion Narrative, Meaning, and Origin," *NTS* 48 [2002]: 30−47), claiming that Matthew does not elsewhere infuse resurrection with eschatological import. Yet, as noted in the last chapter, resurrection is precisely what Jesus repeatedly says will be meted out in the eschaton.

of Man will appear in heaven, and then all the tribes of the earth will
mourn, and they will see 'the Son of Man coming on the clouds of heaven'
with power and much glory. And he will send out his angels with a loud
trumpet call, and they will gather his elect from the four winds, from one
end of the heavens to the other. (24:29–31)

All of these signs of the eschaton occur in Matthew's account of the
death and resurrection of Jesus in roughly the same order: first there
is the tribulation and suffering of Jesus' death. Then the heavenly powers fail and darkness settles over the whole land (27:45). Following Jesus'
death, signs appear (27:51–53; 28:2). The nations are gripped with fear
(27:54; 28:4), and an angel is sent to proclaim the news of Jesus' presence (28:2–7). Finally, the Son of Man appears, having been given all
authority in heaven and earth (28:18). The death and resurrection of
Jesus is, therefore, "the end of the world in miniature."[50] But what of
Matthew's emphasis on the Parousia that lies ahead? I would suggest
that the overlapping of realized and unrealized eschatology in Matthew
is best summarized by the final sentence of the Gospel: "And behold, I
am with you always until the end of the age" (28:20). Jesus, who has
already been raised from the dead and given all authority, is present
with the disciples, a fact which relieves some of the unresolved tension
in Markan eschatology. At the same time, however, they await his Parousia at the end of the age.[51] We turn now to analyze the death and
resurrection in greater detail.

5.3.5 The eschatological down payment (27:45–54)

God appears to be silent in 27:32–50. Jesus is mocked for claiming to be
the Son of God and God seems uninterested in doing anything about it.
For three hours preceding Jesus' death, darkness settled over the whole
land (27:45), recalling the failure of the heavenly powers that Jesus had
said would occur after the great tribulation and before the eschaton.
After Jesus dies, however, God himself appears in an explosion of super-
natural occurrences: (1) the veil of the temple is torn (ἐσχίσθη) from top

---

50 Davies and Allison, *Matthew*, 3.639.
51 28:17 provides another convenient summary of Matthean eschatology: the
    eleven see the risen Jesus and worship him, but some of them doubt (οἱ δὲ ἐδί-
    στασαν). The proleptic Parousia has given the eleven a taste of the end, but it
    has not been fully consummated, and so doubt persists.

to bottom; (2) the earth is shaken; (3) the rocks are split; (4) the tombs are opened and "many" holy ones rise.

Καὶ ἰδοὺ τὸ καταπέτασμα τοῦ ναοῦ ἐσχίσθη ἀπ' ἄνωθεν ἕως κάτω εἰς δύο
καὶ ἡ γῆ ἐσείσθη
καὶ αἱ πέτραι ἐσχίσθησαν,
καὶ τὰ μνημεῖα ἀνεῴχθησαν
καὶ πολλὰ σώματα τῶν κεκοιμημένων ἁγίων ἠγέρθησαν,
καὶ ἐξελθόντες ἐκ τῶν μνημείων μετὰ τὴν ἔγερσιν αὐτοῦ εἰσῆλθον εἰς τὴν ἁγίαν πόλιν καὶ ἐνεφανίσθησαν πολλοῖς. (27:51–53)

The breathless series of divine passives indicates that God is on the loose, as it were, rendering proleptic eschatological judgment – both positive and negative – in the aftermath of Jesus' death. Though Jesus seemed to have been abandoned, it was his mission to give his life. God did not respond, therefore, until Jesus had given his life as the ransom-price for the many.

The proleptic eschaton continues on Sunday, when an angel descends from the sky and rolls away the stone covering Jesus' grave, causing an earthquake (28:2).[52] Those guarding the grave are shaken with fear and become like dead men. The angel announces to Mary Magdalene and "the other Mary" that Jesus has been raised from among the dead ones (ἠγέρθη ἀπὸ τῶν νεκρῶν) and that they must go tell his disciples. Here again we see the pattern of an earthquake, the appearance of an angel, and a resurrection from among the dead.

After the risen Jesus appears to the women, he appears to the eleven on a mountain in Galilee and says the following:

All authority in heaven and on earth was given to me (ἐδόθη μοι πᾶσα ἐξουσία ἐν οὐρανῷ καὶ ἐπὶ τῆς γῆς.). Go, therefore, and make disciples of all the nations (πάντα τὰ ἔθνη), baptizing them in the name of the Father and of the Son and of the Holy Spirit, teaching them to observe all that I have commanded you. And behold, I am with you all days until the end of the age.

In Daniel 7:14 the Son of Man is given authority (ἐδόθη αὐτῷ ἐξουσία) and all the nations (πάντα τὰ ἔθνη τῆς γῆς) come to serve him.[53] Jesus' reign as Son of Man has begun, and the disciples are charged with the task of teaching "all the nations" to obey him. Jesus has thus blazed the trail that he calls all who would be his disciples to follow: he gave his life and earned eternal life and eschatological reign.

---

52 Nolland, *Matthew*, 1247.
53 See the discussion of Matthew's use of Daniel 7 in chapter 4.

I have saved the rising of the holy ones in 27:52–53 for last because it is among the most difficult passages in the Gospel. The principal difficulty stems from the words μετὰ τὴν ἔγερσιν αὐτοῦ that govern all of v.53. Matthew appears to say that the holy ones were raised immediately after Jesus' death, which would mean they waited in their tombs for two days before coming out and entering the city.[54] Some have proposed that the problem be solved by means of textual emendation;[55] others admit that no one solution is fully satisfactory.[56] Many have also noted that it seems a bit awkward for an early Christian text to portray a resurrection that takes place before the resurrection of Jesus, who is the "first fruits" of the resurrection (1 Cor 15:20, 23) and the first-born from among the dead (Col 1:18).[57] Others have attempted to deal with these problems by arguing that this little resurrection is an apocalyptic vision of the future resurrection rather than a description of an actual space-time event, a proposal that does not square well with the fact that the resurrected holy ones are said to have come out of the tombs and been made clear (ἐνεφανίσθησαν) to many.[58]

Our analysis of the narrative as a whole may provide a way beyond these questions. The common shortcoming of most attempts to explain this passage is that they have focused on the relationship of the resurrection of the holy ones to Jesus' resurrection; did their resurrection really precede his? What did they do for two days in the tomb while waiting for Jesus' resurrection? Perhaps these problems have remained unsolva-

---

54 Senior, *Matthew*, 334.
55 Troxel ("Matt 27:51–54 Reconsidered," 37) and Davies and Allison, (*Matthew*, 3.634) appeal to the absence of μετὰ τὴν ἔγερσιν from the Diatessaron, the Palestinian Syriac Lectionary, and Egerton Papyrus 3 to suggest it was a later insertion. This is extraordinarily weak manuscript evidence. Moreover, the very difficulty of the text as it stands in ℵ B et al. would create a strong motive for a copyist to omit the phrase.
56 E.g., Luz, *Matthäus*, 4.366–67.
57 Some have attempted to solve this problem by arguing that it was a resuscitation rather than a resurrection. E.g., Craig S. Keener, *A Commentary on the Gospel of Matthew* (Grand Rapids: Eerdmans, 1999), 685–86. See the rebuttal of Brown, *Death of the Messiah*, 2.1132–33. Serge Wüthrich argues that the presence in 27:55–56 of many women, some of whom are mothers, hints that Jesus' death paradoxically leads to his birth as the firstborn from among the dead. "Naître de mourir: la mort de Jésus dans l'Évangile de Matthieu (Mt 27.51–56)," *NTS* 56 (2010): 313–25, 320–22.
58 E.g., Gurtner (*The Torn Veil*, 160–169); Kenneth L. Waters, Sr., "Matthew 27:52–53 as Apocalyptic Apostrophe: Temporal Spatial Collapse in the Gospel of Matthew," *JBL* 122 (2003): 489–515.

ble precisely because they focus on how vv. 52–53 relate to Jesus' resurrection, whereas the story itself is primarily concerned with the effects
of Jesus' obedient death. Before Jesus enters Jerusalem he says he will
give his life and be repaid with (1) resurrection, (2) rule as the Son of
Man, and (3) the price of release for the many in debt-bondage. Matthew clearly depicts the first two of these: Jesus is raised from the
dead and tells the eleven that "All authority in heaven and on earth
was given to me" (28:18), echoing Daniel 7:14. His rule has begun
even as it awaits the final consummation at the Parousia. But what of
the price of release for the many in bondage? I would suggest that
the main thrust of 27:52–53 is to add this essential element: *Jesus
gives his life to earn the ransom-price for the many, so it is after his death
that Matthew portrays the holy ones bursting forth from their graves.* As we
have seen, Jesus saves his people from debt-bondage and exile resulting
from sin, and, for Matthew, debtor's prison – the place where a debtor
waits until his debt is paid – is the realm of the dead.[59] The resurrection
of the holy ones in vv.52–53 shows that Jesus has earned their price of
release. While the timing of their resurrection and entry into Jerusalem
remains unclear, it is in deep continuity with the Gospel as a whole to
connect their resurrection with Jesus' death, for it is in giving his life that
he earns the price of release.

Matthew's use of Scripture reinforces the sense that Jesus has released the holy ones from bondage. Most scholars agree that Ezekiel
37's vision of the reanimation of dry bones is significant here.[60] After
Ezekiel recounts a vision of the reanimation of dry bones he is given
an interpretation:

> And the Lord spoke to me, saying: Son of man, these bones are the whole
> house of Israel, and they say, "Our bones have become dry; our hope has
> perished; we are lost." Therefore, prophesy, and say, This is what the Lord
> says: Behold, I am opening your tombs (ἰδοὺ ἐγὼ ἀνοίγω ὑμῶν τὰ μνήματα)
> and will bring you up out of your tombs and bring you into the land of
> Israel, and you shall know that I am the Lord, when I open your graves
> so that I might bring my people up out of their graves. (37:11–13 NETS)

Note the verbal similarity between God's promise to open the tombs in
Ezekiel (ἰδοὺ ἐγὼ ἀνοίγω ὑμῶν τὰ μνήματα) and the divine passive in
Matthew: "the tombs were opened (τὰ μνημεῖα ἀνεῴχθησαν)." In Ezekiel
the reanimation of corpses signifies the coming end of exile, and later

---

59   See the discussion in chapter 2.
60   E.g., Nolland, *Matthew*, 1214; Davies and Allison, *Matthew*, 3.633.

Jews and Christians read it as a prophecy of the resurrection of the dead.[61] Both readings of the text are equally appropriate to Matthew, which depicts Jesus bringing both eternal life and an end to captivity.[62] The evocative quotation of Isaiah 62 and Zechariah 9 at the triumphal entry also prepares for this moment. In verses 11 – 12 Zechariah says: "because of the blood of my covenant with you, I will set your prisoners free from the waterless pit (מבור אין מים בו/ἐκ λάκκου οὐκ ἔχοντος ὕδωρ). Return to your stronghold, O prisoners of hope; today I declare that I will repay you double." The thematic coherence of this passage with Matthew could hardly be greater; because of the blood of the covenant, God will set the prisoners free, repaying them double. As noted above, the pit (בור/λάκκος) could refer to the realm of the dead, and this passage was frequently read this way by early Christians.[63] Cyril of Jerusalem made this connection explicit while discussing the phenomena that followed Jesus' death: "Tombs were opened, and the dead arose, because of him who was free among the dead; he sent forth his prisoners out of the waterless pit."[64]

---

61 E.g., 4Q385.

62 Davies and Allison (*Matthew*, 3.629) suggest that Zech 14:4–5, another text that was read as a prophecy of resurrection, is also significant here.

63 In addition to the evidence cited above see the link between "the pit" and ransoming in Job 33:24, 28 MT and Ps 49:8–10.

64 *Catechetical Lecture* 13.34. It was common for early interpreters of the New Testament to read 27:52–53 in light of Christ's decent into Hades. For instance, Ignatius of Antioch said that Jesus' crucifixion was witnessed by those in heaven, those on the earth, and those under the earth (*Trall.* 9:2). A later, perhaps fourth century, expansion of Ignatius' letter explains that "those under the earth" refers to "the multitude that arose along with the Lord. For says the Scripture, 'Many bodies of the saints that slept arose, their graves being opened.' He descended, indeed, into Hades alone, but He arose accompanied by a multitude." Likewise Cyril of Jerusalem says that Jesus "descended into hell alone, but ascended thence with a great company; for He went down to death, and many bodies of the saints which slept arose through Him." Most if not all modern scholars have been unimpressed with this view, in part because Matthew says nothing of Jesus himself personally entering the realm of the dead (though see 28:7; 12:40). Moreover, in Matthew it appears that Jesus did not ascend with the multitude; rather, they came up from their graves immediately after his death, or at least because of his death. Nevertheless, the analysis presented here offers partial corroboration of the early interpretation. Matthew may not say unequivocally that Jesus descended to the dead, but he does pay their ransom-price. Like a kinsman redeemer, he generates the currency required to bring the holy ones up from their graves.

From this angle one can see the importance of this difficult passage in the narrative. The events occurring after Jesus' death are a foretaste of what is to come; the Jerusalem temple is set aside, the holy ones are given eternal life, and Gentiles fear greatly and come to belief. The church lives in the time between Jesus' initial enthronement as Son of Man and the end of the age when he will return to "repay everyone according to their deeds" (16:27). The resurrection of the holy ones is, therefore, what one might call a down payment; Jesus told the disciples that cross-bearers would be repaid with life and that his cross-bearing would earn the price of release for the many in bondage. In Matthew's day this had not yet come to pass, but the rising of the holy ones is "proof" that it would. The fourth century bishop Ambrose (ca. 339–397), speaking on the occasion of his brother's death, expresses this well:

> [Elijah and Peter] purchased (*redemerunt*) the resurrection of another by their tears. Shall we doubt that our resurrection was purchased by the Passion of Christ? When he gave up his spirit to show that he had died for our resurrection, he exemplified the course of the resurrection itself. For, as soon as he cried out with a loud voice and gave up his spirit, the earth quaked, and the rocks were rent, and the tombs were opened, and many bodies of the saints who had fallen asleep arose, and, coming forth out of the tombs after his resurrection, they came into the holy city and appeared to many. If these things occurred when he gave up his spirit, why should we think them incredible when he returns for the judgment, especially since this earlier resurrection is a proof (*documentum*) of that future resurrection, a pattern (*exemplum*) of the reality to come? Indeed, it is less a pattern than it is the truth itself (*Minus autem exemplum est quam veritas*).[65]

Seeking to convince his auditors that Christ, by his passion, had purchased their resurrection, he says that the resurrection of the holy ones is a *documentum* or *exemplum* of the reality to come.[66] They have, as it were, already been given a receipt or proof of purchase that ensures them that they will receive the resurrection purchased by the passion of Christ. Then, correcting himself, Ambrose notes that this little resurrection is less an *exemplum* than it is the reality itself, an observation that accords perfectly with Matthew's mix of realized and unrealized eschatology; the resurrection of the holy ones is an eschatological event sig-

---

65   *Exc.* II.83–84. Translation altered from John J. Sullivan, C. S. Sp. and Martin R. P. McGuire, *Funeral Orations by Saint Gregory Nazianzen and Saint Ambrose* (FC 22; Washington, D. C.: Catholic University of America, 1953), 233–34.
66   See also Chrysostom *Hom.* 87

naling the in-breaking of the kingdom, not merely an eschatological sign. I would contend that Ambrose accurately captures the significance of 27:52–53; Jesus had said he would, by his passion, earn the ransom-price for "the many" in exile and debt-bondage. At the conclusion of his passion, the initial payment is made and holy ones who had been dead are given eternal life, just as all the righteous will be when the final settling of accounts (16:27; 18:23; 25:14–30) occurs.[67]

In response to all this, one may object that Matthew does not actually say that the little resurrection in 27:52–53 is the proof that by his obedient death Jesus earned the ransom-price to redeem captive debtors, including those in the realm of the dead. Have we left the realm of exegesis and wandered into patristic speculation? In response, it is necessary to point out that this is a reading of the events following Jesus' death in light of the preceding narrative. One can only guess what the significance of this tradition might have been prior to its current place in Matthew. Attempts to make sense of this passage by focusing on its relationship with Jesus' resurrection have, it is safe to say, largely failed. In its current context, however, it rounds out the series of eschatological events following Jesus' death, demonstrating that everything Jesus had said would come to pass: he gives his life and is raised from the dead, given authority over heaven and earth, and his wages overflow to the many. Matthew places the full realization of this repayment of wages firmly in the eschatological future while also depicting the proleptic fulfillment of this tripartite promise. Readers of Matthew are told to follow Jesus in bearing crosses in order to store up treasure in heaven for themselves and for others; Jesus' death and resurrection function as the proof that the divine economy is, one might say, credible.[68]

---

67 Cf. the Pauline notion of the Spirit as the ἀρραβών (ערבון) – the pledge or down payment – that ensures that full payment will be made in the eschaton. In 2 Corinthians 5:4–5 the ἀρραβών of the Spirit is the down payment prior to mortal bodies being "swallowed up by life." See also 1:22. In Ephesians 1:13–14 the Holy Spirit is the "ἀρραβών of our inheritance, for the redemption of the possession."

68 In light of the preceding it is worth noting one other possible link between 27:52–53 and the preceding narrative. In 20:28 the price of release is said to be paid for the "many" (ἀντὶ πολλῶν). In 26:28 Jesus says his blood is poured out to cancel the sins of the many (περὶ πολλῶν). Then, after Jesus' death the "many" (πολλά) bodies of the holy ones who had fallen asleep are raised and enter the holy city, appearing to "many" (πολλοῖς). The word πολύς is very common and would probably not, of itself, recall 20:28 and 26:28. On the other hand, if these verses exist primarily to show that Jesus' wage earning re-

5.3.6 A final note on inference and redaction

As noted in the introduction to this chapter, there is no explicit economic language in the passion and resurrection narrative. Matthew never stops the action to remind the readers that when Jesus endures abuse and gives his life he is doing the very things he had said earn treasure in heaven. Again, one might object that any exegetical proposal that moves beyond the explicit details of the text is too speculative. Yet, such inferences are a *sine qua non* of even the simplest narratives; though the gospels tend to be episodic and do not always evince clear, logical progression from one pericope to the next, they all have plots, which means later events sometimes presuppose earlier ones.[69] The use of irony in the passion narrative is a good example of this. For instance, in Matt 27:40–42 the crucified Jesus is mocked with the words "He saved others; he cannot save himself!" Commentators routinely note that it precisely by not saving himself that he saves others. Matthew does not actually say this of course; one must make an inference based on what has already been said.[70] The question, then, is not whether it is legitimate to make inferences; it is indisputable that the passion narrative implies things beyond what is stated explicitly. The question is whether a particular inference is justified on the basis of the preceding narrative. In this study we have seen that while he is on the way to Jerusalem Jesus claims that he will give his life and be repaid with resurrection, rule as Son of Man, and the ransom-price for his people in debt-bondage. In the proleptic eschaton of 27:45–28:20 Matthew portrays Jesus' resurrection, rule as Son of Man, and the rising of holy ones from among the dead. It takes no great interpretive subtlety to make a connection between what Jesus said would happen when he went

---

dounds to "the many," including the captive dead, then Matthew's use of the word πολύς here may be significant. The many holy ones in the realm of the dead are set free by Jesus' self-giving, appearing to "many" to prove to them that their redemption is also at hand. Unlike passages such as 23:37, Matthew here casts Jerusalem in a positive light, calling it "the holy city." In this passage at least, Jerusalem is not the city that murders the prophets, but the city of the people of God where the proof of the redemption won by Jesus is "made manifest" to all of captive Israel.

69 In contrast to the sayings gospel *Gospel of Thomas*.
70 This inference is also commonly made by readers of the Mark. E.g., Joel Marcus, *Mark 8–16: A New Translation with Introduction and Commentary* (AB 27a; New Haven: Yale University Press, 2009), 1052.

to Jerusalem and what Matthew then portrays happening, particularly when this connection explains why the holy ones rise immediately after Jesus' death, rather than after his resurrection.

Once again, a brief comparison with the other canonical gospels may be helpful. As noted above, Matthew alone stresses that cross-bearers are repaid with participation in the rule of the Son of Man, and Matthew alone fleshes out the meaning of the ransom saying against the backdrop of debt-bondage and divine repayment for cross-bearing. The two most important details in the passion and resurrection narrative that pick up these earlier ideas are the rising of the holy ones, and then the depiction of the risen Jesus in language drawn from Daniel 7. Neither of these passages has any parallel in the other gospels; the rising of the holy ones is unattested anywhere else and, though Luke and John feature resurrection appearances, only Matthew describes the risen Jesus in the language of Daniel 7.[71] Thus, even while Matthew sticks closely to the Markan passion narrative, from a redaction-critical angle one can discern an attempt to bring the tradition into conformity with his own unique vision.[72]

5.4 Conclusion

As we saw in the preceding chapter, before he ascended to Jerusalem, Jesus had explained to his disciples that he would go there to give his life, but that he would be repaid with resurrection, exaltation as Son of Man, and the price of release for the many in debt-bondage. Jesus also claimed that this was the path that all his followers must take. He

---

71 Also note that only Matthew says that Jesus gives his life to be poured out "for the forgiveness of sins" (26:28).

72 On Matthew's loyalty to tradition and ability to shape the traditions creatively see Ulrich Luz, "Fiktivität und Traditionstreue im Matthäusevangelium im Lichte griechischer Literatur," *ZNW* 84 (1993): 153–77. Some of the details relevant to the argument are also found in the Markan passion narrative, but even in these cases Matthew provides unique preparation for them. For instance, in Mark 14:56 many people bear false witness against Jesus before the Council, and in 15:32 the brigands crucified with Jesus taunt him (ὠνείδιζον). Matthew adopts this narrative, buts precedes it with the promise, only found in Matthew, that those who endure taunting and others speaking falsely against them earn a great wage in the heavens (5:11–12). Matthew also expands Mark's parodic coronation (27:29), and redacts the request of James and John in 20:21 to match the description of the brigands crucified with Jesus (27:38).

then enters Jerusalem, fulfilling Isa 62 and Zech 9, as the king who comes with his wages to redeem his people from the pit for the sake of the blood of the covenant. In Jerusalem he clashes with the leaders of the people and warns them that their debt is about to be called due. Then, during the Last Supper another aspect of Jesus' coming death is revealed: it is a covenant sacrifice. Thus, Jesus gives his life not only to redeem the people from the debt of sin but also to create the covenant bond. During his trial and execution, Jesus' role as earner of heavenly wages par excellence begins to come into sharper focus. Those who endure insults and persecution have "great wages in the heavens" (5:11–12); Jesus endures insults and persecution (26:67–68; 27:27–44). Those who confess Christ before authorities are rewarded with Christ's corresponding confession of them before the Father (10:32); Christ confesses his own identity before the Sanhedrin (26:64). Those who pray privately will receive a wage from their Father in the heavens (6:1, 5–6); Jesus withdraws to pray alone (26:36). Those who give their lives will be repaid with eternal life, rule with the Son of Man, and a ransom-price for the many (16:24–27; 19:16–29; 20:17–28). When Jesus dies, his cross-bearing is repaid just as he said it would be: the many holy ones are raised up from the dead, and he himself is given eternal life and all authority as the Son of Man. The disciples are sent forth to make disciples of all the nations, teaching them to follow Jesus in storing up treasure in the heavens.

Conclusion

1. Summary

A sizeable stream of Matthean scholarship has been at pains to show that, like a good Kantian, Jesus did not use the hope of heavenly treasure to motivate his followers; that Matthew's *Lohngedanken* can be fitted into a Pauline framework; that the parable of the workers in the vineyard is the hermeneutical key to everything else Jesus says – or, at the very least, that the parable of the workers in the vineyard was central for the historical Jesus. I have sought to show how unhelpful these claims are for understanding Matthew. The central burden of this study, however, has not been to rectify previous misunderstandings but to articulate Matthew's vision of the divine economy in its late first-century Jewish context and also to show that some of the Gospel's central claims about Jesus emerge from this conceptual matrix and should be understood in light of it.

In chapter 1 we surveyed the rich variety of economic tropes found in early Jewish and Christian discussions of divine recompense. Righteous deeds were frequently thought to earn heavenly wages that were stored up in heaven. These heavenly wages are sometimes described as signs of honor or achievement in the life to come. In other cases, they are said to redeem one from sin, deliver from death and punishment, or acquit one on the day of judgment. Indeed, numerous texts closely associate treasure in heaven with the promise of future resurrection. We also saw that, despite the widespread belief that God will "repay to everyone according to their deeds," the meting out of heavenly treasure is generally not depicted as rigidly mechanistic. Frequently one finds frank admissions that divine repayment goes far beyond what one actually deserves. Moreover, heavenly treasures are sometimes said to benefit people other than those who earned them.

In Chapter 2 we turned to investigate heavenly wages and debts in Matthew. Matthean scholars, especially in previous generations, have frequently argued that Jesus wanted the disciples to forsake any thought of recompense. On the contrary, Matthew's depiction of heavenly wages and debts is in most respects not unusual in comparison to the early Jewish and Christian texts surveyed in chapter 1. For Matthew sin is debt. Those who sin against God or against another person are in danger of being thrown into debtor's prison (i.e., Gehenna). One's "account" with God determines one's fate in the judgment – that is, it determines whether one enters the kingdom. Heavenly wages can benefit people other than those who actually earned them (10:41–42). Also, as in most early Jewish and Christian texts, Matthew's economic language does not entail a description of God as coldly calculating in meting out justice, like some distant bank manager. God cancels the debts of those who ask him and repays righteous deeds far more than they are worth. A convenient summary of Matthew's *Lohngedanken* can be found in 25:29 along with 6:12 and 6:19–24: God repays righteous deeds generously and cancels the debts of those who ask him. But those who refuse to earn wages or refuse to cancel the debts of others will be punished. To store up treasure in heaven is to be generous to the poor, rather than clinging to ephemeral earthly possessions.

Though Matthew's depiction of divine recompense is very similar to other early Jewish and Christian texts, a few special emphases emerge that prove significant in the remaining chapters of the study. First, for Matthew, wages are stored up "in the heavens with God" to be repaid at the Parousia. This is a common image in other texts, but, as the recent work of Jonathan Pennington has shown, Matthew is unusually clear in his description of "the heavens" as an actual space, the invisible realm where God's will is done, and where the wages of righteousness are kept until all are repaid for their deeds. Second, Matthew describes the fate of insolvent sinners (i.e., "debtors") in terms of debt-bondage. Third, Matthew repeatedly describes the coming judgment as a settling of accounts. Fourth, time and again Matthew describes Jesus himself doing the things that earn heavenly treasure.

In chapters 3–5 the study turned from a thematic investigation of heavenly wages and debts to an analysis of the light this language sheds light on the narrative. Chapter 3 analyzes the prologue's presentation of Jesus as the one born to save his people from their sins (1:21). It is well-known that the prologue (1:1–4:22) sets out many of the main themes to be developed in the Gospel. Matthew begins with a genealogy and birth narrative that repeatedly emphasizes that the end of exile is at hand with the birth of Jesus, the Davidic messiah. Woven into this story is a series of biblical quotations that deal with the coming restoration of the Davidic monarchy or the end of exile (Isa 7:14; Micah 5:1–3; 2 Sam 5:2; Hos 11:1; Jer 31:15; Isa 40:3; Isa 8:23–9:1). These evocative quotations name the history of God's faithfulness to Israel and the

house of David as Jesus' "back-story" as well as the template for understanding the redemption that is at hand. Moreover, the citation of Jeremiah 31 and Isaiah 40 associates the end of exile with the "wages" due
for works and the repayment of the debt of sin. John the Baptist, whom
Matthew identifies as the herald of the end of exile and of the repayment of works, arrives on the scene announcing Jesus as the coming
mighty one (3:11; Isa 40:10). Jesus' encounter with John the Baptist
in 3:13–17 nuances this picture to include Jesus' vicarious action for
others. John tries to prevent Jesus' baptism, but Jesus explains that in
doing this they will "fill up all righteousness" – a statement that parallels
both the ransom saying in 20:28 and, antithetically, Jesus' words to the
scribes and Pharisees in 23:32. Jesus is the beloved son who goes beyond
what is required of him to fill up all righteousness, thereby liberating
those trapped by the debt of sin.

Chapter 4, which focuses on three key passages that occur when
Jesus begins predicting his death and resurrection (16:13–28; 19:16–
29; 20:17–28), is central for the argument. These three passages indicate that Jesus and his followers must give their lives in order to be repaid with resurrection and the reign spoken of in Daniel 7. In 16:13–28
Jesus announces his coming death and resurrection and then explains
that any who would follow him must also take up their crosses and
lose their lives because the Son of Man is about to repay those who
have given their present lives with eternal life. Then, in 19:16–29
Jesus says that those who renounce their possessions, give the money
to the poor, and follow Jesus will be repaid with eternal life and a
share in the rule of the Son of Man. The emphasis in these passages
is on finding eternal life by imitating Jesus' obedient self-giving. Yet,
as noted in chapter 3, Matthew describes the people as in exile or
debt-bondage due to sin and Jesus as the one who would save them.
In 20:17–28 these two motifs finally converge and illuminate each
other.

Scholarly discussion of 20:17–28 and the "ransom for many" has
been distracted by an erroneous equation of λύτρον with the verb
λυτρόω and by neglect of the considerable light that the preceding narrative sheds on the saying. The word λύτρον always denotes some sort of
price, frequently the price paid to free a captive. Jesus' claim to give his
life as a λύτρον for many thus raises two obvious questions: why do "the
many" need to be ransomed, and how does Jesus' gift of his life accomplish this? The prologue shows that "the many" are in exile because of
the debt of sin, and the narrative subsequently describes the punishment

for "debts" (i.e., sins) as debt-bondage. He earns the ransom-price for them by doing the very thing he taught his followers to do to earn heavenly treasure: he gives his life. According to the logic of the divine economy, it is Jesus' obedient cross-bearing that earns the price of release rather than the mere fact of his suffering and death.

Finally, chapter 5 examines Jesus' final week, especially his death and resurrection. At the triumphal entry Matthew uses the same method of evocative quotation used in the prologue to portray Jesus entering Jerusalem as the king who comes with his wages to redeem his people for the sake of the blood of the covenant. It was argued in chapter 4 that those who give their lives will be repaid with eternal life, rule with the Son of Man, and a ransom-price for the many (16:24–27; 19:16–29; 20:17–28). Matthew's passion and resurrection narrative, unlike the other gospels, depicts this three-fold repayment: the many holy ones are raised up from the dead, and Jesus is given eternal life and all authority as the Son of Man.

In concluding I shall address a lingering question that is raised by Matthew's depiction of the economy of heaven and then indicate a few issues that merit further research.

2. Debt-Captivity and the Price of Release Revisited

As we have seen, according to Matthew, heavenly treasure is necessary to enter the kingdom, and debts with God land one in prison. Those who do not cancel the debts of others will be thrown into debt-prison "until [they] repay all that is owed" (18:34). Similarly, even the smallest of unresolved debts against a brother will be repaid in Gehenna (5:26). At the same time, however, Matthew's Gospel is a story about Jesus, the one who "saves his people from their sins" (1:21), who "fills up all righteousness" (3:15), and who gives his life and earns the price of release (λύτρον) for the many (20:28). After Jesus gives his life, Matthew even provides a proleptic realization of this redemption, depicting the "many" holy ones emerging from their graves (27:52–53). One must ask, then, if Jesus earns the ransom-price for others, should not Gehenna be entirely emptied of its prisoners? Why would anyone need to store up treasure in heaven to acquire eternal life when Jesus has done it for them? Does Jesus' payment on behalf of others render moot all of Jesus' own teaching about heavenly wages and debts?

The great English philosopher Thomas Hobbes exemplifies one possible approach to this question. In Part 4 of his *Leviathan*, entitled "Of Darknesse," Hobbes addresses what he sees as religious errors that have been destructive to the social order, one of which is the belief in purgatory. In his attempt to refute arguments in favor of this doctrine, Hobbes discusses Matthew 5:26, a text that has played a role in the development of thinking about purgatory at least since Tertullian.[1] Like most modern and pre-modern exegetes, Hobbes reads this verse as befits its context in 5:21–26, that is, as a discussion of the effects of the debt of sin, rather than a bit of advice about how to avoid debtor's prison. According to Hobbes, this verse depicts the judge – that is, God – throwing the debtor into prison – that is, death.[2] Prima facie, it would appear that those who do not seek reconciliation for sins against another person will be forced to repay this debt after death. Hobbes, however, counters this conclusion by appealing to another Matthean text: the sinner need not worry about paying back his debt, for Christ paid "the utmost farthing… for him by his Passion, which is a full Ransome for all manner of sin, as well lesser sins, as greater crimes."[3] The logic of Hobbes's argument is plain: if Christ earned the ransom-price, then why would anyone need to repay his debt in Gehenna? Christ has given a gift that exceeds every debt.

The problem with Hobbes's solution to this question is that it cannot account for the complexity of Matthew's depiction of divine recompense and punishment. If entering the kingdom were simply a matter of a heavenly ledger listing debits and credits then yes, Jesus' payment of the ransom-price would erase every debt. There would be no "last penny" to repay, and no need to cancel the debts of others so that God would cancel one's own debts, all debts having been made equally irrelevant. For Matthew, however, entering the kingdom requires actual transformation: "I say to you that unless your righteousness abounds more than the scribes and Pharisees you will never enter the kingdom of heaven" (5:20). One must become perfect (τέλειος) like the heavenly Father (5:48). It is not enough to call Jesus "Lord" and do mighty works in his name; one must do "the the will of my Father who is in heaven" (7:21; see also vv.22–23). Those who do not turn and become like children "will never enter the kingdom of heaven" (18:3). Those who do

---

1   See the discussion of Matt 5:21–26 in chapter 2.
2   *Leviathan* (ed. C. B. Macpherson; London: Penguin, 1968), 655.
3   Ibid.

not imitate God's willingness to cancel the debts of others will not have their debts canceled (18:23−35). As the narrative moves closer to its conclusion it becomes clear that disciples must imitate Jesus by giving their very lives in order to be repaid with resurrection (16:24−28; 19:16−29). Even when Jesus says that he will give his life as the ransom-price for the many he is demanding that the disciples do likewise. For Matthew, "entering the kingdom" is not the result of a financial transaction between Jesus and God that leaves "the many" as mere by-standers in their own salvation; it requires one to become like a child, like Jesus, like God. To maintain Hobbes's reading of 5:26, therefore, one would have to reread these and other texts rather audaciously not as actual demands but as mere preparation for the gift of the ransom-price: Jesus said you would never get out until you repaid the last penny and that you would never enter the kingdom unless you become like a child, but − appearances to the contrary − he says this only to show you your inadequacy so you would receive the gift of Jesus' own treasure in heaven.[4] Such a reading belies the seriousness of Jesus' teaching in Matthew, a Gospel that ends with the risen Jesus sending the apostles to teach all nations "to obey all that I have commanded you" (28:20).

From this angle we can see a potential weakness of Matthew's economic language: it lends itself to describing salvation as a reality that is extrinsic to the people who are saved. The many exiles languish in the debt of their sin. Jesus pays the ransom-price. If sin and righteousness were simply a matter of one's heavenly bank account, this would be the end of the story, but for Matthew it obviously is not: it is necessary not just to receive the payment Jesus earns but also to follow him in storing up heavenly treasure. It may be that the Evangelist himself never paused to balance the heavenly checkbook, as it were, and realize that if Jesus "fills up all righteousness" then his followers have no more debts to ask God to cancel. As noted in chapter 4, Matthew's Gospel provides a coherent account of how Jesus saves his people from their sins, but it is not a work of systematic theology. The Matthean Jesus both teaches his followers how to get out of debt and earns their

---

4   One detects the possible influence of Luther, a great hero of Hobbes. E.g., in his *Historia Ecclesiastica* Hobbes speaks of Luther in the highest panegyrical terms. Cf. Luther on Matt 5:19: "We cannot be justified or saved through the teaching of the Law, which only brings us to the knowledge of ourselves, the knowledge that by our own ability we cannot properly fulfill an iota of it" (*The Sermon on the Mount and the Magnificat* [ed. J. Pelikan; LW 21; St. Louis, Missouri: Concordia, 1956], 72).

price of release for them, but the Gospel never addresses the question of why Jesus' followers still have debt at all. At the level of a historical description of the narrative one must admit that this remains a loose end.

There is more to be said, however, if one is permitted to move beyond bare historical description to think *with* Matthew. As in other early Jewish texts, the divine economy in Matthew does not work by the logic of strict necessity. For instance, those who receive itinerant missionaries into their homes will be repaid at the Parousia as if they themselves had left everything behind (10:40–42), and those who leave everything behind are repaid "a hundred times as much" (19:29). The divine economy is less like a zero-sum game, therefore, than a family in which the parents enjoy enabling their children to be full participants in the family's day-to-day tasks.[5] This can be seen even more clearly in Matthew's description of Jesus' self-giving, which – far from precluding the wage earning of the disciples – is the ground and example of their own cross-bearing. Thus, it is not a matter of God's needing to generate the heavenly currency to release the many from debt-bondage; instead, it is a matter of pulling the disciples into the ambit of Jesus' own self-giving, multiplying heavenly treasure for themselves and for others.[6] In light of all this, it would be very strange indeed if the Matthean Jesus had not told his followers how to have their debts canceled and how to store up treasure in heaven; they are to become τέλειος as God is τέλειος, and the heavenly treasure that Jesus earns for them is not so much the end of this process as it is the beginning.

A second point builds on the first. Matthew's description of divine recompense, when considered in its entirety, invites a second-order distinction between two kinds of debt: the debt that Jesus' payment of the price of release eliminates, on the one hand, and the debt that remains insofar as a disciple has not yet become "complete" as the heavenly Father, on the other. In 5:21–26 Jesus emphasizes that even the smallest

---

5   It was noted in chapter 1 that many of the texts surveyed use tropes drawn from the world of "balanced reciprocity," i. e., reciprocity which aims for strict *quid pro quo* accuracy, especially when it comes to market exchange. Yet, these same texts frequently lapse into "general reciprocity," i. e., the open and less defined exchange found in families and between close friends. See Marshall Sahlins, *Stone Age Economics* (2nd ed.; London/New York: Routledge, 2004). The same could be said of Matthew, which occasionally uses the language of balanced reciprocity (e. g., 7:2), while assuming general reciprocity in other passages.

6   Cf. 2 Cor 5:16–21.

sin against another person, such as calling someone a rude name, must be dealt with. Left unresolved, the debt of this sin will land a person in captivity from which he "will never go out until he repays the last penny." As Hobbes correctly noted, Jesus' ransom-price should be more than enough to pay the debt incurred by calling someone a "fool," not to mention any other treasure in heaven earned by the offender and by others on his behalf. Why should he be forced to repay such a paltry debt? The answer, I would suggest, flows from the observation that the divine economy does not operate according to strict necessity. God does not *need* this person to repay his debt so that his heavenly account will be in the black. Nevertheless, God requires that this person make peace with his "brother" and become like God. Thus, one might say that there is a duality in Matthew's economic language: on the one hand, absolute financial solvency and strict accounting is demanded. Unresolved debts must be paid. On the other hand, God repays even the smallest acts of righteousness with fantastic generosity, and Jesus earns a wage that redounds to all debtors. It is this duality that invites a distinction in how the metaphor of debt is understood. Debts – in the sense of damage that sin does to one's "brother" and oneself – must be repaid. For Matthew it simply is not possible to enter the kingdom with such debts left outstanding. At the same time, Matthew depicts the cancellation of every debt because of Jesus' self-giving, vividly illustrated by the rising of the holy ones in 27:52–52. Indeed, the rising of the holy ones illustrates both sides of this duality: though it was the gift of the ransom-price that freed them from prison, it is not all the dead who emerge from the grave, not "those who murdered the prophets," but "the holy ones," those who, one might say, did the will of the Father.

3. Issues for ongoing research

In addition to ongoing work on Matthew's economic language, more work needs to be done on this language throughout the New Testament and other early Christian literature, especially in fleshing out the hints of a salvation schema similar to Matthew's.[7] For instance, it was noted in

---

7   Gary Anderson (*Sin: A History* [New Haven: Yale University Press, 2009]) describes related understanding of heavenly treasure in the rabbis, Syriac Christianity, and even Anselm.

chapter 4 that Paul repeatedly speaks of Christ "redeeming" (ἀγοράζω) the church with a price (τιμή), and Colossians speaks of a bond of indebtedness (χειρόγραφον) that was destroyed at the cross (2:14) and Paul's own participation in Christ's death, "filling up" (ἀνταναπληρῶ) what is lacking for the sake of the church (1:24). One of the most suggestive things about these passages is the fact that Paul never pauses to explain what he means. Rather, he appeals to a story of Christ's redemption of his people while attempting to convince his churches of some other point. It is worth investigating, then, whether a narrative not unlike Matthew's may have shaped the narrative substructure of Paul's letters.[8]

One other example may suffice to show the need for further study in this area. The *Epistle to Diognetus*, which is commonly dated to the second century,[9] sets out to explain why the "new race or practice" of the Christians came into the world so late, rather than at an earlier time (1:1). The author goes on to say that God wanted the human race to see that it was unable to "enter into the kingdom of God (εἰσελθεῖν εἰς τὴν βασιλείαν τοῦ θεοῦ) on our own" (9:1), and so God waited to send his Son until the moment "when our unrighteousness was filled up (πεπλήρωτο ... ἡ ἡμετέρα ἀδικία) and it had been made completely obvious that the wages of unrighteousness – punishment and death – was expected (ὁ μισθὸς αὐτῆς κόλασις καὶ θάνατος προσεδοκᾶτο)" (9:2). Here again, we see the language of a debt filling up until the creditor steps in and casts the debtor into prison.[10] According to *Diognetus*, God waited until the last possible moment, the time when the wages of unrighteousness were about to be dispensed, and only then did he step in to pay the price to redeem humanity:

> When our unrighteousness was filled up and it had been made completely obvious that the wages of unrighteousness – i. e., punishment and death –

---

8 This proposal would find support from Richard B. Hays's argument that the story of Jesus' obedient self-giving on the cross was central for Paul (*The Faith of Jesus Christ: The Narrative Substructure of Galatians 3:1–4:11* [2nd ed.; Grand Rapids, MI.: Eerdmans, 2002]).

9 *Diognetus* is not mentioned by any ancient author, and its only manuscript, which dated from the 13th or 14th century, was destroyed in 1870. Nevertheless, its similarities to other second-century apologists, lack of use of what would become the NT, and the absence of any hint of the Marcionite controversy lead many scholars to be confident that it dates from the second century. See Bart D. Ehrman, *The Apostolic Fathers* (LCL) II, 127.

10 See the discussion of Matt 3:15 in chapter 3.

was expected, then the time came which God had decided he would
henceforth manifest his generosity (χρηστότητα) and power – O, the sur-
passing benevolence and love of God (φιλανθρωπίας καὶ ἀγάπης τοῦ θεοῦ)!
He did not hate us nor reject us, nor keep a record of our wrongs (ἐμνησι-
κάκησεν), but was patient and forbearing. Having mercy (ἐλεῶν) on us, he
received our sins; he himself paid his own Son as the ransom-price for
us (αὐτὸς τὸν ἴδιον υἱὸν ἀπέδοτο λύτρον ὑπὲρ ἡμῶν), the holy one for the lawless, the guiltless for the guilty, the righteous one for the unrighteous, the
incorruptible for the corruptible, the immortal for the mortal. For what else
but the righteousness of that person (ἐκείνου δικαιοσύνη) was able to cover
our sins? In whom was it possible for us, the lawless and ungodly, to be
justified, except by the Son of God alone? O the sweet exchange (ἀνταλ-
λαγῆς), O the inscrutable work, O the unexpected benefaction (εὐεργε-
σιῶν), that the lawlessness of many should be hidden in a single righteous
one, and the righteousness of one should justify many lawless people (ἀνο-
μία μὲν πολλῶν ἐν δικαίῳ ἑνὶ κρυβῇ δικαιοσύνη δὲ ἑνὸς πολλοὺς ἀνόμους
δικαιώσῃ). (9:2–5)

When the debt of humanity's sins was about to reach its fullness, God
sent his Son as the ransom-price in "exchange" for their sins. This act
is described in the language of almsgiving and benefaction: God mani-
fests his generosity (χρηστότης), benevolence (φιλανθρωπία), and benefaction (εὐεργεσία) by having mercy – or, one might say, by giving
alms (ἐλεέω). The alms given by God are his own Son, which he paid
(ἀποδίδωμι) as the ransom-price (λύτρον) in exchange (ἀνταλλαγή) for
the sins of "many" (πολλοί).

The author then goes on to invite the addressee to become like God
by giving to whomever is in need:

Do not be surprised that a person can become an imitator of God. One is
able if he is willing. For it is not in exploiting one's neighbors, nor in de-
siring to have more than weaker people, nor in being rich and using force
against one's inferiors that prosperity (εὐδαιμονεῖν) is found, nor by these
things can one imitate God. Rather, these things are foreign to his majesty.
But whoever takes up the burden of his neighbor, who desires to do good
in whatever way he is superior to another who is deficient, who, whatever
he has received from God, these things he provides to those in need, this
person becomes a god to those who receive. This person is an imitator
of God (οὗτος μιμητής ἐστι θεοῦ). (10:4–6)

By giving alms, one becomes like God, who sent his Son as the ransom-
price to pay the debts of humanity. Interestingly, the focus here is not, as
it is in Matthew and arguably in Paul, on the self-giving of Jesus and the
corresponding need for his followers to take up their crosses, but on the
beneficence of God in sending the Son, and the corresponding need for

imitators of God to give what they have to those in need. Though considerable attention has been given to the soteriology of *Diognetus*, no one, to my knowledge, has noted the letter's use of the language of debt, ransom, and almsgiving.[11]

4. Conclusion

The purpose of this study has been to situate Matthew's depiction of God's repayment of deeds in its late first-century Jewish-Christian context. Matthew draws on images of exile and debt-bondage – images that were already intertwined in Israel's Scriptures – to depict the people Jesus came to save, as well as individual sinners, as captives because of the debt of their sins. Jesus is introduced as the one born to save his people from their sins (1:21), and throughout the Gospel he does this by teaching them how to find debt forgiveness and store up treasure in the heavens in order to acquire eternal life. From the time Jesus begins predicting his death and resurrection he also teaches his disciples to follow him in giving their lives and being repaid with resurrection (16:24–28; 19:29), participation in the rule of the Son of Man (19:27–28), and the price of release for others who are in captivity. The passion narrative portrays the very repayment Jesus told the disciples that both he and they would receive: Jesus is raised from the dead, given all authority as Son of Man, and earns the ransom-price for the many. The end of the age remains in the future, and so suffering and doubt persist. Nevertheless, God's repayment of Jesus' self-giving is a foretaste or down-payment of the coming settling of accounts.

---

11 E.g., the otherwise helpful article of Brandon D. Crowe, "The Soteriological Significance of the Incarnation in the *Epistle to Diognetus*," *ZNW* 102 (2011): 96–109.

Bibliography

Albright, W. F. and C. S. Mann. *Matthew: A New Translation with Introduction and Commentary.* Anchor Bible 26. Garden City, NY: Doubleday, 1971.

Allison, Dale C. Jr. "The Eye is the Lamp of the Body." *New Testament Studies* 33 (1987): 61–83.

_____. *The New Moses: A Matthean Typology.* Minneapolis: Fortress Press, 1993.

_____. *Testament of Abraham.* Commentaries on Early Jewish Literature. Berlin/New York: Walter de Gruyter, 2003.

_____. *Constructing Jesus: Memory, Imagination, and History.* Grand Rapids, MI.: Baker, 2010.

_____. "Structure, Biographical Impulse, and the *Imitatio Christi*." Pages 135–55 in *Studies in Matthew: Interpretation Past and Present.* Grand Rapids, MI: Baker Academic, 2005.

Anderson, Gary A. *Sin: A History.* New Haven: Yale University Press, 2009.

_____. "How Does Almsgiving Purge Sins," forthcoming in *Hebrew in the Second Temple Period: The Hebrew of the Dead Sea Scrolls and of Other Contemporary Sources.* Edited by S. E. Fassberg, M. Bar-Asher, and R. Clements; Studies on the Texts of the Desert of Judah; Leiden: Brill, 2012.

Arneson, Hans. "Vocabulary and Date in the Study of Wisdom: A Critical Review of the Arguments." Paper presented at the SBL annual meeting, New Orleans, 23 November 2009.

Arzt-Grabner, Peter. "Gott als verlässlicher Käufer: Einige papyrologische Anmerkungen und bibeltheologische Schlussfolgerungen zum Gottesbild der Paulusbriefe." *New Testament Studies* 57 (2011): 392–414.

Aune, David. *The New Testament in its Literary Environment.* Philadelphia: Westminster Press, 1987.

Balz, H. G. and G. Schneider eds. *Exegetical Dictionary of the New Testament.* ET. Grand Rapids: Eerdmans, 1990–1993.

Barrett, C. K. "The Background of Mark 10:45." Pages 1–18 in *New Testament Essays.* Edited by A. J. B. Higgins. Manchester: Manchester University Press, 1959.

Barth, Gerhard. "Law and Christology." Pages 125–59 in *Tradition and Interpretation in Matthew.* Philadelphia: The Westminster Press, 1963.

Barth, Markus and Helmut Blanke. *Colossians: A New Translation with Introduction and Commentary.* Translated by A. B. Beck. Anchor Bible 34B. New York, New York: Doubleday, 1994.

Bauschatz, John. "Ptolemaic Prisons Reconsidered." *The Classical Bulletin* 83 (2007): 3–47.

Bauckham, Richard. "For Whom Were Gospels Written." Pages 9–48 in *The Gospels for All Christians: Rethinking the Gospel Audiences*. Edited by Richard Bauckham. Grand Rapids: Eerdmans, 1998.

———. "Is there Patristic Counter-Evidence? A Response to Margaret Mitchell," Pages 68–110 in *The Audience of the Gospels: The Origin and Function of the Gospels in Early Christianity*. Edited by Edward W. Klink III. Library of New Testament Studies. London: T & T Clark, 2009.

Baur, F. C. *Vorlesungen über neutestamentliche Theologie*. 1864. Repr., Darmstadt: Wissenschaftliche Buchgesellschaft, 1973.

Bazzana, Giovanni Battista. "*Basileia* and Debt Relief: The Forgiveness of Debts in the Lord's Prayer in the Light of Documentary Papyri." *Catholic Biblical Quarterly* 73 (2011): 511–25.

Beasley-Murray, G. R. *Jesus and the Kingdom of God*. Grand Rapids, MI: Eerdmans, 1986.

Bellinger, William H. Jr. and William R. Farmer, eds., *Jesus and the Suffering Servant: Isaiah 53 and Christian Origins*. Harrisburg, PN.: Trinity, 1998.

Ben Shalom, Yael Wilfand. "Poverty, Charity and the Image of the Poor in Rabbinic Texts from the Land of Israel." Ph.D. diss., Duke University, 2011.

Benoît, P., J. T. Milik, and R. de Vaux. *Les grottes de Murabba'ât*. Discoveries in the Judean Desert II. Oxford: Clarendon Press, 1961.

Bergsma, John Sietze. *The Jubilee from Leviticus to Qumran: A History of Interpretation*. VTSup 115. Leiden: Brill, 2007.

Betz, Hans Dieter. *The Sermon on the Mount: A Commentary on the Sermon on the Mount*. Minneapolis; Fortress Press, 1995.

———. "Matthew 6:22–23 and Ancient Greek Theories of Vision." Pages 71–87 in *Essays on the Sermon on the Mount*. Philadelphia: Fortress: 1985.

Bird, Mike. "Bauckham's *The Gospel for All Christians* Revisited." *European Journal of Theology* 15 (2006): 5–13.

Blackman, Philip. *Mishnayoth*. 6 vols. London: Mishna Press, 1954.

Blenkinsopp, Joseph. *Isaiah 40–55: A New Translation with Introduction and Commentary*. Anchor Bible 19 A. New York: Doubleday, 2002.

———. *Isaiah 56–66: A New Translation with Introduction and Commentary*. Anchor Bible 19B. New York: Doubleday, 2003.

Blomberg, Craig. "Degrees of Reward in the Kingdom of Heaven?" *Journal of the Evangelical Theology Society* 35 (1992): 159–72.

Boring, Eugene. "The Gospel of Matthew." Pages 87–505 in *The New Interpreter's Bible* 8 Nashville: Abingdon, 1995.

Bornkamm, Günther. "Der Lohngedanke im Neuen Testament." Pages 2.69–92 in *Studien zu Antike und Urchristentum: Gesammelte Aufsätze*. 2 vols. Munich: Kaiser Verlag, 1963.

Broshi, M., et al. *Qumran Cave 4.XIV: Parabiblical Texts, Part 2*. Discoveries in the Judean Desert XIX. Oxford: Clarendon Press, 1995.

Brown, Raymond. "The Pater Noster as an Eschatological Prayer," *Theological Studies* 22 (1961): 175–208.

———. *Death of the Messiah*. 2 vols. Anchor Bible Reference Library. New York: Doubleday, 1994.

Bultmann, Rodolph. *History of the Synoptic Tradition*. Translated by John Marsh. Oxford: Blackwell, 1972.

Burridge, Richard. *What Are the Gospels? A Comparison with Greco-Roman Biography*. 2d ed. Grand Rapids: Eerdmans, 2004.

Cadbury, Henry J. "The Single Eye." *Harvard Theological Review* 46 (1954): 69–74.

Carey, Holly J. *Jesus' Cry from the Cross: Towards a First-Century Understanding of the Intertextual Relationship between Psalm 22 and the Narrative of Mark's Gospel*. Library of New Testament Studies 398. Edinburgh: T & T Clark, 2009.

Carroll, John T. and Joel B. Green. *The Death of Jesus in Early Christianity*. Peabody, Mass.: Hendrickson, 1995.

Carter, Warren. *Households and Discipleship: A Study of Matthew 19–20*. Journal for the Study of the New Testament: Supplement Series 103. Sheffield: JSOT Press, 1994.

⸻. *Matthew: Storyteller, Interpreter, Evangelist*. Peabody, Mass.: Hendrickson Publishers, 1996.

Charette, Blaine. *The Theme of Recompense in Matthew's Gospel*. Journal for the Study of the New Testament: Supplement Series 79. Sheffield: Sheffield Academic Press, 1992.

Charlesworth, James H., ed. *The Old Testament Pseudepigrapha*. 2 vols. Anchor Bible Reference Library. New York: Doubleday, 1983, 1985.

Chilton, Bruce D. *The Isaiah Targum: Introduction, Translation, Apparatus and Notes*. The Aramaic Bible 11. Wilmington, DE: Michael Glazier, 1987.

Clark, Kenneth W. "The Meaning of κατακυριεύειν." Pages 100–105 in *Studies in New Testament Language and Text: Essays in Hour of George D. Kilpatrick on the Occasion of his sixty-fifth Birthday*. Novum Testamentum Supplements 44. Edited by J. K. Elliot. Leiden: Brill, 1976.

Collins, Adela. *Mark: A Commentary*. Hermeneia; Minneapolis: Fortress Press, 2007.

Collins, J. J., ed. *Apocalypse: The Morphology of a Genre*. Semeia 14. Missoula, MT: Scholars Press, 1979.

⸻. *Daniel: A Commentary on the Book of Daniel*. Hermeneia. Minneapolis: Fortress Press, 1993.

Collins, John J. and Peter W. Flint. *The Book of Daniel: Composition and Reception*. 2 vols. Leiden/Boston: Brill, 2001.

Couroyer, B. "De la mesure dont vous mesurez il vous sera mesuré." *Revue biblique* 77 (1970): 366–70.

Crowe, Brandon D. "The Soteriological Significance of the Incarnation in the Epistle to Diognetus. *Zeitschrift für die neutestamentliche Wissenschaft und die Kunde der älteren Kirche* 102 (2011): 96–109.

Cullman, Oscar. *Die Tauflehre des Neuen Testaments: Erwachsenen- und Kindertaufe*. Abhandlungen zur Theologie des Alten und Neuen Testaments 12. Zürich: Zwingli Verlag, 1948.

Dalman, Gustaf. *The Words of Jesus*. Translated by D. M. Kay. Edinburgh: T&T Clark, 1902.

Danby, Herbert. *The Mishnah: Translated from the Hebrew with Introduction and Brief Explanatory Notes.* Oxford: Oxford University Press, 1933; repr., 1983.

Davies, W. D. *Paul and Rabbinic Judaism: Some Rabbinic Elements in Pauline Theology.* Philadelphia: Fortress, 1948; repr., 1980.

————. *The Setting of the Sermon on the Mount.* Brown Judaic Studies 186. Atlanta: Scholar's Press, 1989.

Davies, W. D. and Dale C. Allison. *A Critical and Exegetical Commentary on the Gospel according to Saint Matthew.* 3 vols. International Critical Commentary. Edinburgh: T&T Clark, 1988–1997.

Davis Ellen F. "Exploding the Limits: Form and Function in Psalm 22." Pages 135–46 in *The Poetical Books.* The Biblical Seminar 41. Edited by David J. A. Clines. Sheffield, 1997.

Deissmann, Gustav A. *Light from the Ancient East: The New Testament Illustrated by Recently Discovered Texts of the Graeco-Roman World.* Translated by Lionel R. M. Strachan. New York: George H. Doran, 1927.

————. *Bible Studies: Contributions Chiefly from Papyri and Inscriptions to the History of the Language, the Literature, and the Religion of Hellenistic Judaism and Primitive Christianity.* Translated by Alexander Grieve. Edinburgh: T & T Clark, 1903.

De Jonge, M. "Jesus' Death for Others and the Death of the Maccabean Martyrs." Pages 142–52 in *Text and Testimony: Essays on New Testament and Apocryphal Literature in Honour of A. F. J. Klijn.* Edited by T. Baarda et al. Kampen: Kok, 1988.

Derrida, Jacques. *The Gift of Death and Literature in Secret.* 2d ed. Translated by David Wills. Chicago: University of Chicago Press, 2008.

de Ru, G. "The Conception of Reward in the Teaching of Jesus." *Novum Testamenum* 8 (1966): 202–22.

deSilva, David A. *4 Maccabees.* Guides to Apocrypha and Pseudepigrapha. Sheffield, Eng.: Sheffield Academic Press, 1998.

Diamond, Eliezer. *Holy Men and Hunger Artists: Fasting and Asceticism in Rabbinic Culture.* New York: Oxford University Press, 2004.

Dodd, C. H. *The Parables of the Kingdom.* New York: Scribner, 1961.

————. *New Testament Studies.* Manchester, Manchester University Press, 1968.

Drazin, Israel. *Targum Onkelos to Exodus: An English Translation of the Text with Analysis and Commentary.* Hoboken, NJ: Ktav Publishing, 1990.

Dupont, Jacques. *Les Béatitudes.* 3 vols. Bruges: Abbaye de Saint-André, 1973.

Edwards, J. Christopher. "Pre-Nicene Receptions of Mark 10:45//Matt. 20:28 with Phil. 2:6–8." *Journal of Theological Studies* 61 (2010): 194–99.

Eissfeldt, O. "Πληρῶσαι πᾶσαν δικαιοσύνην in Matthäus 3:15." *Zeitschrift für die neutestamentliche Wissenschaft und die Kunde der älteren Kirche* 61 (1970): 209–15.

Eloff, Mervyn. "Exile, Restoration and Matthew's Genealogy of Jesus Ὀ ΧΡΙΣΤΟΣ." *Neotestamentica* 38 (2004): 75–87.

Eubank, Nathan. "Bakhtin and Lukan Politics: A Carnivalesque Reading of the Last Supper in the Third Gospel." *Journal of Greco-Roman Christianity and Judaism* 4 (2007): 32–54.

_____. "A Disconcerting Prayer: On the Originality of Luke 23:34a." *Journal of Biblical Literature* 129 (2010): 521–36.

_____. "Almsgiving is 'The Commandment': A Note on 1 Timothy 6.6–19." *New Testament Studies* 58 (2012): 144–50.

Evans, Craig A. "Aspects of Exile and Restoration in the Proclamation of Jesus and the Gospels." Pages 299–328 in *Exile: Old Testament, Jewish, and Christian Conceptions.* Edited by James M. Scott. Leiden/New York: Brill, 1997.

Fiore, Benjamin. *The Pastoral Epistles: First Timothy, Second Timothy, Titus.* Sacra Pagina 12. Collegeville, MN.: Liturgical Press,1991.

Foster, Paul. "The Use of Zechariah in Matthew's Gospel." Pages 65–85 in *The Book of Zechariah and its Influence.* Edited by Christopher Tuckett. Burlington, VT: Ashgate, 2003.

France, R. T. *The Gospel of Matthew.* New International Commentary on the New Testament. Grand Rapids: Eerdmans, 2007.

Gamble, Harry. *Books and Readers in the Early Church: A History of Early Christian Texts.* New Haven: Yale University Press, 1995.

Garrett, Susan R. "'Lest the Light in You Be Darkness': Luke 11:33–36 and the Question of Commitment." *JBL* 110 (1991): 93–105.

Garrison, Roman. *Redemptive Almsgiving in Early Christianity.* Journal for the Study of the New Testament: Supplement Series 77. Sheffield: Sheffield Academic Press, 1993.

Garrow, A.J.P. *The Gospel of Matthew's Dependence on the Didache.* London/New York: T&T Clark, 2004.

Gathercole, Simon J. *Where Is Boasting? Early Jewish Soteriology and Paul's Response in Romans 1–5.* Grand Rapids: Eerdmans, 2002.

Goldstein, Jonathan A. *2 Maccabees: A New Translation with Introduction and Commentary.* Anchor Bible 41 A. Garden City, NY: Doubleday, 1983.

Goodacre, Mark. *The Case Against Q: Studies in Markan Priority and the Synoptic Problem.* Harrisburg, PA: Trinity Press International, 2002.

_____. "The Rock on Rocky Ground: Matthew, Mark and Peter as Skandalon." Pages 61–7 in *What Is It That the Scripture Says?: Essays in Biblical Interpretation, Translation, And Reception in Honour of Henry Wansbrough OSB.* Edited by Philip McCosker. Library of New Testament Studies. London & New York: Continuum, 2006.

Goulder, Michael Douglas. *Midrash and Lection in Matthew.* The Speaker's Lectures in Biblical Studies 1969–71. London: SPCK, 1974.

Gray, Sherman W. *The Least of My Brothers: Matthew 25:31–46: A History of Interpretation.* SBLDS 114. Atlanta: Scholars Press, 1989.

Gray, Timothy C. *The Temple in the Gospel of Mark: A Study in Its Narrative Role.* Grand Rapids: Baker, 2010.

Gregory, Bradley C. *Like an Everlasting Signet Ring: Generosity in the Book of Sirach.* Deuterocanonical and Cognate Literature Studies 2. Berlin: Walter de Gruyter, 2010.

Grindheim, Sigurd. "Ignorance is Bliss: Attitudinal Aspects of the Judgment according to Works in Matthew 25:31–46." *Novum Testamentum* 50 (2008): 313–31.

Gundry, Robert Horton. *Matthew: A Commentary on his Handbook for a Mixed Church under Persecution.* 2d ed; Grand Rapids, MI: Eerdmans, 1994.

Gurtner, Daniel M. *The Torn Veil: Matthew's Exposition of the Death of Jesus.* Society of New Testament Studies Monograph Series 139. Cambridge: Cambridge University Press, 2007.

Hagner, Donald A. "Law, Righteousness, and Discipleship in Matthew." *Word and World* 18 (1998): 364–71.

_____. *Matthew 14–28.* Word Biblical Commentary 33b. Dallas: Word Books, 1995.

Hamilton, Catherine Sider. "His Blood Be upon Us": Innocent Blood and the Death of Jesus in Matthew." *Catholic Biblical Quarterly* 70 (2008): 82–100.

Hamilton, James M. Jr. "'The Virgin Will Conceive': Typological Fulfillment in Matthew 1:18–23." Pages 228–47 in *Built Upon the Rock: Studies in the Gospel of Matthew.* Edited by Daniel M. Gurtner and John Nolland. Grand Rapids, MI.: Eerdmans, 2008.

Harrington, Daniel J. *The Gospel of Matthew.* Sacra Pagina 1. Collegeville, MN.: Liturgical, 1991.

Hart, David Bentley. "A Gift Exceeding Every Debt: An Eastern Orthodox Appreciation of Anselm's *Cur Deus Homo.*" *Pro Ecclesia* 7 (1998): 333–49.

_____. *The Beauty of the Infinite: The Aesthetics of Christian Truth.* Grand Rapids, MI: Eerdmans, 2003.

Hartin, Patrick J. *James.* Sacra Pagina 14. Collegeville, Minnesota: Liturgical Press, 2003.

Hays, Richard B. *Echoes of Scripture in the Letters of Paul.* New Haven: Yale University Press, 1989.

_____. *First Corinthians.* Interpretation. Louisville, KY: John Knox, 1997.

_____. *The Faith of Jesus Christ: The Narrative Substructure of Galatians 3:1–4:11.* 2nd ed. Grand Rapids, MI.: Eerdmans, 2002.

_____. "The Gospel of Matthew: Reconfigured Torah." *Hervormde teologiese studies* 61 (2005): 166–90.

_____. *The Conversion of the Imagination: Paul as Interpreter of Israel's Scripture.* Grand Rapids, MI.: Eerdmans, 2005.

Hayward, Robert. *The Targum of Jeremiah: Translated, with a Critical Introduction, Apparatus, and Notes.* The Aramaic Bible 12. Wilmington, DE: Michael Glazier, 1987.

_____. *Targum Neofiti 1: Leviticus. Translated, with Apparatus.* The Aramaic Bible 3. Collegeville, MN: Liturgical Press, 1994.

Heinemann, H. "The Conception of Reward in Mat. XX. 1 16." *Journal of Jewish Studies* 1 (1948): 85–9.

Hezser, Catherine. *Lohnmetaphorik und Arbeitswelt in Mt 20,1–16.* Novum Testamentum et Orbis Antiquus 15. Göttingen: Vandenhoeck & Ruprecht, 1990.

Hill, David. *Greek Words and Hebrew Meanings: Studies in the Semantics of Soteriological Terms.* Society for New Testament Studies Monograph Series 5. Cambridge: Cambridge University Press, 1967.

Hobbes, Thomas. *Leviathan.* Edited by C. B. Macpherson. London: Penguin, 1968.

Hogan, Karina Martin. *Theologies in Conflict in 4 Ezra: Wisdom, Debate, and Apocalyptic Solution.* Supplements to the Journal for the Study of Judaism. Leiden: Brill, 2008.

Holmes, Michael W. ed. and tran. *The Apostolic Fathers: Greek Texts and English Translations.* 3rd ed. Grand Rapids, MI: Baker Academic, 1992; repr., 2007.

Hooker, Morna. *Jesus and the Servant: The Influence of the Servant Concept of Deutero-Isaiah in the New Testament.* London: S.P.C.K., 1959.

Huizenga, Leroy. *The New Isaac: Tradition and Intertextuality in the Gospel of Matthew.* Novum Testamentum Supplements 131. Leiden: Brill, 2009.

Hultgren, Stephen. *Narrative Elements in the Double Tradition: A Study of Their Place within the Framework of the Gospel Narrative.* Beihefte zur Zeitschrift für die neutestamentliche Wissenschaft und die Kunde der älteren Kirche 113. Berlin/New York: Walter de Gruyter, 2002.

Jeremias, Joachim. *Die Gleichnisse Jesu.* Göttingen: Vandenhoeck & Ruprecht, 1954.

———. *Abba: Studien zur neutestamentlichen Theologie und Zeitgeschichte.* Göttingen: Vandenhoeck & Ruprecht, 1966.

———. *Neutestamentliche Theologie.* 2 vols. Gütersloh: Gütersloher Verlagshaus, 1971.

Juel, Donald. *Messianic Exegesis: Christological Interpretation of the Old Testament in Early Christianity.* Philadelphia: Fortress, 1988.

Kähler, Martin. *Der sogenannte historische Jesus und der geschichtliche biblische Christus.* Leipzig: Deichertsche Verlagsbuchhandlung, 1896.

Kant, Immanuel. *Grundlegung zur Metaphysik der Sitten.* Philosophische Bibliothek 41. Leipzig : Felix Meiner, 1925.

———. *Metaphysik der Sitten.* Philosophische Bibliothek 42. Leipzig: Dürr'schen, 1907.

Keener, Craig. *A Commentary on the Gospel of Matthew.* Grand Rapids, MI.: Eerdmans, 1999.

———. "'Brood of Vipers' (Matthew 3.7; 12.34; 23.33)." *Journal for the Study of the New Testament* 28 (2005): 3–11.

Kim, Kyoung-Shik. *God will Judge Each One According to Works: Judgment According to Works and Psalm 62 in Early Judaism and the New Testament.* Beihefte zur Zeitschrift für die neutestamentliche Wissenschaft und die Kunde der älteren Kirche 178. Berlin/New York: Walter de Gruyter, 2011.

Kingsbury, Jack Dean. *Matthew: Structure, Christology, Kingdom.* Philadelphia, Fortress, 1975; repr., 1991.

Kippenberg, Hans G. *Religion und Klassenbildung im antiken Judäa.* Studien zur Umwelt des Neuen Testaments 14. Göttingen: Vandenhoeck und Ruprecht, 1978.

Kittel, G., and G. Friedrich, eds. *Theological Dictionary of the New Testament.* Translated by G. W. Bromiley. 10 vols. Grand Rapids: eerdmans. 1964–1976.

Klijn, A. F. J. *Der Lateinische Text der Apokalypse des Esra.* Texte und Untersuchungen zur Geschichte der altchristlichen Literatur 131. Berlin: Akademie-Verlag, 1983.

Kloppenborg, John S. *Excavating Q: The History and Setting of the Sayings Gospel.* Minneapolis: Fortress, 2000.

_____. "Agrarian Discourse and the Sayings of Jesus: 'Measure for Measure' in Gospel Traditions and Agricultural Practices." Pages 104–28 in *Engaging Economics: New Testament Scenarios and Early Christian Reception.* Edited by Bruce W. Longenecker and Kelly D. Liebengood. Grand Rapids, MI: Eerdmans, 2009.

Koch, Klaus. "Der Schatz im Himmel." Pages 47–60 in *Leben angesichts des Todes: Beiträge zum theologischen Problem des Todes: Helmut Thielicke zum 60. Geburtstag.* Edited by Berhard Lohse and H. P. Schmidt. Tübingen: Mohr Siebeck, 1968.

Krentz, Edgar. "The Extent of Matthew's Prologue: Toward the Structure of the First Gospel." *Journal of Biblical Literature* 83 (1964): 409–14.

Lagrange, Marie-Joseph. *Évangile selon Saint Matthieu. Etudes bibliques.* Paris: Gabalda, 1927.

Lakoff, George and Mark Johnson. *Metaphors We Live By.* Chicago: University of Chicago Press, 1980.

Lam, Joseph. Review of Gary A. Anderson, *Sin: A History, Review of Biblical Literature* http://www.bookreviews.org 2010.

Lang, T. J. "'You will desire to see and you will not see it': Reading Luke 17.22 as Antanaclasis." *Journal for the Study of the New Testament* 33 (2011): 281–302.

Lauterbach, Jacob Z. *Mekhilta Ishmael: A Critical Edition, Based on the Manuscripts and Early Editions, with an English Translation, Introduction, and Notes.* 2 vols. Philadelphia: JPS, 1933; repr., 2004.

Levenson, Jon D. *The Death and Resurrection of the Beloved Son: The Transformation of Child Sacrifice in Judaism and Christianity.* New Haven: Yale University Press, 1993.

Lightfoot, J. L. *The Sibylline Oracles: With Introduction, Translation, and Commentary on the First and Second Books.* New York/Oxford, Oxford University Press: 2007.

Lightfoot, R. H. *Locality and Doctrine in the Gospels.* London: Hodder & Stoughton, 1938.

Ljungman, Henrik. *Das Gesetz erfüllen.* Lund: C. W. K. Gleerup, 1954.

Luomanen, Petri. *Entering the Kingdom of Heaven: A Study on the Structure of Matthew's View of Salvation.* Wissenschaftliche Untersuchungen zum Neuen Testament 11/101. Tübingen: Mohr Siebeck, 1998.

Lust, J. *Greek-English Lexicon of the Septuagint.* Stuttgart: Deutsche Bibelgesellschaft, 2003.

Luther, Martin. *The Sermon on the Mount and the Magnificat.* Edited by J. Pelikan. Luther's Works 21. St. Louis, Missouri: Concordia, 1956.

Luttenberger, Joram. "Der gekreuzigte Schuldschein: Ein Aspekt der Deutung des Todes Jesu im Kolosserbrief." *New Testament Studies* 51 (2005): 80–95.

Luz, Ulrich. *Das Evangelium nach Matthäus.* 4 vols. Evangelisch-katholischer Kommentar zum Neuen Testament. Düsseldorf: Benziger, 1985–2002.

_____. "Fiktivität und Traditionstreue im Matthäusevangelium im Lichte griechischer Literatur." *Zeitschrift für die neutestamentliche Wissenschaft und die Kunde der älteren Kirche* 84 (1993): 153–77.

_____. *The Theology of the Gospel of Matthew.* Cambridge; New York: Cambridge University Press, 1995

_____. "Eine thetische Skizze der matthäischen Christologie." Pages 221–35 in *Anfänge der Christologie: Festschrift für Ferdinand Hahn zum 65. Geburtstag.* Edited by Ferdinand Hahn et al. Göttingen: Vandenhoeck & Ruprecht, 1991.

Lyonnet, Stanislas and Léopold Sabourin. *Sin, Redemption, and Sacrifice: A Biblical and Patristic Study.* Rome: Biblical Institute Press, 1970.

Marböck, Johannes. *Jesus Sirach 1–23.* Herders theologischer Kommentar zum Neuen Testament. Freiburg im Breisgau: Herder, 2010.

Marcus, Joel. *Mark 1–8: A New Translation with Introduction and Commentary.* Anchor Bible 27a. New Haven: Yale University Press, 2000.

_____. "Crucifixion as Parodic Exaltation." *Journal of Biblical Literature* 125 (2006): 73–87.

_____. *Mark 8–16: A New Translation with Introduction and Commentary.* Anchor Bible 27a. New Haven: Yale University Press, 2009.

Marguerat, Daniel. *Le Jugement dans L'Évangile de Matthieu.* 2nd ed. Le Monde de la Bible 6. Genève: Labor et Fides, 1995.

Martyn, J. Louis. *History and Theology in the Fourth Gospel.* 3d ed. New Testament Library. Louisville: Westminster John Knox Press, 2003.

Massaux, E. *The Influence of the Gospel of Saint Matthew on Christian Literature before Saint Irenaeus.* 3 vols. New Gospel Studies 5. Macon, GA: Mercer University Press, 1990.

Matera, Frank. *Galatians.* Sacra Pagina 9. Collegeville, MN.: Liturgical Press, 1992.

McDonald, James I. H. "The Concept of Reward in the Teaching of Jesus." *Expository Times* 89 (1978): 269–73.

McKnight, Scot. *Jesus and His Death: Historiography, the Historical Jesus, and Atonement Theory.* Waco, TX: Baylor University Press, 2005.

Meier, John P. *Law and History in Matthew's Gospel.* Analecta biblica 71. Rome: Biblical Institute Press, 1976.

_____. *Matthew.* Collegeville, Minn.: Liturgical Press, 1990.

Meyers, Carol L. and Eric M. Meyers. *Zechariah 9–14: A New Translation with Introduction and Commentary.* Anchor Bible 25C. New York: Doubleday, 1992.

Michaels, J. Ramsey. "Almsgiving and the Kingdom Within: Tertullian on Luke 17:21." *Catholic Biblical Quarterly* 60 (1998): 475–83.

Milbank, John. "Can a Gift be Given?" *Modern Theology* 11 (1995): 119–61.

Mitchell, Margaret. "Patristic Counter-evidence to the Claim that 'the Gospels were Written for All Christians.'" *New Testament Studies* 51 (2005): 36–79.

Moffitt, David M. "Righteous Bloodshed, Matthew's Passion Narrative, and the Temple's Destruction: Lamentations as a Matthean Intertext." *Journal of Biblical Literature* 125 (2006): 299–320.

Mohrlang, Roger. *Matthew and Paul: A Comparison of Ethical Perspectives.* Society of New Testament Studies Monograph Studies 48. Cambridge: Cambridge University Press, 1984.

Moss, Candida R. "Blurred Vision and Ethical Confusion: The Rhetorical Function of Matthew 6:22–23." *Catholic Biblical Quarterly* 73 (2011): 757–76.

Moxnes, Halvor. *The Economy of the Kingdom: Social Conflict and Economic Relations in Luke's Gospel.* Overtures to Biblical Theology. Philadelphia: Fortress Press, 1988.

Minear, Paul S. *And Great Shall Be Your Reward: The Origins of Christian Views of Salvation.* Yale Studies in Religion 12. New Haven: Yale University Press, 1941.

Nolland, John. *The Gospel of Matthew: A Commentary on the Greek Text.* New International Greek Testament Commentary. Grand Rapids, MI.: Eerdmans, 2005.

Novick, Tzvi. "Wages from God: The Dynamics of a Biblical Metaphor." *Catholic Biblical Quarterly* 73 (2011): 708–22.

Orlov, Andrei A. *The Enoch-Metatron Tradition.* Texte und Studien zum antiken Judentum 107. Tübingen: Mohr Siebeck, 2005.

Pennington, Jonathan T. *Heaven and Earth in the Gospel of Matthew.* Novum Testamentum Supplements 126. Leiden: Brill, 2007.

———. "Refractions of Daniel in the Gospel of Matthew." Pages 65–86 in Early Christian Literature and Intertextuality. Edited by Craig A. Evans and H. Daniel Zacharias. Vol. 14 of Studies in Scripture in Early Judaism and Christianity. Library of New Testament Studies 391. London: T & T Clark, 2009.

Pesch, Wilhelm. *Der Lohngedanke in der Lehre Jesu: Verglichen mit der religiösen Lohnlehre des Spätjudentums.* Munich: Karl Zink, 1955.

Philo. Translated by F. H. Colson and G. H. Whitaker. 10 vols. Loeb Classical Library. Cambridge: Harvard University Press, 1929.

Pitre, Brant. *Jesus, the Tribulation, and the End of the Exile.* Grand Rapids: Baker, 2005.

Ploner, Maria Theresia. *Die Schriften Israels als Auslegungshorizont der Jesusgeschichte: eine narrative und intertextuelle Analyse von Mt 1–2.* Stuttgarter biblische Beiträge 66. Stuttgart: Bibelwerk, 2011.

Powell, Mark Allan. *What is Narrative Criticism.* Minneapolis: Augsburg Fortress, 1990.

Propp, William H. C. *Exodus 19–40: A New Translation with Introduction and Commentary.* Anchor Bible 2 A. New York: Doubleday, 2006.

Przybylski, Benno. *Righteousness in Matthew and His World of Thought.* Society for New Testament Studies Monograph Series 41. Cambridge: Cambridge University Press, 1980.

Reicke, Bo. "The New Testament Conception of Reward." Pages 195–206 in *Aux sources de la tradition chréttienne: Mélanges offerts à M. Maurice Goguel.* Edited by P. H. Menoud and Oscar Cullman. Bibliothèque théologique. Paris: Delachaux and Niestlé, 1950.

Repschinski, Boris. "For He Will Save His People from Their Sins Matthew 1:21: A Christology for Christian Jews." *CBQ* 68 (2006): 248–67.

Riches, John Kenneth. *Conflicting Mythologies: Identity Formation in the Gospels of Mark and Matthew.* Studies of the New Testament and Its World. Edinburgh: T&T Clark, 2000.

Ritter, Christine. *Rachels Klage im antiken Judentum und frühen Christentum*. Arbeiten zur Geschichte des antiken Judentums und des Urchristentums 52. Leiden: Brill, 2003.

Rowe, C. Kavin. *Early Narrative Christology*. Beihefte zur Zeitschrift für die neutestamentliche Wissenschaft und die Kunde der älteren Kirche 139. Berlin: Walter de Gruyter & Co., 2006.

Sahlins, Marshall. *Stone Age Economics*. 2nd ed. London/New York: Routledge, 2004.

Sanders, E. P. *Paul and Palestinian Judaism: A Comparison of Patters of Religion* Philadelphia: Fortress Press, 1977.

_____. "Did Paul's Theology Develop?" Pages 325–50 in *The Word Leaps the Gap: Essays in Scripture and Theology in Honor of Richard B. Hays*. Edited by J. Ross Wager et al. Grand Rapids: Eerdmans, 2008.

Sanders, E. P. and Margaret Davies. *Studying the Synoptic Gospels*. London: SCM Press, 1989.

Sandt, Huub van de and Jürgen K. Zangenberg eds. *Matthew, James, and Didache: Three Related Documents in Their Jewish and Christian Settings*. Society of Biblical Literature Symposium Series 45. Atlanta: Society of Biblical Literature, 2008.

Schechter, Solomon. *Aspects of Rabbinic Theology*. New York: Macmillan, 1909; repr., New York, Schocken Books, 1961.

Schwartz, Daniel R. *2 Maccabees*. Commentaries on Early Jewish Literature. Berlin/New York: Walter de Gruyter, 2008.

Schwartz, Seth. *Imperialism and Jewish Society, 200 B.C.E. to 640 C.E.* Princeton: Princeton University Press, 2001.

Senior, Donald. *The Passion Narrative According to Matthew: A Redactional Study*. Bibliotheca ephemeridum theologicarum lovaniensium 39. Leuven: Leuven University Press, 1982.

_____. *Matthew*. Abingdon New Testament Commentaries. Nashville: Abingdon, 1998.

Sim, David C. "The Meaning of παλιγγενεσία in Matthew 19.28." *Journal for the Study of the New Testament* 50 (1993): 3–12.

_____. "Christianity and Ethnicity in the Gospel of Matthew." Pages 171–95 in *Ethnicity and the Bible*. Edited by G. Brett. Biblical Interpretation Series 19. Leiden: Brill, 1996.

_____. *The Gospel of Matthew and Christian Judaism: the History and Social Setting and Social Setting of the Matthean Community*. Edinburgh: T&T Clark, 1998.

_____. "The Gospel for All Christians?" A Response to Richard Bauckham." *Journal for the Study of the New Testament* 84 (2001): 3–27.

Snodgrass, Klyne R. *Stories with Intent: A Comprehensive Guide to the Parables of Jesus*. Grand Rapids, MI: Eerdmans, 2008.

Stanton, Graham. *A Gospel for a New People: Studies in Matthew*. Louisville: Westminster John Knox, 1993.

_____. "The Fourfold Gospel." *New Testament Studies* 43 (1997): 317–46.

Strack, H. L., and P. Billerbeck. *Kommentar zum Neuen Testament aus Talmud und Midrasch*. 6 vols. Munich, C. H. Beck, 1922–1961.

Streeter, Burnett Hillman. *The Four Gospels: A Story of Origins.* London: Mac-Millan, 1924.

Stuhlmacher, Peter. "Vicariously Giving His Life for Many, Mark 10:45 Matt 20:28." Pages 16–29 in *Reconciliation, Law, and Righteousness.* Philadelphia: Fortress Press, 1986.

Sugranyes de Franch, Ramon. *Études sur le droit palestinien à l'époque évangélique* Fribourg: Librairie de l'Université, 1946.

Talbert, Charles. *What is a Gospel? The Genre of the Canonical Gospels.* Philadelphia: Fortress Press, 1977.

_____. *Ephesians and Colossians.* Paideia Commentaries on the New Testament. Grand Rapids, MI: Baker Academic, 2007.

_____. *Matthew.* Paideia Commentaries on the New Testament. Grand Rapids, MI: Baker Academic, 2010.

Thompson, J. A. *The Book of Jeremiah.* New International Commentary on the Old Testament. Grand Rapids, MI: Eerdmans, 1980.

Troxel, Ronald L. "Matt 27.51–4 Reconsidered: Its Role in the Passion Narrative, Meaning, and Origin." *New Testament Studies* 48 (2002): 30–47.

Tuckett, Christopher. *Reading the New Testament: Methods of Interpretation.* London: SPCK, 1987.

van Henten, Jan Willem. *The Maccabean Martyrs as Saviours of the Jewish People: A Study of 2 and 4 Maccabees.* Supplements to the Journal for the Study of Judaism 57. Leiden: E. J. Brill, 1997.

Voss, Florian. "Der Lohn der guten Tat: Zur theologischen Bestimmung der Beziehung zwischen Matthäus und Paulus." *Zeitschrift für Theologie und Kirche* 103 (2006): 319–43.

Waltke, Bruce K. *A Commentary on Micah.* Grand Rapids, MI.: Eerdmans, 2007.

Waters, Kenneth L. Sr. "Matthew 27:52–53 as Apocalyptic Apostrophe: Temporal Spatial Collapse in the Gospel of Matthew." *Journal of Biblical Literature* 122 (2003): 489–515.

Watts, Rikki E. "Immanuel: Virgin Birth Proof Text or Programmatic Warning of Things to Come (Isa 7:14 in Matt 1:23)?" Pages 92–113 in *From Prophecy to Testament.* Edited by Craig Evans. Peabody, MA: Hendrickson, 2004.

Weeks, Stuart, Simon Gathercole, and Loren Stuckenbruck eds. *The Book of Tobit: Texts from the Principal Ancient and Medieval Traditions.* Fontes et Subsidia ad Bibliam pertinentes 3. Berlin/New York: Walter de Gruyter, 2004.

Whitters, Mark F. "Jesus in the Footsteps of Jeremiah." *Catholic Biblical Quarterly* 68 (2006): 229–47.

Wilcox, Max. "On the Ransom-Saying in Mark 10:45c, Matt 20:28c." Pages 173–86 in *Geschichte-Tradition-Reflexion: Festschrift für Martin Hengel zum 70. Geburtstag.* Edited by Hubert Cancik et al. 3 vols. Tübingen: Mohr Siebeck, 1996.

Williams, Sam K. *Death as Saving Event: The Background and Origin of a Concept.* Harvard Dissertations in Religion 2. Missoula, Mont.: Scholars Press for Harvard Theological Review, 1975.

Windisch, Hans. *Der Sinn der Bergpredigt: Ein Beitrag zum Problem der richtigen Exegese.* Leipzig: J. C. Hinrichs'she, 1929.

Winston, David. *The Wisdom of Solomon: A New Translation with Introduction and Commentary*. Anchor Bible 43. Garden City, NY: Doubleday, 1979.

Wrede, William. *Das Messiasgeheimnis in den Evangelien: Zugleich ein Beitrag zum Verständnis des Markusevangeliums*. Göttingen: Vandenhoeck und Ruprecht, 1963.

Wright, N. T. *Jesus and the Victory of God*. Minneapolis: Fortress Press, 1996.

———. *The Resurrection of the Son of God*. Minneapolis: Fortress Press, 2003.

Wright, Robert B. *The Psalms of Solomon: A Critical Edition of the Greek Text* New York, New York: T & T Clark, 2007.

Wüthrich, Serge. "Naître de mourir: la mort de Jésus dans l'Évangile de Matthieu (Mt 27.51–56)." *New Testament Studies* 56 (2010): 313–25.

Yinger, Kent L. *Paul, Judaism, and Judgment According to Deeds*. Society of New Testament Studies Monograph Series 105. Cambridge: Cambridge University Press, 1999.

Zahn, Theodor. *Das Evangelium des Matthäus*. Kommentar zum Neuen Testament. 1922. Repr., Wuppertal: R. Brockhaus, 1984.

Index of Modern Authors

Index of Ancient Sources

I. Old Testament

II. Other Jewish Sources

III. New Testament

IV. Early Christian

www.ingramcontent.com/pod-product-compliance
Lightning Source LLC
Chambersburg PA
CBHW070029100426
42740CB00013B/2640